LATIN POETRY AND THE JUDGEMENT OF TASTE

Latin Poetry and the Judgement of Taste

An Essay in Aesthetics

CHARLES MARTINDALE

OXFORD
UNIVERSITY PRESS

OXFORD
UNIVERSITY PRESS

Great Clarendon Street, Oxford OX2 6DP

Oxford University Press is a department of the University of Oxford.
It furthers the University's objective of excellence in research, scholarship,
and education by publishing worldwide in

Oxford New York

Auckland Cape Town Dar es Salaam Hong Kong Karachi
Kuala Lumpur Madrid Melbourne Mexico City Nairobi
New Delhi Shanghai Taipei Toronto

With offices in

Argentina Austria Brazil Chile Czech Republic France Greece
Guatemala Hungary Italy Japan Poland Portugal Singapore
South Korea Switzerland Thailand Turkey Ukraine Vietnam

Oxford is a registered trade mark of Oxford University Press
in the UK and in certain other countries

Published in the United States
by Oxford University Press Inc., New York

© Charles Martindale 2005

The moral rights of the author have been asserted
Database right Oxford University Press (maker)

First published 2005

First published in paperback 2007

All rights reserved. No part of this publication may be reproduced,
stored in a retrieval system, or transmitted, in any form or by any means,
without the prior permission in writing of Oxford University Press,
or as expressly permitted by law, or under terms agreed with the appropriate
reprographics rights organization. Enquiries concerning reproduction
outside the scope of the above should be sent to the Rights Department,
Oxford University Press, at the address above

You must not circulate this book in any other binding or cover
and you must impose this same condition on any acquirer

British Library Cataloguing in Publication Data

Data available

Library of Congress Cataloging in Publication Data

Martindale, Charles.
Latin poetry and the judgement of taste : an essay in aesthetics / Charles Martindale.
  p. cm.
Summary: "This book examines the value of aesthetics. Martindale argues that Kant's analysis of 'the judgement of taste', the judgement that something is beautiful, remains of fundamental importance to the modern critic. He explores the relationship between form and content in poetry and urges the value of aesthetic criticism as pioneered by Walter Pater"—provided by publisher.
Includes bibliographical references (p.) and index.
ISBN 978-0-19-924040-1 (acid-free paper)
1. Latin poetry–History and criticism–Theory, etc. 2. Kant, Immanuel, 1724–1804–Aesthetics. 3. Pater, Walter, 1839–1894–Aesthetics. 4. Aesthetics, Modern. 5. Criticism. I. Title.
PA6047-M27 2004
871'.09001-dc22
2004024300

ISBN 978-0-19-924040-1 (Hbk.)
ISBN 978-0-19-921612-3 (Pbk.)

1 3 5 7 9 10 8 6 4 2

Typeset in 11/12pt MEhrhardt
by SPI Publisher Services, Pondicherry, India
Printed in Great Britain
by
Biddles Ltd, Kings Lynn, Norfolk

To Liz
for introducing me to Kant
and making this book possible

munera et Musarum et Veneris

CONTENTS

Acknowledgements		ix
Prologue		1
1.	Immanuel Kant and Aesthetic Judgement *Horace*	8
2.	Content, Form, and Frame *Catullus, Horace, Propertius*	55
3.	Distinguishing the Aesthetic: Politics and Art *Virgil, Horace*	108
4.	The Aesthetic Turn: Latin Poetry and Aesthetic Criticism *Lucretius, Ovid, Lucan*	167
Epilogue		237
Bibliography		239
Index of Names		257
Index of Subjects		261

ACKNOWLEDGEMENTS

Chapter 1 is a much-expanded version of an essay that appeared in *Arion* (third series, vol. 9, 2001, pp. 63–89). The third section of Chapter 3 reuses parts of 'Green Politics: The *Eclogues*' from *The Cambridge Companion to Virgil*, edited by the author, Cambridge University Press, 1997, pp. 107–24. I am grateful to the publishers for their permission to reuse this material.

The sources of the extracts printed in this book are as follows: C. S. Lewis's poem 'Prayer' is cited from *Letters to Malcolm: Chiefly On Prayer* by C. S. Lewis copyright © C. S. Lewis Pte. Ltd. 1963, 1964. Extract reprinted by permission. The extract from Robert Pinsky's 'Creation According to Ovid' from *After Ovid: New Metamorphoses*, eds. Michael Hofmann and James Lasdun, is reprinted with permission of Faber and Faber Ltd.

The publishers have made every effort to locate copyright holders; where anyone notices a place where this has not been done please apply to the publisher.

In spite of all hostile conditions, man is more human than ever he was before, and he will find out the way to satisfy his imperious need for beauty.
>Bernard Bosanquet, *A History of Aesthetic*

Prologue

This essay issues from my long-standing concern about the apparently inexorable growth, in Classics as generally in the humanities, of what I shall here call 'culturalism' or 'ideology critique'.[1] Characteristic of such work is a hostility to talk about beauty and to aesthetic criticism, usually coupled with an almost complete ignorance of the modern tradition of philosophical aesthetics. The project began, tentatively, in 1997 with a third-year special subject that I co-taught with my friend and colleague Vanda Zajko, entitled 'Homer and Virgil: Language, the Aesthetic, and the Unconscious'. In this we undertook a reading of the two authors at the centre of the ancient canon in the light of questions raised in modern aesthetics from Kant onwards, investigating the reasons for their prestige and the sources of their power. Only three students elected to take the course, and one subsequently withdrew from the University; in the current climate of academic utilitarianism and efficiency gains, the course would doubtless not have taken place. But I, at least, found the wide-ranging, interdisciplinary exchanges immensely fruitful; whether the unpredictable and unpredicted results in the form of this book (no part of the statement of 'aims and objectives' now required within the academy in Britain) justify the venture the reader must judge for herself.

Subsequently, encouraged by William Batstone who was on an exchange visit to Bristol, another friend and colleague, Duncan Kennedy, and I organized an exploratory one-day colloquium on 'The Status of the Aesthetic', with participants drawn from

---

[1] The victory of such criticism was indeed announced by J. Hillis Miller in his famous address to the Modern Language Association of America in 1986: 'As everyone knows, literary study in the past few years has undergone a sudden, almost universal turn away from theory in the sense of an orientation toward language as such and has made a corresponding turn toward history, culture, society, politics, institutions, class and gender conditions, the social context, the material base in the sense of institutionalization, conditions of production, technology, distribution, and consumption of "cultural products", among other products' (Miller (1991) 313). For some good reasons for resisting this new hegemony see Lansdown (2001).

across the humanities and social sciences. Inspired by these discussions I set out some preliminary ideas in a review article for *Arion* on Yun Lee Too's provocative study *The Idea of Ancient Literary Criticism*, and in a lecture I gave at University College, Toronto as Stubbs Lecturer for fall 2000 (subsequently published in *Arion*, and the basis of my first chapter). My aim now was, through a study of Latin poetry, to encourage my fellow Latinists and others in the humanities to take an interest in the modern tradition of Western aesthetics as it applies to literature. Nineteenth-century explorations of aesthetics and Aestheticism were powerfully associated with Greek and Latin literature (think of Hegel's use of the *Antigone*, for example). Classics is now at risk of losing any sort of importance in wider debates about literature and the arts, but I believe, and hope here to show, that classical literature remains a paradigm of special importance for aesthetic issues conceived at their broadest.[2] Indeed, it may be easier to make the judgement of taste—disinterested, making a claim to universality—about a work in a dead language, or so Kant seems to suggest.[3]

In another sense this essay may be said to have been in gestation ever since I was a student. One of the books that had the greatest influence on me at that time was Gordon Williams's magnum opus *Tradition and Originality in Roman Poetry*, which was published in 1968, my first year of study. Here, I felt, was a book that treated Latin poetry in a literary way and which did not shirk the crucial issue of quality. Most importantly it did not collapse literature into something else, whether history, or literary history, or biography, or politics, or ethics, or whatever. But that was in another country... Today the book inevitably seems somewhat dated, and its limitations evident. Its approach to literary value is dependent on assumptions (too often unexamined) deriving from the New Criticism, which in the late 1960s was migrating—rather belatedly—from English literature (where it was already under substantial attack) to Classics. Lurking unacknowledged in the background is

---

[2] Cf. Michael Silk, 'Pindar Meets Plato' in Harrison (2001) 44–5: 'Surprising and unfashionable though it may be to say so, classicists are, or should be, in a special, even privileged, position here, because we have distinctive access both to the most defining literature in the Western tradition and to the full continuum of theory, from Aristotle to Derrida and beyond: the defining literature and the theoretical continuum that, all in all, make the centrality of values so unmistakably plain.'

[3] Kant (1952) 75 §17; 171 §47.

the (inescapable) figure of the poet T. S. Eliot, with his stress on the importance of tradition, classicism, and hierarchy. It will be one of the purposes of this essay to show that the aesthetic has no *necessary* connection with these conservative commitments (however strong those connections may have been in any particular set of historical circumstances).

A number of modern approaches to literature result in a kind of fragmentation of the text. It is worth asking whether aesthetic criticism, without neglecting these powerful critiques and demonstrations, can in some valid sense put—shall we dare to call it?—the literary work together again. Another form of fragmentation has affected the whole discussion of reading and literature. Three separate disciplines—philosophical aesthetics, literary criticism, and the constellation of activities that gets called 'literary theory' or 'critical theory' or just 'theory'—have tended, largely in isolation from each other, to address different audiences, generate different questions, and depend on different views about what constitutes 'knowledge'. Sometimes they share material or terminology, but use it differently. Some attempt to combine the results of these different practices is desirable for an adequate account of what is involved in reading those complex or privileged works that many societies have designated as 'literature' or 'art' (or some equivalent category). So this essay will seek illumination wherever it is to be found, whether in Kant or Pater, Schiller or Derrida.

The structure of the book is easily set forth. In the first chapter I return to Kant's *Critique of Judgement*, the third of his three great Critiques, for a compelling account of the character and conditions of possibility of what he terms 'the judgement of taste' ('X is beautiful'). I am not a philosopher, and I am writing not for philosophers but for students of literature. My concern is thus less with expounding Kant in a merely exegetical or antiquarian spirit than with using him as a guide to the way we might approach the aesthetic today. Part of my purpose is to urge fellow classicists to make more use of the tradition of philosophical aesthetics from Kant to the present. In this respect the book is necessarily synecdochic. I myself have found comparatively little in, say, Hegel, Nietzsche, or Sibley that speaks powerfully to me; but I hope others can start a dialogue with these and other writers. Good accounts of literature generally involve both specific attention to particular texts and wider issues of a broadly theoretical character (even if these are only latent as assumptions). About these wider issues the modern philosophical tradition has much to teach us.[4] Towards the end of this chapter I ask what kind of criticism might be most consonant with the Kantian aesthetic (with an ode of Horace as my example). In pursuit of an answer I look, as I will throughout this work, at aspects of the Aesthetic Movement of the later nineteenth century, a movement largely neglected within philosophical aesthetics— Walter Pater, perhaps our greatest aesthetic critic (who was a philosopher as well as a leading classicist) does not even receive an entry in David Cooper's *A Companion to Aesthetics* (1992), a standard reference work in the field. What might it mean to value art 'for art's sake', more than for something else (for example, morality), and what are the problems this creates, for critic and for artist?

In Chapters 2 and 3 I attempt to counter two commonly made objections to aesthetic judgements about artworks (including works of literature), first that they are formalistic (detaching formal features of the work from the discursive and ideological contexts of their use), and secondly that they are really occluded judgements of other kinds. In the second chapter I argue that the judgement of taste is a judgement of form and content (however construed) *together*. I seek to illustrate this in connection with some odes of Horace and poem 64 of Catullus. I end by examining Derrida's deconstruction of the neo-Kantian notion of the autonomy of art and the issue of the frame (with Propertius 1. 16 as a telling instance). In the third chapter I look at politics and aesthetics as

---

[4] Cf. Duncan Kennedy (1984) 160: 'Modern literary theory is not, as is so often thought, a series of methods or approaches which should or should not be applied to ancient poetry, nor is it something that is merely the pastime of people in "Eng. Lit." with nothing better to do. It is a call to examine the viability of the arguments we employ in talking about literature and the assumptions and preconceptions that are part of *all* the words we use, whatever language we are writing in or about. Our failure to come to grips with this is a symptom of the growing parochialism of the study of Latin in this country.' In his essay 'The Pursuit of Metaphor' Ricks, a leading opponent of what he calls 'theory's empire', seeks, unconvincingly, to distinguish 'principles' (good) from 'theory' (bad) (Ricks (2002) 242–3; cf. 'Literary Principles as against Theory' in Ricks (1996) 311–32). This seems to me little more than juggling with words; the issue is whether we are to think as hard as we can about our wider assumptions. And even if the distinction has its uses, it inflicts no damage at all on theory as such. Of course there is much bad 'theory', just as there is much bad literary criticism. Theory has become, perhaps has always been, a lazy word in the humanities; it remains true that, if as academics we cannot justify our procedures, in ways both particular and general, it is difficult to see why we presume to teach others.

rival discourses, and at the kind of interpretations that each generates, with analyses of Horace *Ode* 2. 7 and Virgil's *Eclogues*. I argue for the legitimacy of aesthetic readings as well as political ones, and show how the notion that the aesthetic is essentially a 'reactionary' category is quite at odds with the history of aesthetics. Both Schiller and Pater accorded a specially privileged importance to the aesthetic, and I end with some thoughts on their arguments. So far, although my eventual concern is with aesthetic criticism, I have to use the language and concepts of ideology critique in order to demonstrate the shortcomings (in the terms of its own arguments) of its attack on the aesthetic.

These obstacles confronted, I turn, in my final chapter, from the past to the future. What might an aesthetic criticism of Latin poetry in the twenty-first century look like? There is a strong body of aesthetic criticism in this country, which, while from a Kantian perspective it should not be regarded as an object of imitation, nonetheless can be construed as exemplary. For both theory and practice I turn to Pater, whose writings sought to isolate the 'virtue', the unique aesthetic character, of artworks. I hope my work may serve as a protreptic towards a new aesthetic criticism, exhorting the rising generation of Latinists to try what might be done. I offer three short essays of my own (on Lucretius, Ovid, and Lucan), for which I claim nothing except that they are gestures, however feeble, towards a revised practice. As in the case of the other Latin poets discussed I have chosen these authors as offering the reader experience of beauty of a unique kind that he or she will find nowhere else. I should perhaps make clear at the outset that such criticism is not primarily concerned with offering 'new' readings, as classicists would normally understand that term (this book is not designed to provide fodder for the next round of specialist journal articles).[5]

A defence of the aesthetic is, to my thinking, timely in a number of ways. Not the least of them is that the Kantian aesthetic, the free judgement of taste, carries a rebuke to the means/end rationality so prevalent and so dangerous in the contemporary West. In this

---

[5] If anyone complains that my accounts of particular poems are not new, my reply would be that novelty as such is not the *goal* of the aesthetic critic (although, as in the case of Pater, novelty may result). Likewise, to forestall possible misunderstanding, I should point out that the analyses of poems in Chapters 2 and 3 are there to support the arguments of those chapters; they are not offered as examples of aesthetic criticism.

country, at least, today's academy has all but abandoned Newman's noble vision of the idea of university education for a managerialism concerned only with targets and measurable outputs, supposedly linked to the performance of the British economy. But, to paraphrase Wilde paraphrasing Swinburne, love knowledge for its own sake, and then all things that you need will be added to you.[6] As Elizabeth Barrett Browning's Aurora Leigh wisely observes:

> We get no good
> By being ungenerous, even to a book,
> And calculating profits...so much help
> By so much reading. It is rather when
> We gloriously forget ourselves, and plunge
> Soul-forward, headlong, into a book's profound,
> Impassioned for its beauty and salt of truth—
> 'Tis then we get the right good from a book.

Although I take most of my examples from Latin poetry (all fully translated—by me, except where otherwise stated), I am not writing for classicists alone. I hope that this book will have something to say to a much wider readership, including those interested in aesthetics, Aestheticism in England, poetry, English Literature, reception, critical theory. I believe that it is only if classicists learn to address those outside as well as within their discipline that the subject has much chance of surviving as a significant element in the general culture. For this reason, in my discussions of Latin poems, I have kept referencing fairly light.[7]

The Leverhulme Trust awarded me a two-year fellowship which allowed me to complete the writing of this book; my thanks to that splendid, unbureaucratic, and philanthropical institution. There could be no better place to write an essay of this kind than in the Classics Department of the University of Bristol, with its inclusive approach to the subject and its commitment to

---

[6] Jackson (1991) 21. For Swinburne see below, pp. 109–10.

[7] One of my readers asked me to clarify my attitude to the modern secondary literature by classicists. For my purposes scholarly articles, useful as they clearly are for those who share their concerns, are part of the general reception of the poems, and, in some important respects, less interesting as receptions than those, say, of the great poets who were inspired by those poems in their own writings. Also, from the perspective of the aesthetic critic, much of this literature, by setting too delimited frameworks of enquiry, frustrates as much as it enables the judgement of taste on the part, say, of student readers.

Prologue

interdisciplinary dialogue and debate. Special gratitude is owed to the following for help of various kinds: Bob Fowler, Miriam Leonard, Aleka Lianeri, Ellen O'Gorman, Carolyn Wilde, Vanda Zajko. Colin Burrow, David Hopkins, Duncan Kennedy, Tony Nuttall, and Richard Thomas kindly read the typescript in its entirety and helped to improve it. I owe most of all to my partner, Liz Prettejohn, for whom, over these last years, my project has been her project; in best Aestheticist fashion I have shamelessly plagiarized her own work on beauty and the aesthetic in art, and no doubt diminished it in the process.

I

Immanuel Kant and Aesthetic Judgement

Shouldn't we abolish aesthetics?
Brecht[1]

I

Listen!—there *never* was an artistic period!—
There *never was* an art loving nation—
In the beginning, man went forth each day—some to do battle—some to the chase—others again to dig and to delve in the field—all that they might gain, and live—or lose and die—until there was found among them, one, differing from the rest—whose pursuits attracted him not—and so he staid by the tents, with the women, and traced strange devices, with a burnt stick, upon a gourd.—
This man, who took no joy in the ways of his brethren, who cared not for conquest, and fretted in the field—this designer of quaint patterns—this deviser of the beautiful, who perceived in nature about him, curious carvings,—as faces are seen in the fire—This dreamer apart—was the *first* artist.—
And when, from the field and from afar, there came back the people, they took the gourd and drank from out of it.

So wrote the avant-garde painter James McNeill Whistler in his famous manifesto 'The Ten O'Clock Lecture'[2], employing what Oscar Wilde characterized, with affectionate ridicule, as 'the style of the minor prophets'.[3] In his novel *The Inheritors*, which offers an anthropological version of the Fall of Man, William Golding devises a similar aetiology for the discovery of the aesthetic, an originary moment for art. Golding's Neanderthal men are apparently unfallen, and they have no art, only a single *trouvaille*, a twisted piece of root which they regard as an image of their

---

[1] Cited Bennett (1990) 165.   [2] Thorpe (1994) 82.
[3] Jackson (1991) 54. Perhaps, for Wilde, Ruskin is the 'major' prophet.

goddess Oa. However among the 'New Men' (*Homo Sapiens*, that is the ancestors of ourselves), who destroy and replace the Neanderthalers, and who are clearly fallen, is an artist, Tuami. He uses his art in two quite distinct ways: magically, totemistically, as when he makes a picture of the animal the New Men hope to kill, but also disinterestedly, creatively. At the end of the book he is making an ivory dagger to kill the leader of his tribe, when he sees the rump of a stolen Neanderthal baby against the head of one of the women:

> The rump and the head fitted each other and made a shape you could feel with your hands. They were waiting in the rough ivory of the knife-haft that was so much more important than the blade. They were an answer, the frightened, angry love of the woman and the ridiculous, intimidating rump that was wagging at her head, they were a password.[4]

In Kantian terms Tuami moves from the judgement that the knife is 'good' (that is, well fitted to its purpose) to one that it is 'beautiful', what Kant calls 'the judgement of taste'.

One might gloss this episode with a passage from the twenty-seventh letter of Friedrich Schiller's *On the Aesthetic Education of Man* describing (or purporting to describe) the origin of art among primitive peoples:

> The things he possesses, the things he produces, may no longer bear upon them the marks of their use, their form no longer be merely a timid expression of their function; in addition to the service they exist to render, they must at the same time reflect the genial mind which conceived them, the loving hand which wrought them, the serene and liberal spirit which chose and displayed them. Now the ancient German goes in search of glossier skins, statelier antlers, more elaborate drinking horns; and the Caledonian selects for his feasts the prettiest shells. Even weapons may no longer be mere objects of terror; they must be objects of delight as well, and the cunningly ornamented sword-belt claims no less attention than the deadly blade of the sword. Not content with introducing aesthetic superfluity into objects of necessity, the play-drive as it becomes ever freer finally tears itself away from the fetters of utility altogether, and beauty in and for itself alone begins to be the object of his striving. Man *adorns* himself. Disinterested and undirected pleasure is now numbered among the necessities of existence, and what is in fact unnecessary soon becomes the best part of his delight.[5]

---

[4] Golding (1979) 233.

[5] Schiller (1967) 211. It is striking how like a theory of surplus value this could be made to sound. In Schiller's system the 'play-drive' harmonizes the 'form-drive' and the 'sense-drive' to restore balance and unity to the individual (on this see further Ch. 3, pp. 159–63). For the development of art among 'primitive' peoples cf. Kant (1952) 155–6 §41.

For Whistler concern with the aesthetic is a mark of the rare individual, of the few like himself; for Schiller, who believed that an education in art would produce integrated individuals and good citizens, a feeling for beauty, if not innate, was at any rate a deeply embedded element in human nature as it had developed and thus an important part of what it means to be fully human (he also anticipates Hegel in assigning a historical dimension to art). Immanuel Kant, the great philosopher of the aesthetic, was more cautious; all he seems to assert is that the conditions exist in all human beings to make 'the judgement of taste'. In that more restricted sense such judgements can be regarded as 'universal', but Kant, as we shall see, is fully aware of the cultural components in any actual taste for the beautiful in nature or in art.

This book will therefore constitute a plea to my fellow Latinists—and indeed all classicists and students of literature in general—to return to the aesthetic, to give aesthetics a turn. My principal opponents here will be those 'enemies of poetry' (to use the title of a book by W. B. Stanford) who are what one might call 'vulgar historicists'—scholars for whom the only legitimate interpretation of a Latin poem is one related to its original historical context, a meaning which they believe, in their positivistic fashion, can be recovered from 'the evidence'. Since 1968—again following in the wake of other humanities disciplines—Classics has experienced a shift towards cultural, political, and neo-historical approaches to literature and the visual arts: this shift is sometimes called the 'cultural turn'. The questions asked of a 'text' are epistemological ones 'what and how does it mean?' rather than aesthetic ones 'is it beautiful, and if so how?' or 'what pleasure does it give, and how?'. It is indeed a bold classicist today who dares publicly to call a Latin poem 'beautiful'—the very word causes us embarrassment.[6] Elsewhere in the humanities there are increasing signs of a certain dissatisfaction with an impoverished aesthetic vocabulary, and I believe that there is both the need for an 'aesthetic turn' and the likelihood of it in the decades to come. It is significant that quite a number of new introductions to aesthetics and new aesthetics readers have been appearing recently, and indeed several

---

[6] For the rejection of beauty by modernist artists see Danto (2003). Tony Nuttall tells me that in the induction week at Oxford students coming to read English are warned against using value terms in their work. So much for the benefits of a humane education.

Immanuel Kant and Aesthetic Judgement

books and essays on beauty.[7] An early sign of what was to come was the publication in 1994 of George Levine's collection *Aesthetics and Ideology*. The contributors to this volume include several writers whom one would not readily associate with a summons to aesthetics; collectively they call, though without much detail or specification, for a rethinking of the aesthetic and a re-imagination of the formal in critical practice—after a period in which 'formalism' has been a particularly deadly critical charge.[8]

Most classicists today, whether they style themselves 'traditional' or 'radical', share in the anti-aesthetic bias of the new culturalism, not least the brightest and best, the liveliest and most innovative. Two works by such, both of which appeared in 1998, may stand for many: Thomas Habinek's *The Politics of Latin Literature* and Yun Lee Too's *The Idea of Ancient Literary Criticism*. Habinek attacks what he calls the 'nostalgia for a realm of the aesthetic untainted by the vulgar concerns of social and material existence', as well as the 'evasion of the exploitative political and economic practices that

---

[7] Examples of the former include: Cooper (1997); Feagin and Maynard (1997) (Oxford Readers Series); Graham (1997); Kivy (1997); Lyas (1997) (the best recent introduction); Kelly (1998); Isobel Armstrong (2000); M. P. Clark (2000); de Bolla (2001); Freeland (2001); Gaut and Lopes (2001); Faas (2002); Hammermeister (2002); Danto (2003); Joughin and Malpas (2003); Matthews and McWhirter (2003); Kivy (2004). On beauty: Regan (1992); Hickey (1993); Beckley (1998); Benezra and Viso (1999); Kirwan (1999); Scarry (1999); O'Hear (2001); Steiner (2001); Donoghue (2003). The Fall 2002 issue of *Daedalus* has essays on beauty by Denis Donoghue, Susan Sontag, Arthur C. Danto, Alexander Nehamas, and four others. In 2003 a major international conference was held in Cambridge, entitled 'Aesthetic Positions'. Whether all this activity amounts to anything yet worth calling 'A New Aestheticism' is, however, open to doubt, in view of the continued dominance of historicism and ideology critique within the academy. 'The New Aestheticism' was so named in an essay in *New Left Review* (Beech and Roberts (1996)), which criticizes the supposed return to aesthetics for offering the 'transcendentally emancipatory' while in actuality helping to secure 'the suppression of bodily wants and needs' (pp. 103–4). The following year the journal published replies by Bernstein (1997) and Bowie (1997). The word 'beauty' is not a locus of dispute in these exchanges. Scientists have long been much less embarrassed about using aesthetic language in connection with what they do, regularly calling equations and theories and the like 'beautiful'; see e.g. Farmelo (2003). Mothersill (1984) is the classic treatment of beauty in the analytic tradition.

[8] Kennedy (1987*b*), recognizing that formalism is unavoidable in literary analysis, gives an unusually nuanced version of the current consensus: 'The point about formalism is not that it should be avoided (can it be?)... but to recognize that it is not an explanation *in itself*... but *is always invoked in the service of some explanatory scheme*, very often serving to mask from those critics who foreground it the ideological underpinnings of that explanatory scheme' (p. 75). But why should one element 'underpin' the other, rather than e.g. vice versa?

could bring such an ideal to realization, if only for the few'.[9] For him Latin literature was subject to 'political and ideological mystifications', constituting 'politics by other means', and he assumes that the aesthetic is necessarily implicated in the evils of formalism.[10] Insisting on 'the inevitable interestedness of all readings', he gives his credo as follows: 'what interests me ... about a literary utterance is not its truth value or its formal features so much as the question *cui bono?*'.[11] To the issue of 'disinterest' I shall be returning. For now it is enough to say that, from an ethical point of view, Habinek's universe of suspicion strikes me as decidedly nightmarish. One may agree with him that poetry for Horace was 'one means of social differentiation'[12] (poets like academics must be allowed their worldly ambitions), but does that exhaust its meaning and significance? Too's book comes very much from the same stable; following the lead of the Marxist critic Terry Eagleton she argues that criticism in antiquity was, and criticism today should be, seen as a form of cultural and political construction: 'criticism in antiquity, far from being a disinterested, aestheticizing, or evaluative project, is central to the production of political identity and the structures which produce the political community.'[13] Like Eagleton then, and indeed the majority of modern theorists, Too reductively collapses aesthetics into politics. Now if the claim of Habinek and Too were merely that a political analysis of literature is a legitimate one, I would have no conceivable quarrel with them—though I would want the word 'political' interrogated with rather more rigour, and not assigned a simplistic and unexamined transhistorical value. But if it is that the aesthetic is merely an occlusion or mystification of the political, or even just that political readings are superior to aesthetic ones, then we are in serious disagreement.

Kant will be the protagonist of this book. His *Critique of Judgement*, and in particular what is its most elegant, compelling, and persuasive section the 'Analytic of the Beautiful', is one of the best places for anyone to start thinking seriously about the aesthetic.[14]

---

[9] Habinek (1998) 167.
[10] Ibid. 5, 13.   [11] Ibid. 10, 8–9.   [12] Ibid. 101.
[13] Too (1998) 282. The present tense in this sentence is interesting in a book which continually wobbles between a reading from the present and a form of historical positivism; see Martindale (2001).
[14] All quotations from Kant are from the exemplary translation of James Creed Meredith, first published in 1911. In the period after the Second World War, and later among

A traditional historicist might say that the appropriate place to ground a discussion of Latin poetry is in the writings of ancient philosophers, rhetoricians, and commentators; but a modern aesthetician is no more bound to confine herself to ancient writing on art than is a modern historian to ancient conceptions of history-writing. Two stories about the history of aesthetics are commonly encountered. The first is one of seamless continuity from the concerns of Plato and Aristotle down to those of modern philosophers and critics. The second insists on rupture, usually located in the eighteenth century, coinciding approximately with the rise of capitalism, the *embourgeoisement* of society, the Industrial Revolution, or any combination of these (that is to say, with some version of Modernity).[15] Of this rupture Kant's Third Critique is regarded as a symptom or cause. I would want to give a more complex story of the continuing dialogue between the ancient and the modern worlds.

In his important recent book *The Aesthetics of Mimesis* Stephen Halliwell advances an anti-Kantian position. He argues, convincingly, that the mimeticist tradition which derives from Plato and Aristotle has continued to inform Western aesthetics since Kant to a degree that is insufficiently recognized. Halliwell's concern is with the history of aesthetics, whereas mine is with the making of aesthetic judgements today and with advancing particular arguments within an aestheticist framework. And underlying Halliwell's account is his conviction that his older mimeticist tradition offers us 'more open-ended, and interpretatively richer ways of thinking and feeling about poetry, painting, or music' than either Kantian or post-Kantian aesthetics.[16] This book rests on the opposite premiss,

---

postmodernists, there was a definite preference for the 'Analytic of the Sublime', largely because of the way that the sublime exceeds the human capacity to encompass it. However, the Kantian sublime is in a sense a sub-category of the beautiful; Kant's most fundamental moves have already been made in the 'Analytic of the Beautiful'. Moreover in his account of the sublime Kant draws back, at least to a degree, from the more radical implications of his account of beauty, by associating the sublime more closely with morality (Kant (1952) 116, 120 §29). Many self-styled 'progressives' today continue to prefer the category of the sublime, which is more easily recuperable for existing discourses. This book by contrast deliberately stresses the beautiful, partly on the basis that it has the potential to be the more 'radical' category.

[15] For this now commoner second view see e.g. Eagleton (1990); Mortensen (1997).

[16] Halliwell (2002) 11. His own brief account of Kant is seriously deficient; e.g. he claims that Kant's analysis of aesthetic judgement wholly excludes 'cognitive and emotional responses that draw on the general understanding of reality' (p. 364)—this ignores, for

that Kant's Third Critique offers us a deeper theoretical understanding of beauty and aesthetic judgement than was ever achieved in antiquity, partly because in theoretical terms the ancients never managed to articulate the specificity of the aesthetic at the same time as acknowledging its power and importance in human life. They either failed to separate the aesthetic from the moral, or, where they did so separate it, they accorded it little more than entertainment value.[17]

It is a trope among interpreters of *The Critique of Judgement* to begin by saying that everyone else has misunderstood it. There is nothing odd about a canonical work being subject to diverse interpretations (indeed some would say that its capacity for reinterpretation is precisely what makes such a work canonical[18]). What I find disturbing about many accounts of Kant's aesthetic views is rather my sense that I have been reading a different work altogether. For example, Wendy Steiner claims that for Kant 'the experience of beauty provides a taste of transcendent freedom from the human condition', and that 'when we judge something beautiful, we do so as beings standing outside the contingencies of flesh-and-blood existence, freed of individual interest, become ideal, pure, almost godlike in our consciousness'.[19] Kant certainly requires a pure judgement of taste to be 'without an interest' (in the special sense we shall be looking at shortly), but otherwise there is nothing vague and lofty as Steiner's formulation implies in Kant's careful analysis. Far from being in any way godlike, we depend, when we judge something beautiful, on features of the human mind and perceptual equipment; the judgement of taste is thus a distinctively human judgement (presumably for Kant God, not having like us a finite mind, knows things-in-themselves and experiences no disjunction between sense/intuition and thought/concept). Repeated sources of confusion reside in the words 'transcendent', 'idealist', 'judgement'. Kant's philosophy is idealist in the sense that in his

---

example, what Kant has to say about 'aesthetic ideas'. Halliwell has his greatest problem with music; his defence, in chapter 8, of the ancient idea of music as a mimetic art (on the grounds that it is 'not a purely formal or abstract art but has its place within a larger cultural network of relationships between human minds and reality as a whole' (p. 355)), despite its panache, is ultimately unconvincing. On this issue see also Scher (1992).

[17] This is roughly the view of Bosanquet (1966), criticized by Halliwell (2000) 12.
[18] So e.g. Kermode (1975*a*).   [19] Steiner (2001) 2.

view the human mind determines what we can know about the world; but the judgement of taste, far from being ideal, general, or transcendent, is, as we shall see, radically local and particular. Similarly Kant uses the word 'judgement' in his special sense. Within his system judgement involves relating an intuition to a function of the mind, or a special case to a concept—'this is a table' and 'this is an instance of injustice' are typical judgements. Unlike theoretical and practical judgements, the judgement of taste, while it involves the faculties of the mind, is peculiar because there is no definite concept involved, and hence no ready closure or determination.

Again, it is repeatedly said that Kant proposed that art inhabited an autonomous aesthetic sphere. But Kant has comparatively little to say about art, his focus being on the beauty of nature, and none of his examples of what he calls 'free beauty' (that is to say the beauty of objects not involved in any concept or end) are taken from the fine arts—instead they are such things as flowers, crustacea, birds of paradise, and free decorative patterns.[20] For Kant there seems to be no special realm in respect of objects for the judgement of taste.[21] His concern is with types of judgement, not with separate spheres. Thus the poet Swinburne coarsens the Kantian position when he writes: 'To art, that is best which is most beautiful; to science, that is best which is most accurate; to morality, that is best which is most virtuous.'[22] Part of the problem is that Kant, cautious to affirm only what he has fully established, says relatively little, less than his readers might like, and they hasten to fill the gaps and attribute their infillings to the master. Many of those readers wish that Kant had written a treatise on art, but *The Critique of Judgement* is very far from being that.

The aim of this chapter, then, is *to explore some of Kant's central and most interesting claims, in the belief that they can help us think productively about the aesthetic today.*[23] The form of the judgement of taste is this: X—'the building we see, the dress that person has

---

[20] Kant (1952) 72 §16.   [21] My terminology here is Kantian (cf. Kant (1952) 14).
[22] Swinburne (1868) 98.
[23] The meaning of almost every one of Kant's principal claims is disputed. The many studies include Crawford (1974); Cohen and Guyer (1982); Caygill (1989); Crowther (1989); Guyer (1993); Savile (1993); Allison (2001). Beginners, however, may do best to start with Cassirer (1970), first published in 1938.

on, the concert we hear, the poem submitted to our criticism'—is beautiful.[24] The statement 'all tulips are beautiful' is for Kant a logical, not an aesthetic one, though it may be based on a number of previous aesthetic judgements.[25] It follows that the judgement of taste is made in a direct encounter with some object, and is never arrived at *a priori*—thus you cannot predict what will please in a work of art, or say that a picture you have not seen or a poem you have not read is beautiful:[26] 'I must present the object immediately to my feeling of pleasure or displeasure, and that too, without the aid of concepts'[27] (it does not matter what the object is or what purpose it might serve). In view of this specificity there is thus a sense in which beauty is 'always a surprise'.[28] Kant retains the ordinary word 'beautiful' (*schön*) rather than coining a new one, but it is clear that beautiful is an umbrella term to describe anything in nature or art that evokes a delight-inducing play of our mental faculties in our response.[29] Mary Mothersill rightly observes that 'a consequence which some may find objectionable is that there is nothing in the world of which we can say in advance that under no circumstances will it ever be discovered to be beautiful'.[30] Far from finding this objectionable, I would argue that it is a major strength of Kant's analysis (though it might mean that beauty could be found in Nazi or Fascist art).

In what can justly be considered (to use Kant's own metaphor) a 'Copernican Revolution' in accounts of beauty, Kant—in this

---

[24] Kant (1952) 52 §7.   [25] Ibid. 140 §33.
[26] Ibid. 32, Introduction VII. So Mothersill (1984) 160: 'So just as the judgment of taste (speech act) presupposes, through the avowal that it implicates, first-personal knowledge of the object judged, for someone who wants to test the truth of a judgment of taste (sentence) the starting point is getting to know the object judged.'
[27] Kant (1952) 55 §8.   [28] Kirwan (1999) 124.
[29] Barbara Herrnstein Smith is wrong to suppose that Kant can be refuted merely by an appeal to 'the historicity of linguistic convention' or that Kant's *schön* simply reflects 'the implicit provincial universalism of the drawingroom conversation with which he was familiar' (B. H. Smith (1988) 67). In general it is unwise for the critic to assume too readily that he or she is obviously much cleverer than Kant.
[30] Mothersill (1984) 365. Admittedly Kant assumes that some things, e.g. wine or food, can only belong to what he calls the 'agreeable', not the beautiful; but, while the distinction between the two different kinds of judgement holds ('I like canary wine' is not a judgement of taste), Kant's restriction of types of object is not an essential entailment of his system, and I would certainly want to make the judgement of taste about, say, a fine wine. Cf. Mothersill (1984) 377.

anticipated by Hume[31]—conceptualizes such judgements not in terms of knowledge of any quality inherent in the object but as a feeling of pleasure or displeasure in the perceiving subject. Kant makes this abundantly clear in the very first sentence of the 'Analytic of the Beautiful': 'If we wish to discern whether anything is beautiful or not, we do not refer the representation of it to the Object by means of understanding with a view to cognition... we refer the representation to the Subject and its feeling of pleasure or displeasure.'[32] According to Kant the mind, possessing the *a priori* categories of time and space, is bombarded with stuff which it organizes into 'representations', from which it then produces conceptual categorizations.[33] It is thus the mind that gives order to the world, and no world is available to us except in human structurings of it (we have no access to what Kant terms the 'thing-in-itself'). Beauty, on Kant's account, is not 'in' the object we judge beautiful; the most we could say is that, in Hume's words, 'there are certain qualities in objects which are fitted by nature to produce those particular feelings'.[34]

Kant's stress on the non-conceptual character of the judgement of taste leads him to distinguish between two kinds of beauty, which he calls 'free' beauty (*pulchritudo vaga*) and 'dependent' beauty (*pulchritudo adhaerens*).[35] When we find a flower beautiful, we are not concerned by any purpose that it may serve (Kant thinks this would be true even for a botanist who understands its function in reproduction[36]): 'A flower..., such as a tulip, is regarded as beautiful, because we meet with a certain finality, which, in our estimate of it, is not referred to any end whatever.'[37] By contrast, we have 'dependent' beauty where the beauty of an object is related to its

---

[31] Hume (1996) 136: 'Beauty is no quality in things themselves: it exists merely in the mind which contemplates them.' Beauty is not 'in' the object in the sense that, say, a circle might be 'in' a painting.

[32] Kant (1952) 41 §1.

[33] Here I follow Lyas (1997) ch. 1.

[34] Hume (1996) 141. Cf. Kant (1952) 92 §23, on the sublime: 'All that we can say is that the object lends itself to the presentation of a sublimity discoverable in the mind.'

[35] Kant (1952) 72 §16.

[36] Ibid. 72 §16: 'Hardly any one but a botanist knows the true nature of a flower, and even he, while recognizing in the flower the reproductive organ of the plant, pays no attention to this natural end when using his taste to judge of its beauty.'

[37] Kant (1952) 80 n. 1 §17.

purpose, for example in the case of a building or an animal or a human being (these are Kant's examples). When I judge a palace beautiful I also know it was built for certain ends (in connection with which it matters whether it keeps out water and the various spaces serve their purposes effectively). One can see why Kant introduces this distinction. It allows beauty to be part of experiences that might otherwise be disqualified, and thereby saves a whole range of objects from being dismissed from consideration. But it also raises a problem about which Kant perhaps never quite made up his mind. If there are two sorts of beauty, are there also two sorts of aesthetic judgements appropriate to different objects? If so, we might make a free judgement of taste about a rose or Bach's *Goldberg Variations*, but a compound judgement about a palace or the *Aeneid* (where moral reactions and hermeneutic considerations are also in play). Since literature—in comparison with, say, music—seems a relatively impure form of art (this might be more true of a novel than of a lyric poem), it would be reasonable to argue that the judgements we make are more likely to be compound judgements. The danger of this is that beauty and pleasure become in practice increasingly subsumed under other categories, as in Leavisite criticism, while the distinctiveness and utility of the aesthetic is diluted. On occasion Kant writes as if we might make a two-stage judgement:

> Abundant proof has been given above to show that the judgement of taste by which something is declared beautiful must have no interest *as its determining ground*. But it does not follow from this that after it has once been posited as a pure aesthetic judgement, an interest cannot then enter into combination with it.[38]

This, however, seems rather artificial. There is an important unresolved issue here, and we shall be returning to it.

The judgement of taste is paradoxically both subjective and universal ('subjective universality'). It is subjective because it is particular to a perceiving subject, it is universal because it makes a claim on the agreement of all. Saying that something is beautiful is not like saying 'I like peas or the colour green' (which is a purely subjective claim that cannot be challenged and that Kant calls judgement of 'the agreeable', *das Angenehme*).[39] This is not to say

---

[38] Kant (1952) 154 §41. For the meaning of an interest here see pp. 21–4 below.
[39] Kant (1952) 52–3 §7.

that there is necessarily any agreement in practice.[40] Disagreement is indeed part of the aesthetic, since the agreement of others is, in Kant's terms (or rather his translator, Meredith's rendering of them), 'imputed', not 'postulated'.[41] We are, as he says, 'suitors for agreement'.[42] This is the conditional 'ought' of aesthetic judgements,[43] later encapsulated in F. R. Leavis's formulation 'This is so, isn't it?'.[44] Kant offers no systematic account of why such disagreements occur, but he does suggest some possibilities: one or more judgement may not be fully disinterested;[45] there may be a confusion of the agreeable and the beautiful;[46] a 'free' beauty may be confused with a 'dependent' beauty.[47] Kant is certainly much more sceptical about particular objects being found beautiful by all[48] than, say, Hume, whose account of these matters in his essay 'Of the Standard of Taste' of 1757 is grounded in such normative agreements (for Hume 'the true standard of taste and beauty' is provided by 'the joint verdict' of critics who show 'strong sense, united to delicate sentiment, improved by practice, perfected by comparison, and cleared of all prejudice').[49] For Kant by contrast no critical authority, however majestic, can force you to find an object beautiful:

If any one reads me his poem, or brings me to a play, which, all said and done, fails to commend itself to my taste, then let him adduce *Batteux* or *Lessing*, or still older and more famous critics of taste, with all the host of rules laid down by them, as a proof of the beauty of his poem; let certain passages particularly displeasing to me

---

[40] Ibid. 54 §8.   [41] Ibid. 56 §8. The German verbs are *sinnen* and *postulieren*.
[42] Ibid. 82 §19.   [43] Ibid. 82 §19.
[44] Leavis (1972) 62. Leavis, having stated that 'A judgment is personal or it is nothing', continues: 'The question is an appeal for confirmation that the thing *is* so; implicitly that, though expecting, characteristically, an answer in the form, "yes, but—" the "but" standing for qualifications, reserves, corrections.' It is true that the Leavisite formula seems more of an act of will than the Kantian imputation of universality.
[45] As in the case of our liking for birdsong, where we may confuse the beauty of the song with 'our sympathy with the mirth of a dear little creature' (Kant (1952) 89 §22).
[46] Kant (1952) 66 §14.
[47] Ibid. 74 §16.
[48] 'Much less is it inferable from universality of experience.... For, apart from the fact that experience would hardly furnish evidences sufficiently numerous for this purpose, empirical judgements do not afford any foundation for a concept of the necessity of these judgements' (Kant (1952) 81 §18).
[49] Hume (1996) 147. Hume gives as reasons for difference in taste 'the different humours of particular men' and 'the particular manners and opinions of our age and country' (p. 149).

accord completely with the rules of beauty, (as set out by these critics and universally recognized): I stop my ears....[50]

Any claim for universalism (even one as putative as Kant's in the Third Critique) is today out of fashion (it is coercive, essentializing, disrespectful of the Other, and all that). But might not the value of the aesthetic be that it offers the possibility (without, of course, the guarantee) of a common humanity? Beauty is not a purely private matter. If I take delight in a beautiful object, I want to share that delight. Alexander Nehamas puts the point well:

> The judgment of taste... is more like hearing something call me, a guess or a hope that if that thing were part of my life it would somehow make it more worthwhile. But when I find something beautiful, even when I speak only to myself, I expect others to join me and make that beautiful thing part of their own lives as well.

And he concludes that 'the judgment of beauty, which is a judgment of value, implicates you in a web of relationships with people and things'.[51] So it is unsurprising that for Kant the aesthetic is indeed a prime site for sociability:

> The empirical interest in the beautiful exists only in *society*. And if we admit that the impulse to society is natural to mankind, and that the suitability for and the propensity towards it, i.e. *sociability*, is a property essential to the requirements of man as a creature intended for society, and one, therefore, that belongs to *humanity*, it is inevitable that we should also look upon taste in the light of a faculty for estimating whatever enables us to communicate even our *feeling* to every one else, and hence as a means of promoting that upon which the natural inclination of every one is set.[52]

Later aestheticians including Schiller will take these ideas much further, though at the cost of blurring the distinction between the aesthetic and the political or moral.[53]

---

[50] Kant (1952) 140 §33.
[51] Nehamas (2002) 57, 61; cf. Steiner (2001) 92–3. Of course the judgement of taste is not merely like spreading one's good humour—it implies an invitation to others to look, to read, to listen.
[52] Kant (1952) 155 §41.
[53] It is significant that this is the aspect of Kant's theory that most appeals to Eagleton: 'Against a social philosophy founded upon egoism and appetite, Kant speaks up for a generous vision of a community of ends, finding in the freedom and autonomy of the aesthetic a prototype of human possibility equally at odds with feudal absolutism and possessive individualism. If there is no way in which this admirable ideal of mutual respect, equality and compassion can enter upon material reality, if it is necessary to rehearse in the mind what cannot be enacted in the world, this is hardly the responsibility of Kant himself' (Eagleton (1990) 100).

Crucially for Kant the judgement of taste does not involve a definite concept or universal criterion.[54] An object is not beautiful because it can be assimilated to a pre-existing rule—if that were the case we could reach such judgements *a priori* without a direct encounter with that object. There are no proofs of beauty by which we can be compelled to recognize something as beautiful.[55] So, at a stroke, Kant puts an end to centuries of fruitless attempts to define the beautiful in a general formula (for example, Plato's attempt to connect beauty and proportionality), and to such claims as those advanced by the Scottish Enlightenment philosopher Francis Hutcheson in *An Enquiry Concerning Beauty, Order, Harmony, Design* of 1725 that a square is more beautiful than an equilateral triangle or that beauty comes from 'uniformity amidst variety'.[56]

The claim of Kant's that has perhaps proved most controversial in our time is that a pure judgement of taste must be 'disinterested' (*uninteressiert*). As we have seen, Habinek, in common with most modern theorists and postmodernists generally, denies the very possibility of such a judgement. Kant defines an 'interest' as 'the delight which we connect with the representation of the real existence of an object', and proceeds to give an example:

> If any one asks me whether I consider that the palace I see before me is beautiful, I may, perhaps, reply that I do not care for things of that sort that are merely made to be gaped at. Or I may reply in the same strain as that Iroquois *sachem* who said that nothing in Paris pleased him better than the eating-houses. I may even go a step further and inveigh with the vigour of a *Rousseau* against the vanity of the great who spend the sweat of the people on such superfluous things. Or, in fine, I may quite easily persuade myself that if I found myself on an uninhabited island, without hope of ever again coming among men, and could conjure such a palace into existence by a mere wish, I should still not trouble to do so, so long as I had a hut there that was comfortable enough for me. All this may be admitted and approved; only it is not the point now at issue. All one wants to know is whether the mere representation of the object is to my liking, no matter how indifferent I may be to the real existence of the object of this representation.[57]

---

[54] Kant (1952) 75 §17.   [55] Ibid. 56 §8.

[56] Hutcheson (1994) 15; for Hutcheson and early British aesthetics see Kivy (2003). One way of reading Komar and Melamid's *Painting by Numbers* (Wypijewski (1997)) is as a deconstruction of the idea that beauty can be produced by following rules, though the multiple ironies are hard to pin down.

[57] Kant (1952) 42–3 §2.

If I call a poem beautiful because I hope to make money out of it, or because I am proud that it was written by a member of my family, or because I happen to share the politics of the writer, the judgement clearly would not be disinterested. For the judgement of taste I have to try to get my needs and wants out of the way.[58] There is not necessarily anything wrong with an interest (many interests are beneficial); one may legitimately share the moral disapprobation of Rousseau or the preferences of the Iroquois sachem. One may judge a knife 'good' and justly value it for that reason, but that is not an aesthetic matter.[59]

Moreover disinterest does not imply any sort of detachment—as Kant has it, 'A judgement upon an object of our delight may be wholly *disinterested* but withal very *interesting*'[60]—and is quite consistent with a passionate attention to the object. It is partly because a pure judgement of taste is disinterested that its maker readily assumes its universality. If I have removed the effects of needs and wants that are purely personal to myself, there seems no reason why someone else should disagree with me, or so Kant argues:

> For where any one is conscious that his delight in an object is with him independent of interest, it is inevitable that he should look on the object as one containing a ground of delight for all men. For, since the delight is not based on any inclination of the Subject... but the Subject feels himself completely *free* in respect of the liking he accords to the object, he can find as reason for his delight no personal conditions to which his own subjective self might alone be party. Hence he must regard it as resting on what he may presuppose in every other person; and therefore he must believe that he has reason for demanding a similar delight from every one.[61]

One has to ask anyone who denies the possibility of a disinterested judgement of taste—a view that seems very much a product of late capitalism[62] (to adopt for the moment the discourse of the ideology

---

[58] So Crawford (1974) 41.

[59] The Bauhaus, of course, attempted to elide the notions of beauty and utility. As a general theory of art, this is indefensible, but, like many other false theories, this one led to the making of many beautiful objects.

[60] Kant (1952) 43 n. 1 §2. There are thus some analogies between Kant's disinterest and Dr Johnson's account, in the Preface to his edition of Shakespeare, of the nature of dramatic allusion: the members of the audience are fully involved despite being fully 'in their senses' (Wimsatt (1969) 70–2).

[61] Kant (1952) 50–1 §6.

[62] For Adam Smith all the different self-interests combine harmoniously in a market; this is not the same as the cynical late-capitalist view that no-one acts *except* out of self-interest.

critic)—to explicate the claim being made.[63] Is the claim an empirical one that in practice aesthetic judgements are never disinterested (this would be the view of the French sociologist Pierre Bourdieu of whom more in a moment)? Or is it that disinterested judgement is untheorizable?—but, as we have just seen, Kant seems to have theorized it. Following Kant, one can explore the notion of the beautiful as being valuable 'for itself', not as a means towards a gratification, and of a response to the beautiful as being non-instrumental, a rejection of 'means-end' rationality (one might compare Newman's conception of the Idea of a University with its stress on 'knowledge for its own sake'). In his influential book *Distinction* Bourdieu argues that aesthetic preferences are mystifications of social exclusion and class hegemony.[64] He attempts to refute Kant with a barrage of statistics; there is something circular about Bourdieu's methods since he decides which works of art are middlebrow or whatever and then triumphantly claims that the results of his taxonomy of those works exactly fit his class analysis. But whether you accept his statistics or not is beside the point, for the fact (if fact it is) that some, even the great majority, of supposedly aesthetic judgements are occluded judgements of other kinds leaves the theory unaffected; Kant's point that there is a kind of knowledge which is neither rational nor ethical remains unrefuted. In effect Bourdieu wholly elides interest and judgement, so that nothing is left after the interest has been subtracted.[65] There is also an irritating snobbism rather evidently at work. As Thomas Crow well observes:

Museum exhibitions of uncompromisingly advanced and demanding art continue to draw large numbers of people. It would be an abuse of language to describe these audiences—swelled by curious and intrigued visitors of distinctly modest means—as an elite.... Such people evidently find sustenance within the boundaries of fine art that is available nowhere else, and they would doubtless be dismayed to find

---

[63] To say that there is no sphere where good and bad are not presupposed is like saying that there is a sphere where good and bad are absolute. In other words it is essentializing, and, in aesthetic terms, 'pre-Copernican'.

[64] Bourdieu (1984), especially introduction and part 1 and postscript. So Bourdieu writes 'Kant's analysis of the judgement of taste finds its real basis in a set of aesthetic principles which are the universalization of the dispositions associated with a particular social and economic condition' (p. 493). This view has become a new orthodoxy.

[65] For this view that the purity of judgement would leave *nothing* see B. H. Smith (1988) 64–9: 'the residue is nothing at all' (p. 69).

their adventurousness swept aside by academic commentators whose notion of 'the popular' is far more restricted and conventional.[66]

Kant anyway does not claim that our judgement of art should be aesthetic only; indeed, as we have seen, the implication of his analysis may be that a pure judgement of taste in the case of a work of literature would be difficult and not necessarily desirable. Certainly at times he argues that human beings and their artistic representation cannot elicit a pure judgement of taste. This is partly because our ideas about human beings are influenced by norms which are purely local and contingent, different for different races: 'For this reason a negro must necessarily (under these empirical conditions) have a different normal idea of the beauty of forms from what a white man has, and the Chinaman one different from the European.'[67] It follows from this that the supposedly exemplary beauty of Polyclitus' Doryphorus—the so-called 'canon'—is in fact culture-specific. This is a radical conclusion since the human body and its representation in Graeco-Roman art was regularly accorded central significance within eighteenth-century aesthetics (for example, in the writings of Winckelmann). To some extent Kant seems to vacillate between two positions. One is that only a very limited range of objects can evoke a pure judgement of taste (virtually all the works of art we admire most would evince only 'dependent' beauty). The other is that you can make a pure judgement of taste about any object at all, but only if you remove all interest ('In respect of an object with a definite internal end, a judgement of taste would only be pure where the person judging either has no concept of this end, or else makes abstraction from it in his judgement'[68]). But even if a pure judgement is rarely or even never achieved (and thus exists only as a thought experiment), that would hardly of itself abolish the category of the aesthetic.[69]

Politicizing critics are almost all suspicious of the aesthetic (aesthetics thus becomes the demonized Other of politics). The love of beauty seems to them at best an evasion or escape from the

---

[66] Crow (1996) p. vii; of course one is entitled to ask what sort of sustenance is being received.
[67] Kant (1952) 78 §17.
[68] Ibid. 74 §16.
[69] So Guillory (1993) 336: 'the *specificity* of aesthetic experience is not contingent upon its "purity"... It may well be impossible, for example, to experience "just sex", exclusive of the social meanings of sexual acts. But it would be incorrect on that account to deny the specificity of the sexual.'

problems of social reality, at worst a way of shoring up the status of the rich and powerful. Aesthetics is seen as hierarchical and complicit with political conservatism. It is claimed to be an essentializing, timeless discourse which denies historical contingency. From a Kantian perspective none of these charges seems persuasive. Aesthetics on this Kantian model does not involve any hierarchy, and is thus egalitarian, not elitist. No special knowledge is necessary in order to make 'the judgement of taste' (indeed it may get in the way). There are no canons in the aesthetic, since for comparative judgements an overarching logic would be required. Such judgements are always singular and about a particular object, not about ranking. As Benedetto Croce, the great Italian aesthetician put it: 'A short poem is aesthetically equal to a long poem; a tiny little picture or sketch, to an altar picture or a fresco. A letter may be no less artistic than a novel. Even a beautiful translation is as original as an original work!'[70] When Walter Pater, inventor and supreme exponent of 'aesthetic criticism' in England, distinguishes 'good' from 'great' art, he does so on non-aesthetic criteria: 'It is on the quality of the matter it informs or controls, its compass, its variety, its alliance to great ends, or the depth of the note of revolt, or the largeness of hope in it, that the greatness of literary art depends, as *The Divine Comedy*, *Paradise Lost*, *Les Misérables*, *The English Bible*, are great art.'[71] Hierarchy then belongs not with the aesthetic, but with history and pedagogy, with politics and ethics.[72]

Likewise it is not true that the aesthetic is *inherently* a conservative discourse, even if recently political conservatives like the philosopher Roger Scruton have tended to dominate it. Pure beauty is not instrumentalist, but it might be transformative, and is thus at least compatible with 'progressive' politics. There is a sense in which a utopia is created whenever a judgement of taste is made. Schiller regarded an aesthetic education[73] as a propaideutic towards a transfigured commmunity. Similar radical political stances were adopted

---

[70] Croce (1995) 46.   [71] From 'Style' in Pater (1973) 78.

[72] Nehamas (2002) 68 suggests that our desire to rank beautiful objects is an aspect of our selfishness: 'The passion for ranking and judging, the fervor for verdicts, which has for so long dominated our attitude toward the arts, and our lives, is simply another manifestation of selfishness.'

[73] Of course, in practice, as soon as the aesthetic becomes involved in education, the political/ethical is likely to be involved. But by 'aesthetic education' Schiller means an exposure to objects of beauty to be responded to non-instrumentally.

by William Morris and Oscar Wilde in England. Paul Crowther, following Theodor Adorno, draws attention to the 'socio-political explosiveness'[74] of the idea of aesthetic autonomy (instanced by the hostility such ideas provoked from the conventional). Eagleton himself recognizes the basis for a left-wing argument for the aesthetic, when he writes: 'The goal of Marxism is to restore to the body its plundered powers; but only with the supersession of private property will the senses be able to come into their own. If communism is necessary, it is because we are unable to feel, taste, smell and touch as fully as we might.'[75] I shall pursue these matters in much more detail in the third chapter.

In general politicizing critics try, in Manichaean vein, to force us to make a choice between politics and aesthetics, on the supposition—surely incorrect—that if a 'thing' has, or might have, a political function, it could not have an aesthetic function. At the very least it should be acknowledged that many philosophers, critics and theorists down the centuries have supposed that 'art' could be appreciated according to both categories. Indeed the claim that aesthetic judgements are occluded and mystified political judgements can easily be reversed. For example, the favourable ethical account of Manet's *Olympia*—as a politically radical and honest representation of a naked prostitute—might be portrayed as just such a mystified aesthetic judgement. Something similar might be said of the present enthusiasm for the poetry of Ovid and Lucan, or the writings of de Sade. The aesthetic appeal of the radical political life is, it may be, a compelling one, and academic radicals could be seen as modern dandies. As Geoffrey Galt Harpham puts it, 'If the aesthetic is always already ideological, so, too, is ideology always already aesthetic.'[76]

The issue of whether aesthetics is a timeless, universalizing (as opposed to historicizing) discourse is a complex one. On the one hand there is no progress or regress in the aesthetic (many people think that the *Iliad*, the earliest work of Western literature, is still

---

[74] Crowther (1996) 82.   [75] Eagleton (1990) 201.
[76] 'Aesthetics and Modernity' in Levine (1994) 138. Cf. Beckley (1998) p. xviii: 'It could be that every aesthetic choice is political. But it is equally possible that every political choice is ultimately aesthetic'. It is of course a commonplace of poststructuralism to point out that categories depend on occluded traces of their others. If everything was political, in the words of the old slogan, nothing would be.

the most beautiful). On the other the judgement of taste is always made from 'the present';[77] and Kant nowhere implies that such judgements stand for eternity. Works of art transcend their context in the sense that they continue to arouse a response in the receiver *now*. As Jeanette Winterson puts it: 'All art belongs to the same period. The Grecian drinking horn sits beside Picasso's bulls, Giotto is a friend of Cézanne.'[78] Michael Tanner suggests that this phenomenon might imply some continuity in human nature: 'It may even be one of the most powerful arguments for a persisting set of human characteristics that we are still so affected by works which were created in circumstances which have so little, superficially, in common with ours.'[79] Kant, as we have seen, is well aware of cultural differences. He is a universalist only in the more rigorous sense that in his view all human beings have the potential to make the judgement of taste.[80] After all we might be surprised to encounter someone who found *nothing* beautiful, and might regard this as a significant defect in his humanity.[81] Feminists often accuse Kant of

---

[77] Duncan Kennedy *per litteras* suggests that this aesthetic present is timeless. It is true that different discourses work with different temporalities, and that time in aesthetics differs from time in history. The aesthetic present is like the lived present of ordinary experience, the time of modernity—I see no reason why it should be taken as timeless or transcendent. See further pp. 28–9 below.

[78] Winterson (1995) 67.

[79] Tanner (1997) 31. One reply would be to argue that we are not really responding to 'the same' works: the Homer Plato read is not the same as ours, just as *The Last Supper* does not look the same as when it was first painted (see below).

[80] Thus Kant notes that while all have the faculty to judge something sublime, that faculty is not fully developed in the majority of cases (Kant (1952) 115–16 §29). To account for the communicability of aesthetic judgements Kant posits what he calls a *sensus communis*, a 'common sense'—but it is unclear whether such a common sense actually 'exists', or is simply a theoretical requirement (pp. 82–4 §§20–1). At the Cambridge conference 'Aesthetic Positions' (note 6) Thierry de Duve argued that Kant is more sceptical about the existence of a *sensus communis* than is generally recognized; rather we need the idea of a *sensus communis*, and therefore we posit its existence. Even if there were no *sensus communis* we ought to act as if it existed, granting to others the faculty of taste which we recognize in ourselves. This would mean that an unstated moral imperative would underlie Kant's aesthetic system, something I would want to resist. But clearly the agreement presupposed in the judgement of taste is a transcendental principle, and has nothing of the empirical about it.

[81] Cf. Mothersill (1984) 176 and 277: 'What makes the concept of beauty indispensable is the fact that there is a particular complex capacity, that of taking various items to be beautiful, which is central to our form of life. In support of this claim, I have argued that a description of a person who lacked that capacity would find its natural place, if anywhere, in the literature of psychopathology'.

basing his theory on the idea of a universal human subject who is male. It may be that, on specific occasions, men and women make the judgement of taste differently, but that would not necessarily affect the theory given that universal agreement is not demanded but imputed. There is comparatively little for the student of gender politics in the Kant of the Third Critique,[82] certainly in comparison with other eighteenth-century aestheticians, for many of whom (including the radical Hume) taste is closely involved with being a 'gentleman' and having received a particular sort of education. Kant's system is even-handed, and in a pure judgement of taste there would presumably be no place for the special experience of the embodied man or woman (gender would then become an 'interest', perfectly legitimate in itself but incompatible with the purity of the judgement).[83] To these issues about aesthetics and gender I shall return shortly.

In *Redeeming the Text* I emphasized the contingency and situatedness of all interpretations of art, something which might, at first glance, seem a long way from the universal claims of the Enlightenment. However, that view of reception and the Kantian judgement of taste have a crucial element in common—they both start from the present, from what is experienced now (the contingency of the reception theorist is thus like Kant's singularity). Indeed Kant's emphasis on subjectivity can be seen to entail an aesthetics of reception.[84] In his essay 'Notes on Leonardo da Vinci' Pater presents *The Last Supper*, which early started to fade and decay, as a symbol of the ebbing of faith:

Vasari pretends that the central head was never finished. Well; finished or unfinished, or owing part of its effect to a mellowing decay, this central head does but consummate the sentiment of the whole company—ghosts through which you see the wall, faint as the shadows of the leaves upon the wall on autumn afternoons; this figure is but the faintest, most spectral of them all. It is the image of what the history it symbolises has been more and more ever since, paler and paler as it recedes from us.[85]

---

[82] *Pace* Jane Kneller, 'Feminism and Kantian Aesthetics' in Kelly (1998), iii. 55–7 (Kneller has to import sexist statements made by Kant elsewhere into her reading of the Third Critique). See below.

[83] This seems to be the point of the comment on gender in Kant (1952) 73 §16.

[84] So Cheetham (2001) 8. Hammermeister (2002) 97 quotes Hegel's dictum that 'every work of art is a dialogue with whoever stands in front of it'.

[85] This is the text as it appeared in *Fortnightly Review*, NS 6, November 1869, 494–508, p. 505. Pater cautiously removed the last sentence from the version in *The Renaissance*.

This response would be anathema to the historicist, but is perfectly acceptable both to the reception theorist and to the aesthetic critic. My own 'aesthetic turn' might then be seen as a further move in my war against the determination of classicists to ground their discipline in 'history'—I would like to see 'history' giving place to 'reception', and historical to aesthetic criticism. This is not to argue for a two-dimensional presentism. The time of the aesthetic, far from ignoring the past, is what Walter Benjamin calls *Jetztzeit*, 'not homogeneous, empty time, but time filled by the presence of the now'.[86]

One of Kant's most radical moves is the severing from morality of the judgement of taste. Aesthetic judgement is an activity of the mind, part of the way that human beings experience the world, and in that sense a kind of knowledge, but it is not a moral form of knowing. For many such a claim is an unsettling one, since the desire to link Beauty and Goodness is deeply rooted within Western civilization (as often in the discussions of ancient philosophers). Many later aestheticians, even those in the Kantian tradition, have proved recidivist on this issue. Kant himself makes some concession to convention by describing the beautiful as a symbol of morality,[87] a claim that is quite hard to understand. It perhaps has something to do with the way that, within Kant's larger system, aesthetic judgement mediates between the practical and the intellectual.[88] The aesthetic imagination helps us to comprehend abstractions and things we cannot see. In *On Beauty and Being Just*, Elaine Scarry's beautiful book on beauty, two arguments are advanced to link the ethical and the aesthetic: first, that both involve 'proportionality' (as we have seen, Kant would reject this), and secondly that aesthetic response requires an attentiveness to the beautiful object

---

Ironically the painting has now been 'restored' to nearer its supposed original state. Paintings obviously change in colour relations over time, and poems change too during the course of their reception history. Thus aesthetic judgements require constant revision—in this case Pater's response is no longer open to us, at least not directly (though our judgements may be informed by a work's reception history). For a full discussion of Pater's account of *The Last Supper* see C. Williams (1989) 94–102.

[86] Benjamin (1992) 252–3 (from *Theses on the Philosophy of History*).

[87] Kant (1952) 221.

[88] We may say, with Paul Guyer (in Kelly (1998) iii. 30), that 'the beautiful can serve as a symbol of the morally good because of analogies between the freedom of the imagination inherent in the experience of beauty and the freedom of the will that is the essence of morality, but which can never be directly experienced'.

that causes a radical decentring of the self (this seems like a stronger version of Kantian disinterestedness). Seductive though this second suggestion may be, we may prefer to look for some distinctive virtue in the aesthetic. For me that virtue resides precisely in its freedom from concepts. Within the aesthetic good and bad are not predetermined. The aesthetic could thus be described as the sphere of the revolutionary and of pure modernity: every judgement of taste is a fresh event; every new art object presents an unpredictable and unpredicted opportunity for beauty.[89] Kant himself talks about a free play of imagination and understanding within the judgement of taste.[90] Scarry gives an illuminating gloss on what this might mean in practice: 'what is beautiful prompts the mind to move chronologically back in the search for precedents and parallels, to move forward into new acts of creation, to move conceptually over, to bring things into relation, and does all this with a kind of urgency as though one's life depended on it.'[91] This free play is *inter alia* a free play over time. As Scarry puts it:

> The material world constrains us, often with great beneficence, to see each person and thing in its time and place, its historical context. But mental life doesn't so constrain us. It is porous, open to the air and light, swings forward while swaying back, scatters its stripes in all directions, and delights to find itself beached beside something invented only that morning or instead standing beside an altar from three millennia ago.

That is one precise sense in which the judgement of taste involves an experience of temporal transcendence.

II

The 'Analytic of the Beautiful' is concerned with beauty, not with art. The arts feature rather more prominently in the much less tightly organized remainder of the 'Critique of Aesthetic Judgement'. But even in this section there is no sustained analysis of the question 'what is art?' (a conceptual, not an aesthetic matter, of course). In his discussion of the division of the 'fine' (beautiful) arts, Kant sets out his taxonomy: poetry, drama, oratory, sculpture,

---

[89] For some of the consequences of the radical modernity of the aesthetic, in relation to music, see Rosen (1994) ch. 1.
[90] Kant (1952) 58 §9.   [91] Scarry (1999) 30. The subsequent quotation is from p. 48.

architecture, painting, landscape gardening, music. Most contemporary critics would argue that the definition of the arts is a contingent and historical matter,[92] not one of transhistorical essences (though in practice Platonism, like nature according to Horace, is apt to run back, however much you drive it out with a pitchfork). As a result of a famous essay by Paul Oskar Kristeller 'The Modern System of the Arts', it has become a commonplace to say that the present organization of the arts was not formed until the eighteenth century, partly under the influence of the Abbé Batteux's celebrated treatise *Les Beaux Arts Réduits à un Même Principe* first published in 1746. 'The various arts', writes Kristeller, 'are certainly as old as human civilization, but the manner in which we are accustomed to group them and to assign them a place in our scheme of life and of culture is comparatively recent'[93] (indeed there have been further subsequent changes, not least the introduction of new media such as photography and film; many would not share Kant's view that landscape gardening is a fine art, while the status of the novel as art has risen substantially since the eighteenth century). Others would go further and argue that the first part of Kristeller's sentence reifies the various arts and ideas of art and fails to acknowledge their radical cultural specificity.[94]

Certainly it is widely agreed that the ancients had nothing like our present system. In Kristeller's words, 'We have to admit the conclusion, distasteful to many historians of aesthetics but grudgingly admitted by most of them, that ancient writers and thinkers, though confronted with excellent works of art and quite susceptible to their charm, were neither able nor eager to detach the aesthetic quality of these works of art from their intellectual, moral, religious and practical function or content, or to use such an aesthetic quality as a standard for grouping the fine arts together or for making them

---

[92] So Mortensen (1997), with full bibliography. Compare Paul Veyne (quoted Kennedy (1993) 98): 'there is no essence of art, just an infinity of styles. Every aesthetic has merit, and excludes and misjudges all others.'

[93] Kristeller in Feagin and Maynard (1997) 101. Kristeller's essay was first published in two parts in the *Journal of the History of Ideas*, 12 (1951) 496–527 and 13 (1952) 17–46. See Halliwell (2002) 7–9 for the view that Kristeller's thesis is historically simplifying.

[94] See, for example, the disputes over the exhibition *'Primitivism' in Twentieth-Century Art: Affinity of the Tribal and the Modern*, held at the Museum of Modern Art in New York in 1984, between those who saw the tribal objects as art and those who did not (Beckley (1998) pt. 2, 'Ownership').

the subject of a comprehensive philosophical interpretation.'[95] Classicists of a historicizing bent have taken up such claims with enthusiasm. For Yun Lee Too, as we have already seen, the body of works traditionally grouped together under the rubric 'ancient literary criticism' should be understood not as contributions to aesthetics or criticism of literature as these terms are commonly understood today but rather as political interventions. The aim was to distinguish texts that were acceptable from those which were not, acceptability being defined in terms of the good of the elite citizen body. Too starts off her discussion with an ingenious allegorization of the myth of Typhon from Hesiod's *Theogony*: Typhon with his myriad voices is figured as the dangerous text that requires censorship, Zeus as the critic who controls what may be said, by imposing exclusions and inclusions. For Simon Goldhill the use of the word 'literature' in connection with the Greeks or Romans is anachronistic, since no such term existed in antiquity. We are urged to jettison it along with 'Art' and 'the other shibboleths of Romantic aesthetics': 'That "literature" is not a category in the ancient world is clear enough.'[96] As with all such tough-minded historical claims, this one depends on a strategy of constructing difference and rupture rather than continuity and sameness (all history, as its condition of possibility, depends on a combination of sameness and difference, for if the past were wholly other, how could we know anything about it, or even know that this was so?). If I were constructing a different sort of narrative from Goldhill's, I could point out that in the *Poetics* Aristotle's concern is wholly with works like Homer's epics and the tragedies of Sophocles and Euripides, so that, even if he did not have a concept of literature, all the texts he discusses fall easily into our category (perhaps then poetics is the Greek for literature). Similarly for the elder Pliny the artistry of a work of art is more valuable than the material from which it is made (*Natural History* 34. 5, 35. 50) which suggests he had something like our concept of fine art, while in practice his detailed categories for such works are

[95] Feagin and Maynard (1997) 94–5.
[96] Goldhill (1999) 57. Goldhill begins his essay with the ringing assertion that '"Literature" began, as Auden might have put it, in 1823'. Like Larkin's (in)famous claim that sexual intercourse began in 1963, which Goldhill presumably echoes, this is fine as paradox or provocation but bad as 'history'. Goldhill's formulation anyway oddly assumes the status of the category of literature.

quite 'like' ours.[97] After all it is noteworthy that both Too and Goldhill are happy to use words like 'elites' about both antiquity and the modern world, evidently without feeling that they are guilty of reifying the term into a transcendental and ahistorical category. All this depends on the issue of the translatability of cultures, on what we accept as a valid translation in our accounts of the past. The argument that some terms are untranslatable is hard to get off the ground since to claim, for example, that *ars* does not mean the same as 'art' implies that you have already translated it. I would prefer to say that, given the differences both between words and within words, translation of anything is always and never possible—any translation will have elements of difference from and similarity to what is being translated.

Kant makes two important presumptions about fine art. The first is that art involves an element of design, of human intentionality. Otherwise it would not be art but nature (this would be true even of a *trouvaille*, since such an object has to be selected by a human consciousness, often because it resembles an artefact). The second is that the artist produces (and presumably designs to produce) something that is beautiful. To explain how this is possible and consistent with his theory of beauty Kant introduces the notion of genius: '*Fine art is the art of genius*'[98] (I shall return to the reasons for this shortly). Kant here takes a concept that one can trace back to ancient notions of inspiration, and gives it his own special inflection (there are a number of occasions when he prefers to retain a word in common usage and give it a specially defined sense, rather than invent a new 'jargon' term, something that, however, easily gives rise to misunderstanding). Kant has come under considerable fire from feminists and others for his theory of genius which has been attacked as both elitist (since few can be geniuses) and misogynistic (since those historically identified as geniuses have almost always been biologically male, and the word is indelibly tainted with sexism). Indeed the whole discourse of the aesthetic is seen as undesirably saturated with gendered language (though the same is equally true of most other discourses).[99] Thus aesthetics as a whole

---

[97] See Barkan (1999) 70–80.

[98] Kant (1952) 168 §46 (chapter heading). For the history of the word genius see the essays in Murray (1989); and cf. Kris and Kurz (1979) on the image of the artist.

[99] See e.g. Battersby (1989); Brand and Korsmeyer (1995); Isobel Armstrong (2000); Freeland (2001) ch. 5; Steiner (2001).

is feminine, and excluded from the masculine world of significant political action; the beautiful is associated with women, whereas the sublime is associated with men; form and content often become another gendered pair; woman becomes the most characteristic instance of the beautiful, and women associated with self-beautification and decoration. The emphasis on the lone genius also downplays the collaborative efforts involved in art-making (this is one justification of the current preoccupation with intertextuality).

It should not surprise anyone that, in her finely polemical study *Gender and Genius*, Christine Battersby has no difficulty in demonstrating the prevailing depths of misogyny evinced by the Western tradition in relation to the concept of genius. Gerard Manley Hopkins, writing to a friend in 1886, claimed that 'masterly execution' is 'a kind of male gift, and especially marks off men from women, the begetting of one's thoughts on paper, on verse, or whatever the matter is', concluding 'The male quality is the creative gift.'[100] In his book of 1903 translated into English as *Sex and Character*, the Austrian Otto Weininger is equally offensive: 'The man of genius possesses, like everything else, the complete female in himself; but woman herself is only a part of the Universe, and the part never can be the whole; femaleness can never include genius.'[101] Madame de Staël may have introduced a female genius as protagonist of her novel *Corinne, or Italy* (1807), but even Corinne has in the event to choose between art and love, with foreseeably fatal results.[102] All this is as depressing as it is predictable.[103] In 1989 the Guerilla Girls posted an advertisement in New York, with the legend 'Do women have to be naked to get into the Met. Museum? Less than 5% of the artists in the Modern Art Sections are women, but 85% of the nudes are female.'[104] And doubtless Kant shared many of the 'commonsense' judgements of his time about men and women. In the largely empirical *Observations on the Feeling of the Beautiful and Sublime* (1764) Kant, like Edmund Burke in his *Philosophical Inquiry into the Origin of our*

---

[100] Battersby (1989) 38. [101] Ibid. 113. [102] Ibid. 99–100.
[103] There were, however, other views. For example, both Dante Gabriel Rossetti and Ruskin thought that Elizabeth Siddall, despite her lack of craft skill, displayed all the marks of genius. Further exceptions are noted by Battersby herself ((1989) 83). Above all Sappho was regarded as the very type of the inspired artist throughout antiquity, though Horace does call her *mascula Sappho* (*Epistle* 1. 19. 28).
[104] Reproduced in Freeland (2001) 124.

Ideas of the Sublime and the Beautiful (1757) by which he may have been influenced, makes extensive use of gendered language. For example, he writes, 'The fair sex has just as much understanding as the male, but it is a *beautiful understanding*, whereas ours should be a *deep understanding*, an expression that signifies identity with the sublime.'[105] Some of his observations have a distinctly sexist cast: 'A woman who has a head full of Greek, like Mme Dacier, or carries on fundamental controversies about mechanics...might as well even have a beard.'[106] Likewise much that today passes as 'common sense' will be the object of derision in after times. But when Kant, following his earlier 'dogmatic slumbers', turned to his transcendental method for the three Critiques, he thought at a level of abstraction that enabled him to pass beyond such empirical niceties.

Battersby's uncompromising approach to the history of genius and its connection with gender was, and still is, entirely justified in terms of current politics; but it is possible to give a more complicated, and less austere, account of the matter, which could also be liberating. Peter Kivy argues that there are two models for genius, both connected to antiquity: the one derives from Plato,[107] and presents the artist as the wholly passive recipient of the divine (and in some versions therefore comparable to a child), of which the type for Kivy is Mozart; the other derives from Longinus, and makes the artist with his natural talent more active and heroic (and hence more like God in some versions), of which the type is Beethoven.[108] The first model clearly could be gendered female, the second male.[109] In practice the two types can often blur or coalesce.

---

[105] Kant (1960) 78.

[106] Ibid. 78. Similarly in section four Kant employs racial discourses: 'Of the peoples of our part of the world, in my opinion those who distinguish themselves among all others by the feeling for the beautiful are the Italians and the French, but by the feeling of the sublime, the Germans, English, and Spanish' (p. 97).

[107] See in particular the *Ion*: 'a poet is a light, winged, holy creature, and cannot compose until he is possessed and out of his mind, and his reason is no longer in him' (Russell and Winterbottom (1972) 43). Plato of course wishes to show that poets have no knowledge or art (*technē*); it follows that it is not poets but philosophers who must explain how we should live and justify those explanations.

[108] Kivy (2001) 21 ('So antiquity gave us two notions of creative genius in the arts: the genius of the possessed and the genius of the possessor; the passive genius, possessed by the God, and the active genius, a God himself...; a genius to which creation happens and a genius who makes creation happen.') and *passim*.

[109] Kivy (2001) 221.

Moreover in Goethe, Coleridge, and many others the poet is figured as an androgyne, which complicates the issue of gender.[110] One may recall too that in antiquity it is often a female deity, the Muse, who is said to inspire the artist. The gendering of genius is certainly not a straightforward matter.

A good example of this complexity is *Ode* 3. 25 where Horace, in excitedly dithyrambic mode, describes his experience of inspiration:

> Quo me, Bacche, rapis tui
> plenum? quae nemora aut quos agor in specus
>   velox mente nova? quibus
> antris egregii Caesaris audiar
>
>   aeternum meditans decus   5
> stellis inserere et consilio Iovis?
>   dicam insigne, recens, adhuc
> indictum ore alio. non secus in iugis
>
>   exsomnis stupet Euhias
> Hebrum prospiciens et nive candidam   10
>   Thracen ac pede barbaro
> lustratam Rhodopen, ut mihi devio
>
>   ripas et vacuum nemus
> mirari libet. o Naiadum potens
>   Baccharumque valentium   15
> proceras manibus vertere fraxinos,
>
>   nil parvum aut humili modo,
> nil mortale loquar. dulce periculum est,
>   o Lenaee, sequi deum
> cingentem viridi tempora pampino.   20

Where, Bacchus, are you snatching me, who am possessed by you? Into what woods or caverns am I driven swiftly with a new mind? In what caves shall I be heard practising to set Caesar's eternal glory into the stars and Jupiter's council? I shall tell something outstanding, fresh, not spoken by other mouth. Just as on the mountain ridges a wakeful Maenad is amazed as she looks out over the [river] Hebrus and Thrace white with snow, and [Mount] Rhodope traversed by wild feet, so as I wander it is my pleasure to marvel at the banks and empty grove. O powerful over the Naiads and the Bacchants strong at overturning tall ash-trees with their hands, I shall say nothing small or of lowly mode, nothing mortal. Sweet is the danger, o Bacchus, to follow the god wreathing his temples with green vine-tendrils.

---

[110] See MacLeod (1998).

In one sense this ode is about self-empowerment, always a prime concern of the Roman elite male. Horace declares and enacts his ability to create sublime and original poetry (*recens, indictum ore alio, nil parvum aut humili modo*). But at the same time he is feminized by losing his self-control; like Ion in Plato's dialogue, he is outside himself. So too he is penetrated and made pregnant by the god (*rapis, plenum*).[111] A hauntingly visionary image (which suggests that Horace has partly been inspired by reading Euripides' *Bacchae*) figures him as a female worshipper of Bacchus, alone and at night, amazed at the snow-clad landscape of Thrace. *Nil admirari*, 'to marvel at nothing', Horace was to assure Numicius (*Epistle* 1. 6. 1–2), is the best course to keep one's happiness, but in this poem astonishment is at the heart of an inspirational Bacchic poetics. Horace's experience pre-echoes one of Kant's descriptions of the sublime: 'The *astonishment* amounting almost to terror, the awe and thrill of devout feeling, that takes hold of one when gazing upon the prospect of mountains ascending to heaven, deep ravines and torrents raging there, deep-shadowed solitudes that invite to brooding melancholy...'.[112] David West thinks that Horace puts an ironic gap between the Maenad and himself by softening the language he uses about himself (*mirari* contrasted with *stupet*, *devio* with *pede barbaro lustratam*, *vacuum* with *nive candidam*).[113] This reading seems to me out of keeping with the fiery onrush of the poem (however little that suits our comfortable and comforting image of Horace), and to treat the relationship of tenor and vehicle in the operation of the simile as a kind of cryptogram. But, whatever view we take of the matter, this remarkable poem suggests that poetic inspiration cuts across conventional gender lines in thought-provoking ways.

Thus one might wish to give a rather more positive account of the relationship between aesthetics and gender than Battersby's. The association of women, femininity, sociability, beauty, and the aesthetic does not have to be seen as a necessarily negative one. The

---

[111] See D. Fowler (2002) 149, 150–1, 159: inspired poets 'are filled with strength to tackle the most elevated or repugnant of subjects, and that strength is figured as masculine semen-like force that through the green fuse drives the flower of their verse. At the same time, however, they lose that control of the self which is essential to ancient masculinity and the same empowering flow of force places them in the female subject position, penetrated and overborne.'

[112] Kant (1952) 120–1 §29.   [113] West (2002) 209–10.

account by the eighteenth-century aesthetician Lord Shaftesbury of the 'harmonizing' effects of the feminine may strike us as somewhat quaint in expression but it offered a new 'feminized' model for human character and behaviour: 'I have often observed that this enchanting turn in conversation prevails only in those of our own sex who have conversed much with the more sensible part of the other... for let a man's erudition be ever so profound, his fancy lively and judgement solid, this grace, which is not to be described, will be wanting, if his soul has not been refined and his tongue attuned to this sweet melody by an habitual intercourse with these fair preceptors.'[114] Wendy Steiner remarks that 'the problem is how to imagine female beauty, in art or outside it, without invoking stories of dominance, victimization, and false consciousness',[115] and she later quotes some lines of Dutch feminist poet and painter Marlene Dumas:

> (They say) Art no longer produces Beauty.
> She produces meaning
>   But
> (I say) One cannot paint a picture of
> or make an image of a woman
> and not deal with the concept of beauty.[116]

One might reverse the usual argument and say that hostility to the aesthetic can be construed as misogynistic ('The aesthetic is a woman. That is the second thing wrong with it.'[117]). One of the least attractive features of Modernism is its macho tendency to gender art as masculine.[118] In one of his manifestos the Italian futurist and opponent of feminism, F. T. Marinetti, declared, with characteristic phallocentrism, that a roaring motorcar was more beautiful than the 'Winged Victory of Samothrace'.[119] There is of course no reason why men and women should not both be found beautiful. The founder of modern art history, J. J. Winckelmann, enthused with sensitive attention over the beauty of ancient nudes of both sexes, though he thought the naked male

---

[114] Quoted by Kramnick (1998) 69 from *Characteristics of Men, Manners, Opinions, Times* etc. (1711).
[115] Steiner (2001) p. xviii.
[116] Steiner (2001) 216.
[117] Isobel Armstrong (2000) 31 (the first thing wrong with it is that it is ideology).
[118] Beckley (1998) 1.   [119] Steiner (2001) 38.

body the paradigm of beauty[120] (as we have seen, the traditional paradigmatic beauty of the human body is something Kant specifically rejects as too bound up with local cultural prejudices). As for genius, despite all the disadvantages of their situation, there is no shortage of women, either now or in the past, who can be said to have possessed it. One of the poets whom Longinus most conspicuously praises for sublimity is Sappho, regularly deified in antiquity as 'the tenth Muse'. Of a famous poem (fragment 31) he writes:

> Do you not admire the way in which she brings everything together—mind and body, hearing and tongue, eyes and skin? She seems to have lost them all, and to be looking for them as though they were external to her. She is cold and hot, mad and sane, frightened and near death, all by turns. The result is that we see in her not a single emotion, but a complex of emotions. Lovers experience all this; Sappho's excellence, as I have said, lies in her adoption and combination of the most striking details.[121]

The sublime has conventionally been gendered male, yet one of Longinus' prime instances of sublimity is by a female poet. Hers is an instance of Coleridge's 'esemplastic power', that power which combines ideas together into a new whole.

In the Third Critique Kant largely avoids the gendered language and gendered assumptions so prevalent in eighteenth-century aesthetics (for example, in Burke, Lessing, and Winckelmann and indeed his own earlier writings on the subject). He uses the idea of genius to solve a particular problem in his aesthetic system, to theorize a gap. As we have seen, Kant maintains that there are no rules for beauty or concepts under which objects can be subsumed as beautiful (if there were, the judgement of taste would be logical, not aesthetic). When we pronounce a flower or a landscape beautiful, we do so because of a pleasurable, lively, and fruitful free play of our mental faculties; the natural object satisfies us but in a way that does not seem purely random but is free from specific determination ('purposiveness without a purpose', the special form

---

[120] 'A beautiful male body is the precondition for valuing great art, and...only men stirred by male comeliness possess the true sense of beauty' (cited Steiner (2001) 22). Steiner's book ends with an eloquent peroration (p. 240) in which she calls for 'a time when beauty, pleasure, and freedom again become the domain of aesthetic experience', one in which 'a female subject may symbolize it [beauty], but so may one who is male'. For art, beauty, and gender see also Hickey (1993) ch. 3.

[121] Russell and Winterbottom (1972) 472.

of finality of the beautiful[122]). We have the experience of making sense of the object, but not by wrapping a theory round it. But, unlike nature (at least in our estimation of it), art is clearly not outside determination, since the artist both plans the work and employs rule-bound procedures of making. What we might call the academic is normally needed to organize the production of the artwork.[123] The beautiful work of art thus might appear strictly unmakeable, because of this need that it avoid determinate planfulness (in this sense Kant might be said to have theorized in advance the rationale for such modern artistic practices as automatic composition or *trouvaille*).[124] Successful art needs to be like nature: 'art can only be termed beautiful, where we are conscious of its being art, while yet it has the appearance of nature.'[125]

It is the idea of genius that resolves this aporia. Genius, 'the innate mental aptitude ... through which nature gives the rule to art',[126] is that in an artist which makes it possible for him—or her—to make something new and beautiful, without the use of a concept. Hence Kant's stress, in his account of art, on originality and on the orientation of the artist towards an unknown future. This orientation towards the future is recognized in a semi-humorous scene in Joseph von Eichendorff's romantic, picaresque novella *Life of a Good-for-nothing* (1826). A painter discourses on the discomforts of genius:

We geniuses—for I am one also—care as little for the world as the world cares for us. In our seven-league boots—which in the near future prodigies such as ourselves will be born with—we stride unceremoniously on into eternity. Oh, what a very pitiable, uncomfortable position we are in, with one leg in the future and its

---

[122] In this connection Manning (2001) 212 illuminatingly quotes the final section of Wallace Stevens's *Notes towards a Supreme Fiction*: '... stop just short, | Red robin, stop in your preludes, practicing | Mere repetitions. These things at least comprise | An occupation, an exercise, a work, | A thing final in itself and, therefore, good: | One of the vast repetitions final in | Themselves and, therefore, good, the going round | And round and round, the merely going round, | Until merely going round is a final good, | The way wine comes at a table in a wood. | And we enjoy like men, the way a leaf | Above the table spins its constant spin, | So that we look at it with pleasure, look | At it spinning its eccentric measure.'

[123] Kant (1952) 171 §47: 'there is ... no fine art in which something mechanical, capable of being at once comprehended and followed in obedience to rules, and consequently something academic (*Schulgerechtes*) does not constitute the essential condition of the art.' Cf. Prettejohn (2000) 46–8.

[124] I borrow this formulation from Prettejohn (forthcoming).

[125] Kant (1952) 167 §45.   [126] Ibid. 168 §46.

hope of a new dawn and new life, and with the other leg still in the middle of Rome in the Piazza del Popolo where the children of this world seize the opportunity to hitch their wagons to our star and hang onto our boots until they almost pull our legs out of them.[127]

Kant has been criticized for refusing to assign genius to great scientists and others, but the reason for this determination to restrict the term in his special sense to makers of beautiful art is entirely cogent and has nothing at all to do with the relative value of the arts on the one hand and the sciences (i.e. all forms of conceptual knowledge) on the other:

> all that *Newton* has set forth in his immortal work on the Principles of Natural Philosophy may well be learned, however great a mind it took to find it all out, but we cannot learn to write in a true poetic vein, no matter how complete all the precepts of the poetic art may be, or however excellent its models. The reason is that all the steps that Newton had to take from the first elements of geometry to his greatest and most profound discoveries were such as he could make intuitively evident and plain to follow, not only for himself but for every one else. On the other hand no *Homer* or *Wieland* can show how his ideas, so rich at once in fancy and in thought, enter and assemble themselves in his brain, for the good reason that he does not himself know, and so cannot teach others. In matters of science, therefore, the greatest inventor differs only in degree from the most laborious imitator and apprentice, whereas he differs specifically from one endowed by nature for fine art. No disparagement, however, of those great men ... is involved in this comparison of them with those who on the score of their talent for fine art are the elect of nature. The talent for science is formed for the continued advances of greater perfection in knowledge.... Hence scientists can boast a ground of considerable superiority over those who merit the honour of being called geniuses, since genius reaches a point at which art must make a halt....[128]

The difference between the *Iliad* and Newton's *Principles* is the difference between non-conceptual and conceptual discovery. In vulgar parlance we may call Einstein a genius, but his work does not require genius in this rigorous Kantian sense. One sign of this difference is that, where there can be progress in science, there is none in art.

At one point Kant says specifically that genius is not widely distributed: 'the genius is one of nature's elect—a type that must be regarded as but a rare phenomenon.'[129] He may well also have

---

[127] von Eichendorff (2002) 77–8. [128] Kant (1952) 169–70 §47.
[129] Ibid. 181 §49.

believed, on empirical grounds, that genius was more frequently found in men than in women (though he nowhere says so in the Third Critique). But the structure of his argument does not of itself point to these conclusions. Kant also observes that genius in the making of art corresponds to taste in its reception; both genius and taste involve the free play of imagination and understanding (constituting what in the case of the artist Kant calls 'aesthetic ideas'). Longinus had already noted the way that the receiver of sublime art has a kind of mediated experience of creativity: 'Filled with joy and pride, we come to believe we have created what we have only heard.'[130] In practice a great deal of genius may be wasted on the desert air, as has indeed demonstrably been the case with women and other disadvantaged groups (either because, for social reasons, they were unable to put their genius to use, or because their efforts went unrecognized[131]). But if we all have the capacity to make the judgement of taste, why should we not all also, potentially at least, be gifted with genius? Language use might provide us with an analogy. Many modern versions of linguistics, for example pragmatics, recognize that no speech act is simply a mechanical application of rules (even if rules are always involved), but is always potentially a fresh event, with an orientation towards the future. The word is always worlded, and language always on the move, its meaning never fully predetermined.[132] As Andrew Bowie puts it, 'The individuality that Kant reserved for the genius in art . . . is thus potentially carried over into all areas of linguistic usage and thus into all areas of human activity.'[133] Of course some language uses are much more creative than others, but it does not follow that the potential for such creativity is necessarily restricted to the few. This, however, is no reason for not being grateful when we are presented with the results of genius, which, under present social conditions, are likely to be much rarer than they might be.

[130] Russell and Winterbottom (1972) 467. Winckelmann's responses to his favourite ancient sculptures are often of this kind.
[131] Obviously one invaluable feminist project is the attempt to rediscover neglected artworks made by women. Other potential artworks, of course, were never made because of unsympathetic social conditions.
[132] See Harris (2002): 'Nor do words have meanings whose stability is guaranteed by the internal organization of the system of signs to which they belong culturally... their interpretation is subject to contextual factors that cannot be identified in advance and, in retrospect, are not replicable.' Harris terms this view 'integrationism'.
[133] Bowie (1990) 161.

Kant's account of genius is also consistent with the testimony of a great many artists, both women and men. George Eliot told a friend 'that in all that she considered her best writing, there was a "not herself" which took possession of her, and that she felt her own personality to be merely the instrument through which this spirit, as it were, was acting'.[134] Dan Jacobson in one of his novels has a character, himself a novelist, describe the transition from what Kant called the academic to the operations of genius:

> A fortnight ago he'd felt like a man with a flat tire and a pump in his hand; he had simply been pumping away, almost mechanically. But now there was nothing mechanical about what he was doing: he had to be alert, cautious, obedient to the demands that he could feel the work wanted to make of him.... Once escaped from oneself, one submitted oneself to an impersonal will. And it didn't matter that the will had originated in oneself.[135]

Such accounts often convey a sense of something arriving that the artist could not have predicted or predetermined. In his essay 'Belief and Creativity' William Golding claims that, when he creates, he does not merely rearrange elements already existing in his imagination, but that during the course of composition 'the new thing' comes, mysteriously, into his awareness:

> There is room in the writer's awareness for more than the simulacrum of abundance however that abundance may seem to blaze. Somewhere—shall we say metaphorically?—somewhere in the shadows at the edge of the area stands a creature, an assessor, a judge, a broken-off fragment of the total personality who surveys the interior scene with a desperate calm and is aware how he wishes to proceed. He is all the time controlling things, admonishing them. He is a divided creature. Then it may be, if he has—what? Luck? Grace? Lightning? the new thing appears from nowhere. We will stick to the spatial metaphor that I have used because here it is at the very centre. The new thing appears from a point in the area of his awareness, from a position without magnitude, which is of course quite impossible. Yet this is the occasional operation of creativity.[136]

This mass of testimony cannot, I think, simply be ignored, or dismissed as merely an attempt at self-validation, or mystification (our current word for things we cannot wholly master). Stephen Medcalf observes how prayer, in the religious sphere, can be

---

[134] Cited T. Clark (1997) 5; I am indebted to Clark for this whole section.
[135] Cited Lansdown (2001) 37.   [136] Golding (1982) 196.

conceptualized as something like inspiration in the secular, and he quotes C. S. Lewis's poem 'Prayer':[137]

> They tell me, Lord, that when I seem
>   To be in speech with you,
> Since but one voice is heard, it's all a dream,
>   One talker aping two.
>
> Sometimes it is, yet not as they
>   Conceive it. Rather, I
> Seek in myself the things I hoped to say,
>   But lo! my wells are dry.
>
> Then, seeing me empty, you forsake
>   The listener's role and through
> My dumb lips breathe and into utterance wake
>   The thoughts I never knew.
>
> And thus you neither need reply
>   Nor can; thus, while we seem
> Two talkers, thou art one forever, and I
>   No dreamer, but thy dream.

The notion of genius, then, may seem readily comprehensible to the religious temperament. So Milton in *Paradise Lost* moves easily from invoking the Muse to prayer to the Spirit.[138] But it may make sense too for a secular postmodernism, prepared to acknowledge a poetic text as 'an event that must exceed definition', something that exists 'as a practice of radical contradiction resistant to philosophical conceptualization'. A view like this allows for 'an inspirational poetic' such as Derrida advances in his essay 'Che cos'è la poesia?' as he works with the ancient trope of poetry as dictation.[139] The alternative might be to suppose a grimly determinate world in which Golding's 'new thing' can never appear.

---

[137] For the poem see Hooper (1994) 136–7; it first appeared, with some differences of wording, in *Letters to Malcolm* (Lewis (1964) 290–1), and that is the version I give here.

[138] For the connection of inspiration with both the Spirit and the Son see Sherry (2002); for the theology of beauty see Grace M. Jantzen, 'On Changing the Imaginary', in Ward (2001) 280–93.

[139] T. Clark (1997) ch. 11 'Dictation by Heart' (the quotations are from pp. 260, 261, 266). For Derrida's text in French and English translation see Kamuf (1991) 221–37. The psychoanalytic discourse of the unconscious provides another way of theorizing genius today.

III

What kind of criticism might a Kantian seek to promote? This, in relation to a possible future for writing about Latin poetry, will be the subject of my final chapter; but a few preliminary thoughts may be useful at the outset. For Kant himself the job of the critic is not 'one of exhibiting the determining ground of aesthetic judgements of this kind in a universally applicable formula', since this is impossible, rather it is 'the investigation of the faculties of cognition and their function in these judgements, and the illustration, by the analysis of examples, of their mutual subjective finality'[140], what he elsewhere calls their purposiveness without a purpose. Exemplary lists of objects of aesthetic pleasure occur in Walter Pater, though very far from constituting anything one could call an orthodox canon: for the aesthetic critic 'the picture, the landscape, the engaging personality in life or in a book, *La Gioconda*, the hills of Carrara, Pico of Mirandola, are valuable for their virtues, as we say, in speaking of a herb, a wine, a gem; for the property each has of affecting one with a special, a unique, impression of pleasure.'[141] Matthew Arnold, in his essay 'The Study of Poetry' proposes his theory of touchstones of poetic excellence:

Indeed there can be no more useful help for discovering what poetry belongs to the class of the truly excellent, and can therefore do us most good, than to have always in one's mind lines and expressions of the great masters, and to apply them as touchstones to other poetry. Of course we are not to require this other poetry to resemble them; it may be very dissimilar. But if we have any tact we shall find them ... an infallible touchstone for detecting the presence or absence of high poetic quality, and also the degree of this quality, in all other poetry which we may place beside them. Short passages, even single lines, will serve our turn quite sufficiently. Take the two lines I have just quoted from Homer, the poet's comment on Helen's mention of her brothers;—or take his

> *a deilō, ti sphōi domen Pēlēi anakti*
> *thnētō? humeis d'eston agērō t'athanatō te*
> *e hina dustēnoisi met'andrasin alge' echēton?*

the address of Zeus to the horses of Peleus;—or take finally his

> *kai se, geron, to prin men akouomen olbion einai*

the words of Achilles to Priam, a suppliant before him. Take that incomparable line and a half of Dante, Ugolino's tremendous words—

---

[140] Kant (1952) 141 §34.   [141] Preface to *The Renaissance* (Pater (1980) p. xx).

> *Io non piangeva; si dentro impietrai.*
> *Piangevan elli...*

take the lovely words of Beatrice to Virgil—

> *Io son fatta da Dio, sua mercè, tale*
> *che la vostra miseria non mi tange,*
> *Nè fiamma d'esto incendio non m'assale...*

take the simple, but perfect, single line—

> *In la sua volontade è nostra pace.*

Take of Shakespeare a line or two of Henry the Fourth's expostulation with sleep—

> Wilt thou upon the high and giddy mast
> Seal up the ship-boy's eyes, and rock his brains
> In cradle of the rude imperious surge...

and take, as well, Hamlet's dying request to Horatio—

> If thou didst ever hold me in thy heart,
> Absent thee from felicity awhile,
> And in this hard world draw thy breath in pain
> To tell my story...

Take of Milton that Miltonic passage—

> Darken'd so, yet shone
> Above them all the archangel; but his face
> Deep scars of thunder had entrench'd, and care
> Sat on his faded cheek...

add two such lines as—

> And courage never to submit or yield
> And what is else not to be overcome...

and finish with the exquisite close to the loss of Proserpine, the loss

> ...which cost Ceres all that pain
> To seek her through the world.

These few lines, if we have tact and can use them, are enough even of themselves to keep clear and sound our judgements about poetry, to save us from fallacious estimates of it, to conduct us to a real estimate.[142]

Two of his touchstones in this essay are from Homer; in a similar sample of touchstones, 'eminent specimens of the grand style', in 'On Translating Homer' he quotes one passage each from Homer, Virgil, Dante, and Milton.[143] This might seem an instance of

---

[142] Arnold (1964) 242–3 (I have transliterated the Greek).
[143] Super (1960) 136–7. The passages are *Iliad* 21. 106–7; *Aeneid* 12. 435–6; *Inferno* 16. 61–3; and *Paradise Lost* 1. 591–4.

British pragmatism (the preference for the exemplary over the theoretical), but it could also be read as a more rigorous Kantianism. On such a reading the classics are not models from which universal rules can be taken but examples of objects about which positive aesthetic judgements have been made, and might again be made. For Arnold the classical poems are beyond question the examples to be recited first. Today ideology criticism normally puts some version of 'relevance' before aesthetic exemplarity. As a result the classics have slipped out of our canons.

Pater's famous meditation on Leonardo's *Mona Lisa* offers a different model for the aesthetic critic:

> The presence that rose thus so strangely beside the waters is expressive of what in the ways of a thousand years men had come to desire. Hers is the head upon which all 'the ends of the world are come,' and the eyelids are a little weary. It is a beauty wrought out from within upon the flesh, the deposit, little cell by cell, of strange thoughts and fantastic reveries and exquisite passions. Set it for a moment beside one of those white Greek goddesses or beautiful women of antiquity, and how would they be troubled by this beauty, into which the soul with all its maladies has passed! All the thoughts and experience of the world have etched and moulded there, in that which they have of power to refine and make expressive the outward form, the animalism of Greece, the lust of Rome, the mysticism of the middle age with its spiritual ambition and imaginative loves, the return of the Pagan world, the sins of the Borgias. She is older than the rocks among which she sits; like the vampire, she has been dead many times, and learned the secrets of the grave; and has been a diver in deep seas, and keeps their fallen day about her; and trafficked for strange webs with Eastern merchants: and, as Leda, was the mother of Helen of Troy, and, as Saint Anne, the mother of Mary; and all this has been to her but as the sound of lyres and flutes, and lives only in the delicacy with which it has moulded the changing lineaments, and tinged the eyelids and the hands.[144]

Pater's account is often dismissed as solipsistic, as telling us only about Pater, not about Leonardo. This seems to me quite wrong. Of course this passage has little to do with Leonardo's supposed intentions as they would be construed by a historicizing critic[145]—it is not historical criticism as we understand the term,

---

[144] Pater (1980) 98–9. For a lengthy discussion see C. Williams (1989) 111–23.
[145] Wilde comments: 'Do you ask me what Lionardo would have said had anyone told him of this picture that "all the thoughts and experience of the world had etched and moulded there in that which they had of power to refine and make expressive the outward form, the animalism of Greece, the lust of Rome, the reverie of the Middle Ages with its spiritual ambition and imaginative loves, the return of the Pagan world, the sins of the Borgias?" He

even if, in a sense, it is almost a history of the painting; obviously the language is not the language of a critic of our time. But the passage is clearly about this particular painting, and would not serve as a description of any other. Pater takes an old picture by a famous master, and, in a singular act of judgement, makes its beauty 'modern' again, indeed makes the work 'the symbol of the modern idea'.[146] He starts from specific details: the 'subtle expression' on the face, with 'the unfathomable smile, always with a touch of something sinister in it'; the curious and curiously lit landscape, 'that circle of fantastic rocks, as in some faint light under sea'.[147] Pater's account can thus be seen, in Kantian terms, as a move to making the judgement of taste in a more detailed way and so to help establish its subjective universality. We are invited to look again, and, when we look, may see the beauty that Pater sees. In this case the attempt was successful; the standing of the *Mona Lisa* was immeasurably raised by Pater's meditation.[148] Gilbert, in Wilde's 'The Critic as Artist', murmurs to himself, and says to his friend, Pater's lines whenever he looks upon the painting:

> Who... cares whether Mr. Pater has put into the portrait of Monna Lisa something that Lionardo never dreamed of? The painter may have been merely the slave of an archaic smile, as some have fancied, but whenever I pass into the cool galleries of the Palace of the Louvre, and stand before that strange figure... I murmur to myself, 'She is older than the rocks among which she sits....'[149]

Most responses to the painting since Pater involve a sense of its unfathomability, the woman's smile being regarded as enigmatic. Similarly Pater's short essay on the special virtue of Botticelli changed the painter, almost overnight, from a minor to a major

---

would probably have answered that he had contemplated none of these things, but had concerned himself simply with certain arrangements of lines and masses, and with new and curious colour-harmonies of blue and green' (Ellmann (1970) 367). Intentionality is, of course, a complex matter, for which there are competing models—Leonardo, if he were alive today, might not necessarily take exception to Pater's account. Note too how cunningly Wilde makes his 'historical' Leonardo into an early version of an aestheticist artist like Whistler.

[146] Pater (1980) 99.
[147] Ibid. 97–8.
[148] Not that this was the purpose of Pater's judgement. But a successful judgement of taste may affect canonical arrangements (at which point it becomes involved with the politics of canon making).
[149] Ellmann (1970) 366–7.

Immanuel Kant and Aesthetic Judgement 49

figure in the history of art, a position he has held ever since.[150] We might call Pater's characterizations a kind of aesthetic 'thick description'.[151] Sadly, few critics have had Pater's imagination and precision (I use the word advisedly, because the now unfamiliar nature of Pater's critical idiom has rendered that precision invisible to many moderns), so such criticism is currently as rare as it is precious. The situation might change if more critics were to attempt aesthetic criticism of this kind.

Let us look in this light at an ancient poem, Horace, *Ode* 2. 5, and attempt the judgement of taste. The ideology critic characteristically proceeds by reconfiguring a poem within a pre-established ideological framework, in order to generate a 'new' reading. My aim here will be less to give another such reading, but rather to try, in the mode of the aesthetic critic, to say what this poem is to *me*:[152]

>   nondum subacta ferre iugum valet
>   cervice, nondum munia comparis
>   aequare nec tauri ruentis
>   in Venerem tolerare pondus.
>
>   circa virentes est animus tuae   5
>   campos iuvencae, nunc fluviis gravem
>   solantis aestum, nunc in udo
>   ludere cum vitulis salicto
>
>   praegestientis. tolle cupidinem
>   immitis uvae: iam tibi lividos   10
>   distinguet autumnus racemos
>   purpureo varius colore.
>
>   iam te sequetur: currit enim ferox
>   aetas et illi quos tibi dempserit
>   apponet annos; iam proterva   15
>   fronte petet Lalage maritum,
>
>   dilecta quantum non Pholoe fugax,
>   non Chloris albo sic umero nitens

---

[150] See Weinberg (1987).

[151] For this term see Geertz (1973) ch. 1.

[152] So Pater (1980) pp. xix–xx: 'What is this song or picture, this engaging personality presented in life or in a book, to *me*? What effect does it really produce on me? Does it give me pleasure? and if so, what sort or degree of pleasure? How is my nature modified by its presence, and under its influence? The answers to these questions are the original facts with which the aesthetic critic has to do; and ... one must realise such primary data for one's self, or not at all.' For a more detailed analysis of Pater's aesthetic criticism see Chapter 4 below.

> ut pura nocturno renidet
> luna mari, Cnidiusve Gyges, 20
> quem si puellarum insereres choro,
> mire sagaces falleret hospites
> discrimen obscurum solutis
> crinibus ambiguoque vultu.

Not yet is she broken in and strong enough to bear the yoke, not yet to share duties with a mate, or bear the weight of a bull rushing into Venus. The mind of your calf is on green meadows, now finding relief from oppressive heat in streams, now longing to play with bull calves among the moist willows. Set aside desire for the unripe grape. Soon autumn in all its variety with purple tint will mark out the clusters for you. Soon she will follow you: for fierce time runs on and will credit her with the years it takes from you; soon Lalage will seek a partner with lusty forehead, loved as was not fleeing Pholoe, not Chloris gleaming with white shoulder as the pure moon gleams back on the night sea, or Gyges from Cnidus—if you put him in a dance of girls, wonderfully would even perceptive guests miss the difference obscured by flowing hair and ambiguous face.

A poem like this will probably be read today as part of a discourse of gender and sexuality, an approach which often leads to a sociology of art. By contrast a Paterian, as we have seen, would seek to define the distinctive virtue of the poem, the quality that makes experience of it different from experiencing other poems and other poets. Thus art for art's sake becomes a way of reading and responding to works of art more than it is a way of making them. Pater is concerned for style, stressing the way the writer chooses the word that most precisely conveys what he wants to say, so as to, in Henry James's account of it, 'strain the expression of it so clear and fine that beauty would result';[153] but the virtue of a poem is a matter of the aesthetic effect of both form and content—Pater's criticism is very far from being formalistic. One of Gautier's examples of 'pure' art is Shakespeare's *Othello*, and he accounts for its artistic purity thus:

> L'art pour l'art signifie, pour les adeptes, un travail dégagé de toute préoccupation autre que celle du beau en lui-même. Quand Shakespeare écrit *Othello*, il n'a d'autre but que de montrer l'homme en proie à la jalousie; quand Voltaire fait

---

[153] Preface to the New York edition of *The Aspern Papers and The Turn of the Screw* (James (1986) 39). James later glosses beauty thus: 'putting for the beautiful always, in a work of art, the close, the curious, the deep' (p. 40).

Mahomet, outre l'intention de dessiner la figure du prophète, il a celle de démontrer en général les inconvéniens du fanatisme et en particulier les vices des prêtres catholiques ou chrétiens de son temps: sa tragédie souffre de l'introduction de cet élément hétérogène, et, pour atteindre l'effet philosophique, il manque l'effet esthétique du beau absolu. Quoique *Othello* ne sape pas le moindre petit préjugé, il s'élève de cent coudées au-dessus du *Mahomet*, malgré les tirades encyclopédiques de celui-ci.[154]

Art for art's sake signifies, for initiates, a kind of work that is disengaged from any preoccupation other than that of the beautiful in itself. When Shakespeare writes *Othello*, he has no goal but to show man prey to jealousy; when Voltaire produces *Mahomet*, beside the intention of delineating the figure of the prophet, he has the one of demonstrating the disadvantages of fanaticism in general, and in particular the vices of the Catholic or Christian priests of his own time: his tragedy suffers from the introduction of this heterogeneous element, and in order to obtain the philosophical effect, he misses the aesthetic effect of absolute beauty. Although *Othello* does not undermine the tiniest little prejudice, it rises a hundred cubits above *Mahomet*, despite the encyclopaedic tirades of the latter.

The aesthetic purity of Shakespeare's play clearly does not mean that it has no significant content. To this issue of the relationship between form and content I shall return in the next chapter.

According to the standard modern commentary our poem lacks 'the supreme Horatian virtues of humanity and sense'.[155] But in the lyric Horace other poetic qualities might be more highly valued, and found equally 'Horatian'. As often Horace starts with discontinuous figuring, perhaps on the model of Pindar or Callimachus—the young cow in the meadows, the grapes of autumn turning blue. The discrete metaphors are so sharply defined that they become in effect a series of literal pictures—the distinction between literal and metaphorical is blurred in the reader's mind. The poem is an argument, but, as he does often, Horace argues partly with images, so that only part of the advice is given in straightforwardly paraenetic form. The words, often interlocking in order, are slotted together with monumental precision and economy—making almost any other lyric writing seem carelessly loose and verbose by comparison. No one has described the effect better than Nietzsche:

Up to the present I have not obtained from any poet the same artistic delight as was given me from the first by an Horatian Ode. In certain languages that which is

---

[154] Gautier (1847) 900.   [155] Nisbet and Hubbard (1978) 80.

obtained here cannot even be hoped for. The mosaic of words in which every word, by sound, by position and by meaning, diffuses its force right, left, and over the whole, that *minimum* in the compass and number of signs, that *maximum* thus realised in their energy,—all that is Roman, and if you will believe me, it is *noble par excellence*. All other poetry becomes somewhat too popular in comparison with it—mere sentimental loquacity.[156]

In such writing the gap between signifier and signified seems to contract so to say, and words to become things—an illusory effect no doubt but one experienced by many readers of a certain kind of poetry. In no other Latin writer, except perhaps Lucretius, is there a stronger sense of the physical quality of words, the sheer materiality of language.

The shadow of time and death is everywhere in Horace and falls across the fourth stanza of this ode—time, like a sexual partner, is both urgent and fugitive (*sequetur, currit, ferox, fugax*). The poem ends with a tangent of a 'wilfully supplementary character',[157] a swerve typical of the *Odes*, and with a thickening of the syntax. *Ambiguo* is itself ambiguous, since it can refer either to doubts about someone's sex or to sexual ambivalence (there may also be a reference to the Greek word *lysis* in the sense of the unravelling of a literary problem[158]). The difficulty and involved word order of the final stanza describing the puzzlingly androgynous Gyges may absorb the reader so much that she may forget the poem's abrupt opening and its direct language (this movement from an urgent beginning to more complex and opaque developments is also common in Donne).[159] We have come a long way from 'the bull rushing into Venus'. The effect of the lyrical recall of previous lovers—Chloris imaged in the moon reflected on the surface of the sea, Gyges unnoticed among the girls like Achilles on Scyros—suggests a mind in its circling coming to rest on two brilliant memories of past affairs. This lingering in memory annihilates the difference between past, present, and future on which the poem's logic depends, creating what I would call a poetic

---

[156] Quoted by Charles Tomlinson in Martindale and Hopkins (1993) 244 (from Friedrich Nietzsche, *The Case of Wagner, Nietzsche Contra Wagner, The Twilight of the Idols, The Antichrist*, trans. Thomas Common, London 1899, 233–4).

[157] Oliensis (2002) 99, in a suggestive essay on Horace's use of the motif of hair as a closural device.

[158] So Nisbet and Hubbard (1978), note ad loc. [159] So Commager (1967) 253–4.

'epiphany'. By this I mean a moment when an artist concentrates so intensely on something that, for the time being, it totally engrosses our attention, inducing a moment of reverent stillness which I have had to resort to religious language to describe. In a painting by an artist such as Vermeer it might be a piece of fruit on a dish or light playing on a woman's sleeve. Horace is usually thought of as a distinctly masculinist poet, but these Horatian epiphanies might be compared with *écriture féminine* as described by some feminist writers.[160] Gyges' androgynous character is reinforced by his loosened hair (*solutis crinibus*) in syntax which Romans might well have identified as loose or effeminate, creating a 'conjunction of "weak" form and effeminate content'.[161] A closure like this creates 'a space of lyric delay or dallying' that can be construed as a feminine ending.[162] In short, Horace's ode may not be sensible and humane, but we might want to call it beautiful and to grant it a distinctively Horatian virtue.

IV

The current reign of ideology critique and culturalism not only involves an undesirable narrowing; in my view it also has its dangers for the future of Classics. In the last resort the cultures of antiquity, considered as bundles of signifying practices, are as much—or as little—interesting as any other (moreover ideology critics are preoccupied with issues that seem, somehow, 'relevant' to us today). By contrast for centuries in the West the great works of literature of Greece and Rome, among them Horace's *Odes*, have stood for so many of our ancestors as instances of beauty without peer. (The aesthetic critic of the future will, among other things, want to discover what beauties others have found in the past in such poems, thus employing reception as an appropriate mode of enquiry.) But I do not wish to end this chapter on a pessimistic note. I began with a quotation from Whistler's 'Ten O'Clock', so I will end with its ending:

---

[160] See e.g. Moi (1985), esp. introduction and ch. 6.
[161] Oliensis (2002) 94, 98–9, 104: cf. 104, 'Hair could also stand as an emblem for the centrifugal arguments of these elusive endings.'
[162] Oliensis (2002) 104.

Therefore have we cause to be merry!—and to cast away all care—resolved that all is well, as it ever was—and that it is not meet that we should be cried at, and urged to take measures—...

We have then but to wait—until, with the mark of the Gods upon him, there comes among us, again, the chosen, who shall continue what has gone before—satisfied that even, were he never to appear, the story of the beautiful is already complete—hewn in the marbles of the Parthenon, and broidered, with the birds, upon the fan of Hokusai—at the foot of Fusihama—[163]

[163] Thorpe (1994) 94–5.

2
Content, Form, and Frame

For something can only be called art when it requires that we construe the work by learning to understand the language of form and content so that communication really occurs.

Hans-Georg Gadamer[1]

I

In a piece later entitled 'The Red Rag' (first published in *The World*, 1878) James McNeill Whistler defended his habit of giving his paintings titles of a musical or abstract kind:

Art should be independent of all clap-trap—should stand alone, and appeal to the artistic sense of eye or ear, without confounding this with emotions entirely foreign to it, as devotion, pity, love, patriotism, and the like. All these have no kind of concern with it; and that is why I insist on calling my works 'arrangements' and 'harmonies.'

Take the picture of my mother, exhibited at the Royal Academy as an 'Arrangement in Grey and Black.' Now that is what it is. To me it is interesting as a picture of my mother; but what can or ought the public to care about the identity of the portrait?[2]

Whistler is referring to what is now perhaps his most famous work, one of painting's most compelling portrayals of an old woman, and one of the few non-French pictures deemed worthy to hang in the Musée d'Orsay in Paris (it was bought for the French national collection). Whistler's comments are usually taken as an extreme, and rather crude, statement of formalism, the idea that what matters in a work of art are its formal features, not its subject or content. Such a doctrine, now generally regarded as politically reactionary, was radical and progressive in 1878; and certainly the disposition of shapes in the painting and its austere colour range have been found

---

[1] Gadamer (1986) 52.   [2] Whistler (1967) 127–8.

unusually satisfying by many viewers since. Evidently Whistler is protesting against the kind of ideology criticism widely practised in 1878, which, with a work of such a kind, would be likely to concern itself with the representation of motherhood and the family—with aspects of what Whistler calls 'devotion, pity, love, patriotism'. Such criticism, like most ideology criticism *de nos jours*, was usually intensely moralistic (even if the morals were, or are thought to have been, different from ours). A call to turn from such sentimental and morally suspect preoccupations to concentrate on the formal properties of a work of art was thus as timely then as it is today.

This account seems to force us towards making a choice between form and content. Whistler was never the subtlest of writers, yet perhaps a more complex reading of his words is possible. As we have seen, for Kant a pure judgement of taste, such as could be made in the case of a flower or a shell, would probably be impossible with a representation of a human subject. Nonetheless we might *try* to make such a judgement in the case of Whistler's painting of his mother, and the artist's remarks could be construed as encouraging us so to do. We would then put aside any general concern with the ideology of motherhood or the particular interest we might have in our own or any other mother, so that our response would to that extent cease to be moral or ideological (the judgement 'I like this painting because it reminds me of my mother' is not, of course, an aesthetic one, since it involves an interest[3]). But that would not necessarily entail pretending that we were merely looking at abstract shapes and a particular narrow range of colours, rather than at a portrayal of an old woman who was also, as it happened, the artist's mother. This interpretation receives support from the fact that Whistler, contrary to his claim in 'The Red Rag', in 1872 had exhibited the picture under the title *Arrangement in Grey and Black: Portrait of the Painter's Mother*. In other words Whistler, both in the first title he gave his work and in his comments on it in 'The Red Rag', draws our attention to its status as a portrait, while at the same time directing us against a particular kind of response; the enormous public success of the image is testimony to the likelihood that for most viewers the subject matter was of no irrelevance.[4] But it is

---

[3] Free-floating thoughts about 'maternalness' might, however, be relevant to an aesthetic response.
[4] See MacDonald (2003), esp. ch. 4 on the picture's American tour.

the artistic handling that makes it possible for us to see the portrayal of a wrinkled old woman in dour black against a grey background as something we can pronounce 'beautiful', and thus to make a true judgement of taste that is neither interested nor a disguised moral judgement. In other words the dual title offers us a richer possibility than an apparent stark choice between formalism and ideology; and we are not forced to abstract away the painting's character as a portrait. Whistler, we might say, like Gautier, believes in art for art's sake, not in form for form's sake.[5]

Many of today's critics, hostile to the aesthetic, want to force us back into making a stark choice, and are ever quick to accuse their opponents of that most deadly critical vice, formalism—the abstracting of the formal qualities of artworks from the ideological discourses within which, on this view, they alone have meaning, with the politically reactionary aim of naturalizing art as something autonomous and transcendent. Let us look at another case of apparent formalism where a less hasty reading shows how matters may be more complex than they seem. In his book *Plato and Platonism* (1893)—a work shamefully neglected by modern classicists—Walter Pater declares, in a way that might be found altogether shocking, that in Plato's philosophy the *form* is what is new, concluding: 'But then, in the creation of philosophical literature, as in all other products of art, *form*, in the full signification of that word, is everything, and the mere matter is nothing.'[6] What could be a clearer statement of formalism than that—or, in the eyes of any respectable philosopher, one more ill founded? But Pater is not saying that Plato's writings are not 'about' anything (what they are about is indeed the subject of most of the book). Pater's point rather derives from his observation, a pre-echo of poststructuralism, that—to use a later critical idiom—all texts are sites of intertextuality, everything always already written, nothing

---

[5] Gautier (1847) 901: 'L'art pour l'art veut dire non pas la forme pour la forme, mais bien la forme pour le beau, abstraction faite de toute idée étrangère, de tout détournement au profit d'une doctrine quelconque, de toute utilité directe' ('Art for art's sake does not mean form for form's sake, but rather form for the sake of the beautiful, having excluded any foreign idea, any deviation for the profit of any kind of doctrine, any direct utility').

[6] Pater (1893) 4. Pater is following Schiller: 'In a truly successful work of art the contents should effect nothing, the form everything; for only through the form is the whole man affected, through the subject-matter, by contrast, only one or other of his functions' (Schiller (1967) 155).

originary. We think of Plato's philosophy as foundational, as, in Pater's words 'an absolutely fresh thing in the morning of the mind's history'; but in truth Plato's world was already belated, 'already almost weary of philosophical debate', so that—and here the language comes close to that of Barthes or Derrida—'the seemingly new is old also, a palimpsest, a tapestry of which the actual threads have served before, or like the animal frame itself, every particle of which has already lived and died many times over'.[7] Pater shares Hayden White's realization that there is a content to the form, as well as a form to the content.

The point becomes clearer when Pater turns to the sophists, characterized (with Platonic hostility) as those who value form without content: 'With them art began too precipitately, as mere form without matter; a thing of disconnected empiric rules, caught from the mere surface of other people's productions, in congruity with a general method which everywhere ruthlessly severed branch and flower from its natural root—art from one's own vivid sensation or belief.'[8] The contradiction here with the earlier passage is only seeming: Plato is a better philosopher than the sophists because he is a better artist, who, like any good artist, uses words with precision to express what is to be expressed. The matter is 'nothing' if it is 'mere' matter, that is not formed. For Pater—like Wittgenstein and the post-structuralists—knows that 'From first to last our faculty of thinking is limited by our command of speech'.[9] Language, as Heideggerians like to say, is the house we dwell in; it may be an old house, and much repaired, and perhaps somewhat rickety—but it is the only one we have got. The sophists, then, are the true formalists, not Pater—who, rather, is a modern Plato: lover, aesthete, and philosopher, one in whose productions form and content work together to produce a novel work of art that is also a novel work of philosophy, though, strictly speaking, for reasons we have seen, it is the form and not the matter that is new.

The principal argument of this chapter is a very simple one: *that the judgement of taste is a judgement of what we call 'form' and what we call 'content' (however these terms are defined) in conjunction, and thus is not a species of formalism.* This is not to be confused with the 'Romantic' claim (partly derived from a particular reading of Kant)

---

[7] Pater (1893) 2–3.   [8] Ibid. 105.   [9] Ibid. 129.

that in works of art, or at any rate the greatest works of art, form and content work harmoniously together to create a special 'organic' form of unity. I shall suggest that form and content are most profitably thought of, not as elements 'in' the works of art or objects we judge 'beautiful', as they are in the Romantic view, but rather as categories within the human mind that we use in our exploration of these things. This is in accord with Kant's first move in the 'Analytic of the Beautiful': 'If we wish to discern whether anything is beautiful or not, we do not refer the representation of it to the Object by means of understanding with a view to cognition, but... we refer the representation to the Subject and its feeling of pleasure or displeasure.'[10] Within this model, form and content are treated as heuristic, not as reified entities. Thus if I adjudge the urgent, emotional opening of Horace's Postumus *Ode* (2. 14) beautiful

> eheu fugaces, Postume, Postume,
> labuntur anni nec pietas moram
>   rugis et instanti senectae
>   adferet indomitaeque morti:

Alas fleeing, Postumus, Postumus, glide the years, and goodness will bring no delay to wrinkles and pressing old age and unconquered death

I am not responding merely to the sounds and rhythms and rhetorical effects of the verse but also to feelings about death embodied in those sounds and rhythms and effects[11]—toying with the notion of time as flowing water or perhaps a runaway from battle, of death as the unconquerable enemy or as an uncontrollable sweep of water, with the implications of the iterated name Postumus, suggestive of someone late born, and much more. This is a very different process either from reaching a decision how to live on the basis of our mortality, or from complaining that the poem uses the shortness of human life to advocate a hedonistic quietism rather than political change—neither of which responses is sensitive to the special 'virtue' of this passage and neither of which would be properly part of the judgement of taste.[12]

---

[10] Kant (1952) 41 §1. For example, onomatopoeia requires a prompt from the sense.
[11] For the different possible associations of the words see Nisbet and Hubbard (1978) and West (1998) ad loc.
[12] For some ancient views on the relationship between the words used in poetry and the thoughts they express (*verba/res*, one version of the form/content polarity) see the essays by

Thus belief in 'art for art's sake', a movement that can be said to have begun in the nineteenth century in both France and England, is not, or need not be, a narrowly defined formalism, though it was (mis)represented as such from the first by its opponents. Rather it involves the claim that art is not for the sake of information (science, Kant's pure reason) or for the sake of morality (ethics and politics, Kant's practical reason), but for the sake of beauty.[13] On this view, art tends to be construed as autonomous in respect to its content as well as its form, as containing its own meaning, which is not merely an imitation of a prior real or imagined world. As a result the aesthetic critic will not wish to abstract a content from a work of art and make a moral or other judgement about it (this is what ideology critics characteristically do). Initially art for art's sake was a way of thinking about art, though it led artists to ways of making a more autonomous sort of art, focused on beauty. Ideology criticism is also always possible, but, I would argue, it too should pay attention to form as well as content. In his *Discourses* Sir Joshua Reynolds calls for the most important figure to be immediately identifiable by its position on the canvas.[14] This reflects his commitment to hierarchy in painting (as in life); history painting deals with great men and events from the Bible and the classics, and the disposition of the elements should be organized so as to make visible what is important. In such a case aesthetic form can be clearly seen to have political/ethical entailments.

In his lecture 'The Origin of the Work of Art' (first delivered in 1935) Heidegger argued that we would do better to jettison form and content as foundational terms altogether:

James Porter ('Content and Form in Philodemus: The History of an Evasion') and David Armstrong ('The Impossibility of Metathesis: Philodemus and Lucretius on Form and Content in Poetry') in Obbink (1995) 97–147 and 210–32.

[13] This position is anticipated by Hegel: 'The poetic work of art has no aim other than the production and enjoyment of beauty; in its case aim and achievement lie directly in the work itself, which is therefore independently self-complete and finished; and the artistic activity is not a means to a result falling outside itself but an end which in its accomplishment directly closes together with itself' (Hegel (1975) ii. 992).

[14] Reynolds (1975) 156: 'the principal figure should be immediately distinguished at the first glance of the eye.' Aesthetic form always has implications beyond itself if we want to pursue them. For example, as Loesberg (1991) observes, 'literary and linguistic structures have made history by making our understanding of it' (p. 123). It does not follow, of course, that linguistic structures map readily on to the phenomenal world, a point de Man is always insisting upon.

Content, Form, and Frame 61

The distinction of matter and form is *the conceptual schema which is used, in the greatest variety of ways, quite generally for all art theory and aesthetics*. This incontestable fact, however, proves neither that the distinction of matter and form is adequately founded, nor that it belongs originally to the domain of art and the artwork. Moreover, the range of application of this pair of concepts has long extended far beyond the field of aesthetics. Form and content are the most hackneyed concepts under which anything and everything may be subsumed. And if form is correlated with the rational and matter with the irrational; if the rational is taken to be the logical and the irrational the alogical; if in addition the subject–object relation is coupled with the conceptual pair form–matter; then representation has at its command a conceptual machinery that nothing is capable of withstanding.[15]

Heidegger, who was suspicious of the Kantian distinction between subject and object, sought to 'overcome' the whole Western tradition of aesthetics. For him art belonged to the sphere of truth, not beauty, and the effect of the artwork was to disclose 'Being' (in his special sense of that word). Characteristically he desiderates a wholly fresh start (though in practice form and content may be said to reappear, in new guises, as, for instance 'world' and 'earth'). For all the attractions of this approach there is a heavy price to pay. Great emphasis is restored to the distinction between what counts as art and what does not. One consequence is the disparagement of craft and of the decorative arts (it might seem pretentious to claim that a Morris wallpaper reveals Being?). And on what criteria do we distinguish art from non-art (if from its supposed disclosure of Being, we are clearly in a vicious circle)? Heidegger's own choice of artwork, one of Van Gogh's paintings of shoes (which Heidegger sees as the shoes of the working peasant, and not those of the artist, as others suppose), quite apart from the fact that it is conventionally mimetic, seems worryingly to suggest that taste for earth and blood that was soon to engulf Europe (and thus objectionable on ideological grounds). Elsewhere Heidegger's hostility to modernity leads him to praise a silver chalice for liturgical use, while disparaging the products of technology as inauthentic; by contrast a Kantian could find beauty and worthwhile reflection in an object produced from such a modern synthetic substance as styrofoam.[16]

---

[15] Heidegger (1993) 153.

[16] The silver chalice features in 'The Question Concerning Technology', 1954 (Heidegger (1993) 311–41). For this paragraph I am indebted to a lecture by Jeff Collins. For a

Beauty, as theorized within the Kantian tradition, seems something altogether less hierarchical and more savoury than Being.

Certainly form and content are slippery terms, and critical disagreements sometimes spring from the fact that they are being used in different ways. Writing about a period of only thirty years in nineteenth-century England and only in connection with the art of painting, Elizabeth Prettejohn comments on the striking diversity of usage:

> 'form' could refer to technique or craftsmanship, to eclectic borrowings from the art of the past, to compositional evidence of the artist's intellect, or to traces in the brushwork of the artist's inspiration; 'content' could refer to subject-matter, to the faithful imitation of 'nature', to emotional expressiveness, or to some notion of spiritual depth.[17]

Indeed, as can happen with other polarities (nature and culture, for example), either term can easily flip over into its supposed opposite. For example, on one model form can refer to the superficial appearance, content to the essential thing (this would be the case with versions of 'Realism'). On another model, common in German aesthetics, content is the gross inchoate material mass, form is what gives that matter coherence: so in making a pot the potter gives shape to the unformed clay. Schiller often works with this model, as when he writes that a master in any art '*can make his form consume his material*'.[18] The content can be seen as objective, what is 'out there', the form as subjective, what we do with it. Or content can be the emotional, 'human' aspect, form the 'objective' presentation of it, according to artistic rules. The material and the idea can be differently evaluated. In Neo-classical History Painting it is the painter's idea, expressed in the concrete material of the artwork, that is of crucial importance. By contrast, in the writings of the modernist art critic Clement Greenberg, the central role in art is the matter, the material from which the work is made.[19]

---

sympathetic account of Heidegger's poetics from an ecocritical perspective see Bate (2000) ch. 9 'What Are Poets For?', pp. 243–83 (p. 255 for the styrofoam cup).

[17] Prettejohn (2000) 43.   [18] Schiller (1967) 157.
[19] For Greenberg's aesthetic see O'Brian (1986): 'Avant-garde and Kitsch' (1939), on pp. 5–22, and 'Towards a Newer Laocoon' (1940), on pp. 22–38; for Greenberg and Kant see O'Brian (1993): 'Modernist Painting' (1960), on pp. 85–93 (interestingly, since this is the most famous art-historical essay known under the label 'formalism', Greenberg does not use the word 'form', speaking only of the unique qualities of the medium).

Kant is often described as a formalist, sometimes on the assumption (clearly false) that he is using the word 'form' in the same sense as modern, 'thin' formalists like Greenberg and Roger Fry (the most influential English Modernist art critic). For them form is an attribute of objects, involving such properties as shape, line, and colour. Kant, for whom form is something presented to us by the mind, suggests that our pleasure in the beautiful involves a sense of finality, or purposiveness, that is 'formal' in the sense that it is not directed towards, or constitutive of, a specific end or purpose. If we adjudge a flower beautiful, it is because we 'trace in it' formal finality, not the finality that a botanist might locate (its role in reproduction), but a finality that is non-teleological, for its own sake.[20] Because most of Kant's examples of pure beauty are taken from the visual sphere (flowers, shells, etc.), the formal finality in these cases, the capacity to satisfy the mind, must have something to do with shape;[21] by contrast the formal finality in the experience of a piece of music or a poem would clearly be somewhat different. A number of elements in Kant's system suggest that he is far from being a formalist in the modern sense,[22] among them the emphasis on the free play of imagination and understanding, and the difficult notion of 'aesthetic ideas'[23] (ideas which are not properly speaking concepts, but which are involved in the creation and reception of works of art).

Kant, as we have seen, does not present a developed theory of art in the *Critique of Judgement*, though one might be developed from Kantian premises (which is in part what this book attempts to do). A claim that something is art is not, in Kant's terms, an aesthetic judgement at all, but rather a conceptual one. There is thus nothing Kantian about the famous formalist definition of art given by Clive Bell, associate of Roger Fry, in 1914:

There must be some one quality without which a work of art cannot exist; possessing which, in the least degree, no work is altogether worthless. What is this quality? What quality is shared by all objects that provoke our aesthetic

---

[20] Kant (1952) 61–3 §§10–11.   [21] So Crawford (1974) 99.

[22] For a detailed defence of this position see Crowther (1996) ch. 3, 'Beyond Formalism: Kant's Theory of Art', pp. 56–71.

[23] Kant's definition is as follows: 'that representation of the imagination which induces much thought, yet without the possibility of any definite thought whatever, i.e. *concept*, being adequate to it, and which language, consequently, can never get on level terms with or render completely intelligible' (Kant (1952) 175–6 §49).

emotions? What quality is common to Sta Sophia and the windows at Chartres, Mexican sculpture, a Persian bowl, Chinese carpets, Giotto's frescoes at Padua, and the masterpieces of Poussin, Piero della Francesca, and Cézanne? Only one answer seems possible—significant form. In each, lines and colours combined in a particular way, certain forms and relation of forms, stir our aesthetic emotions. These relations and combinations of lines and colours, these aesthetically moving forms, I call 'Significant Form'; and 'Significant Form' is the one quality common to all works of visual art.[24]

This celebrated and influential passage shows how an aesthetic theory may be false or misleading but still have a massive—and to a large extent beneficial—impact on public taste. With arguments such as these Bell and Fry persuaded people to attend carefully to, and find beautiful, objects which would, or might, otherwise have been dismissed or ignored: non-Western, 'primitive' artefacts such as African sculpture or Aboriginal painting, Byzantine enamels, Islamic pottery, Post-Impressionist painting, and so forth (of course, there was also a price: the disparagement of some other beautiful things, in particular Victorian art[25]). However, as an argument, the passage is extremely weak, with obvious circularity (significant form is what stirs aesthetic emotions, aesthetic emotions are what respond to significant form). 'Significant Form'—even with capital letters—seems mere mystification: how are we to determine whether a particular form is significant or not? There is no reason to believe that all artworks must have a common quality in the first place; what constitutes art is determined within complex discursive practices that differ between one culture and another, one historical period and another. It is better to think of art, non-Platonically, in terms of a Wittgensteinian set of family resemblances (artwork *a* has something in common with artwork *b*, and *b* with *c*, but there is no necessary common factor between *a* and *c*). We should not seek for any single concept which allows us to call all the items in Bell's list 'beautiful'; for the reasons set out in the *Critique of Judgement*, 'anything that has significant form is beautiful' is certainly not a judgement of taste.

The view that, in poetry, good reading attends to form and content together was a central belief of the New Critics, encapsulated

[24] Feagin and Maynard (1997) 15.
[25] Like many art theories Bell's formalism can be seen as a protest against the art practice of the immediately preceding period.

in the familiar slogan 'the heresy of paraphrase'.[26] A historically important and effective statement of this view is contained in A. C. Bradley's inaugural lecture as Professor of Poetry in Oxford, entitled 'Poetry for Poetry's Sake' (1901). Bradley distinguishes content from the subject of the poem (something 'outside' the work, as it were), and dismisses the notion that a paraphrase 'means' the same as the words paraphrased. Only to a coroner, he quips, does 'To be or not to be, that is the question' mean anything like 'What is just now occupying my attention is the comparative disadvantages of continuing to live or putting an end to myself' (the argument is thus a variant of the untranslatability thesis within translation theory).[27] He describes the experience of form and content as follows: 'If you read the line, "The sun is warm, the sky is clear," you do not experience separately the image of a warm sun and clear sky, on the one side, and certain unintelligible rhythmical sounds on the other; nor yet do you experience them together, side by side; but you experience the one *in* the other.'[28] T. S. Eliot has pointed out that poets *think* metrically:

> To create a form is not merely to invent a shape, a rhyme, or rhythm. It is also the realization of the whole appropriate content of this rhyme or rhythm. The sonnet of Shakespeare is not merely such and such a pattern, but a precise way of thinking and feeling.[29]

What this means for the critic is explored in Bradley's rather beautiful discussion of a much admired line from the *Aeneid* (significantly this instance of paraphrase involves translation from one language to another):

> If I take the famous line which describes how the souls of the dead stood waiting by the river, imploring a passage from Charon:
>
> > Tendebantque manus ripae ulterioris amore,
>
> and if I translate it, 'and were stretching forth their hands in longing for the further bank,' the charm of the original has fled. Why has it fled? Partly... because I have substituted for five words, and those the words of Virgil, twelve words, and those my own. In some measure because I have turned into rhythmless prose a line of verse which, as mere sound, has unusual beauty. But much more because in doing

---

[26] The phrase is the title of a chapter in Cleanth Brooks's seminal New Critical study, *The Well Wrought Urn* (Brooks (1974)), first published in 1947.
[27] Bradley (1909) 20.   [28] Ibid. 14–15.
[29] Eliot (1920) 57 (from 'The Possibility of a Poetic Drama').

so I have also changed the *meaning* of Virgil's line. What that meaning is *I* cannot say: Virgil has said it. But I can see this much, that the translation conveys a far less vivid picture of the outstretched hands and of their remaining outstretched, and a far less poignant sense of the distance of the shore and the longing of the souls. And it does so partly because this picture and this sense are conveyed not only by the obvious meaning of the words, but through the long-drawn sound of 'tendebantque,' through the time occupied by the five syllables and therefore by the idea of 'ulterioris,' and through the identity of the long sound 'or' in the penultimate syllables of 'ulterioris amore'—all this, and much more, apprehended not in this analytical fashion, nor as *added* to the beauty of mere sound and to the obvious meaning, but in unity with them and so as expressive of the poetic meaning of the whole.[30]

Bradley here goes beyond the claim I am making in this chapter, to argue for a deeper unity between form and content, a matter to which we shall return, but he is surely right to suggest that when we find a line of poetry beautiful we are not doing so in relation to the sound only or the sense only. Indeed I would argue that this is not only true for poetry but for any language use that we respond to aesthetically.

Like many of his predecessors Bradley appeals to music to provide the clearest example of the fusion he is describing. In music, more than in any other art form, we evidently experience form and content, however we construe them, *together*—in the experience of music it is indeed hardly possible to abstract a content, all such experience of serious listening being intransitive in character (on this term more in a moment). The music critic Eduard Hanslick (supposedly the inspiration for Wagner's Beckmesser) made of this point an ingenious paradox: 'The content of music is tonally moving forms.'[31] Pater has numerous beautiful passages on the matter, including this one from 'The School of Giorgione':

It is the art of music which most completely realises this artistic ideal, this perfect identification of matter and form. In its consummate moments, the end is not distinct from the means, the form from the matter, the subject from the expression; they inhere in and completely saturate each other; and to it, therefore, to the condition of its perfect moments, all the arts may be supposed constantly to tend and aspire.[32]

---

[30] Bradley (1909) 20–1. Compare Croce (1995) 35: 'If the meter, rhythm, and words of a poem are taken away from it, there does not remain beyond them all, as some suppose, its poetic thought. There remains nothing.'
[31] Cited Kivy (1997) 97.   [32] Pater (1980) 109.

Music, we may say, is in that sense a 'purer' art form than literature,[33] though not necessarily for that reason superior (within the model of aesthetics espoused here the relative value of the arts is a matter of little meaning and no moment). But nonetheless form and content remain standard and useful heuristic tools in music analysis.[34]

The philosopher Peter Kivy, in a wholesale critique of Bradley's lecture,[35] maintains that such arguments prove not that form and meaning can be fused but that there is nothing in music that can properly be called content. For him what he terms 'the form–content identity thesis' is simply a mystificatory attempt, by those he calls 'literary types',[36] to suggest that there is a special, 'ineffable' sort of knowledge that only poetry can provide. Meaning, he insists, is no different in poetry from in anything else, and it is absurd to suggest that poetry is unparaphrasable, since paraphrased it clearly has been. This, however, is surely to miss the point. Bradley and those who think like him are not arguing that paraphrase is impossible—indeed it may serve a useful, even an essential pedagogical purpose;[37] rather they deny that such paraphrase, as an abstracted content, can simply replace the poet's own formulations for purposes of understanding, as regularly happens in ideology criticism—the original and the paraphrase do not mean 'the same', even if the paraphrase can help us in the task of construing a meaning for the original. Kivy thus fails in his attempt to refute the case for the heresy of paraphrase. But, despite the philistine tone, he is surely right to query whether fusion of form and content can be used to differentiate poetry from non-poetry (he correctly notes that

---

[33] For the 'purity' of music see Scruton (1997) 478. For Scruton 'music is *intrinsically* aesthetic; and any society that makes music is already taking an interest, however primitive, in something that has no purpose but itself'. Surprisingly this view is shared by so noted a culturalist as Edward Said: 'Unlike the words of a great poem . . . the notes in a piece of music in the end either refer back to themselves or to other music, and are uncorrupted by references or connotations that stand outside the actual sound' (Said (2001) 11). But music in practice can serve many instrumental purposes (e.g. encouragement to valour), and I doubt whether we have access to the intrinsic nature of anything (even supposing that the thing has an intrinsic nature). What is true is that it is easier to make a pure judgement of taste about, say, a Bach concerto than about a poem.

[34] See, for example, Scruton (1999) chs. 10 and 11.

[35] Kivy (1997) ch. 4, 'On the Unity of Form and Content'.   [36] Ibid. 84.

[37] 'We can very properly use paraphrases as pointers and as short-hand references provided that we know what we are doing' (Brooks (1974) 196–7).

Bradley wobbles about whether such fusion is a mark of poetry as such or only of great poetry).

My argument, it will be remembered, is simply that the judgement of taste is a judgement of form and content together. The notion that in poetry there is a profound organic unity between the two is most familiar to English readers from the poet Samuel Taylor Coleridge, who obtained the idea from post-Kantian German aesthetics and who declared 'such as the life is, such is the form'.[38] This conception of poetic diction is an appealing one, and certainly preferable to any notion that poetic language is merely dress to the thought.[39] But nonetheless, in its strong form, it should be rejected. Much of the entire intellectual project of the Yale critic Paul de Man was devoted to comprehensively deconstructing this Romantic theory, which he regarded as evincing ontological bad faith.[40] We may have a yearning for unity, between world and word, object and subject, form and content, but de Man, resisting such sentimental longings, works ceaselessly to prise the pairs apart, to make clear that the movement from one to the other is difficult and treacherous. We have no good reason to suppose that art can reconcile conflicts that are elsewhere unreconciled;[41] or that linguistic forms correspond to prior experiences or to the world outside language. Hence de Man's un-Romantic preference for allegory (a figure of disjunction) over symbolism (a figure of unification);[42] hence too his stress on linguistic aporia in the texts he explores, on their self-deconstructing character. The Coleridgean account ignores the slippage that continually occurs within texts, and which is often evoked with Derrida's term *différance*; for Coleridge poetic language is present to itself and to us, but for Derrida there is a constant traffic between presence and absence:

The play of differences supposes, in effect, syntheses and referrals which forbid at any moment, or in any sense, that a simple element be *present* in and of itself,

---

[38] Cited de Man (1983) 191 (from *Essays and Lectures on Shakespeare and Some Other Old Poets and Dramatists*).

[39] For a useful history of theories of poetic diction in English poetry see Marks (1998).

[40] See in particular his influential essay 'The Rhetoric of Temporality', included in de Man (1983) 187–228.

[41] de Man (1983) 237, 245 ('The Dead-End of Formalist Criticism').

[42] So Geoffrey Galt Harpham, 'Aesthetics and the Fundamentals of Modernity' in Levine (1994) 134; Denis Donoghue, 'Murray Krieger versus Paul de Man' in M. P. Clark (2000) 110; Isobel Armstrong (2000) 35.

referring only to itself.... Nothing, neither among the elements nor within the system, is anywhere ever simply present or absent. There are only, everywhere, differences and traces of traces.[43]

Literary critics often write, particularly in the case of a certain kind of 'gritty' poetry, that the words become like the things described, closing the gap between signifier and signified. In abstract linguistic terms this is probably nonsense—in most cases the signifier is best treated as arbitrary in good Saussurean manner. As Terry Eagleton puts it:

> The celebrated 'materiality' of a poet like Heaney is really a linguistic trompe l'oeil, a psychological rather than ontological affair, a matter of association rather than incarnation. The density of his discourse does not 'embody' material process... it is just that the one phenomenon brings the other to mind.[44]

This may well be right, if rather over-confident ('really' is as ever the give-away). But the 'psychology' surely is important; within a particular tradition readers may become acculturated to respond in this way, so that, in Eagleton's words, 'an awareness of the textures of signs puts us in mind of the textures of actual things'. So there is nothing irrational—unless one supposes that cultural experience is purely irrational—in finding a special materiality in the poetry of Keats or Seamus Heaney or Ted Hughes in English, or of Lucretius or Horace in Latin.

Similarly either a writer or a reader may feel that a particular way of expressing something has a special sense of inevitability and rightness about it. Virginia Woolf describes how such an occasion arises for her Lily Briscoe:

> She looked at her canvas; it was blurred. With a sudden intensity, as if she saw it clear for a second, she drew a line there, in the centre. It was done; it was finished.[45]

Pater thought this perfection happened when a writer removed all 'surplusage' so that each word was exactly the *mot juste* and none could be removed without loss. Flaubert is Pater's master in this 'exact apprehension of what was *needed* to carry the meaning',[46]

---

[43] Derrida (1981) 26. [44] Eagleton (1999) 15.
[45] Cited by Lyas (1997) 70 (from the last chapter of *To The Lighthouse*).
[46] Pater (1973) 76 (from 'Style'). Pater's account is marred by excessive mentalism; he appears to assume a prior meaning for which the right words are then found. Experience suggests that such rightness is only found in the making, that we do not know fully what we wish to say until the process of writing is complete.

which Flaubert finds in the *Aeneid* for example ('There are phrases there which stay in one's head, by which I find myself beset, as with those musical airs which are for ever returning, and cause you pain, you love them so much'[47]). This rightness may proceed from a sense of a particular harmony (or a pointed disharmony) between form and content.[48] John Ruskin has a brilliant passage on the way Pope employs the potential of the end-stopped couplet to fix the character of Sir Plume in *The Rape of the Lock*:

> Sir Plume, of amber snuff box justly vain,
> And the nice conduct of a clouded cane.

'Such writing', Ruskin observes, 'admits...of no careless or imperfect construction, but allows any intelligible degree of inversion'; and he continues:

Thus, 'Sir Plume, of amber snuff-box justly vain' is not only more rhythmic, but more elegant and accurate than 'Sir Plume, justly vain of his amber snuff-box'; first, because the emphasis of rhyme is laid on his vanity, not his box; secondly, because the 'his', seen on full consideration to be unnecessary, is omitted, to concentrate the sentence; and with a farther and more subtle reason,... that a coxcomb cannot, properly speaking, *possess* anything, but is possessed by everything, so that in the next line Pope does not say 'And the nice conduct of *his* clouded cane', but of *a* clouded cane.[49]

Pope, along the lines Eliot suggests, is thinking in the couplet form.

But, of course, none of this puts a stop to *différance*. Indeed one can say that the relationship between content and form changes as the artwork changes, as happens in its reception. This is particularly clear in the case of painting where the physical character of the work including its tonal relationships can change visibly over time. In the first chapter we saw how Pater perceived the subject matter of Leonardo's *Last Supper* (as it became subject to the ravages of time) to be the decay of faith; this meaning perfectly fitted the

---

[47] Pater (1973) 73.

[48] Sometimes a positive effect comes from a perceived *disharmony*. For example, in *Paradise Lost* the classical form and the Christian content seem often to pull in different directions, energizing the poem. Similarly in his sonnet 'On the Late Massacre in Piedmont' the form (normally associated with subjects like love) is put under violent pressure by the power of Milton's denunciations—the result is thrilling but not harmonious. But in these cases too form and content work *together*.

[49] Cited by Marks (1998) 230–1 (from *The Elements of English Prosody*, 1880); Bloom (1969) 351.

decayed and fragile form of the painting as it was in his day. If the title of Whistler's painting of his mother were lost along with all other evidence about the work, its subject might be differently construed (is, then, the title part of the work, as we perceive it?). The subject matter of many artworks is disputed; for example, the painting by Titian usually treated as an allegory of something like *Sacred and Profane Love* has also been taken to be a wedding picture, depicting the clothed bride and the naked goddess Venus. Clearly, with such a divergence, the relationship between form and content will be differently construed.[50]

One of the objections to the Romantic thesis (as to Russian Formalism in the twentieth century) is that it depends upon an absolute divide between the poetic and the non-poetic (or between literature and non-literature), which it sees in terms of qualities *in* the work itself. The difference between poetry and non-poetry is, on such a view, a conceptual matter, and thus could play no part in the Kantian judgement of taste. And indeed one does not need to be a 'radical' critic to find the concept of literature a problematic one. C. S. Lewis, in an argument with E. M. W. Tillyard, made the point long ago, and it would be difficult to improve on his formulation:

> discussions about 'Literature'—as if literature were a single homogeneous thing like water—are discussions about a nonentity. Poetry is not a low nor a lofty, a useful or a mischievous, a grave or a trivial, a 'true' or a 'false' activity, any more than 'saying' is. In that sense there is really no such thing as literature—only a crowd of people using concrete language as well as they can to talk about anything that happens to interest them.[51]

Conservatives today habitually try to ring-fence literature with some notion of 'literarity', usually of a formalist kind (unlike their Victorian predecessors who emphasized content); but there is no great gulf fixed between the language used in canonical texts and, say, complex conversational exchanges, or a fine piece of journalism, or even a cleverly phrased advertisement (which might indeed

---

[50] For the Titian example and other sensible thoughts on this issue see Meyer Schapiro, 'On Perfection, Coherence, and Unity of Form and Content', in Beckley (1998) 3–43. Schapiro points out that perfection is not a prerequisite for artistic greatness (as evidenced, for example, by the unevenness of Shakespeare, even in his finest plays).

[51] Tillyard and Lewis (1965) 112–13.

involve a feedback from 'literature').[52] The frequent claim that 'non-literary' language is purely instrumental, or simply about reference or information exchange, is simply false. (Of course in a more discursive, non-ontological sense, within a series of acts of communal negotiation, we can continue to use the word 'literature' and argue about the forms of attention we want to give texts so designated.) It could be maintained that poetry is a more useful category than literature, on the grounds that in poetry 'normal' grammar, syntax, vocabulary are all subtly transformed by their relocation (this is an aspect of what the Russian Formalist, Victor Shklovsky, called 'defamiliarization'[53]); however the boundary between poetry and prose is notoriously difficult to police, and sooner or later it is conceded that some 'prose' has 'poetic' quality, and vice versa.

Moreover 'ordinary' people, just as much as artists, can produce writings of great beauty. Colin Lyas cites an epitaph for a two-year-old child of a laconic and dignified effectiveness: 'Peace to his dear soul'.[54] Language, one of the greatest achievements of the species in a world aflame with signs, is a collective creation, something that the more democratic students of aesthetics, like the pragmatist John Dewey, have always recognized.[55] Thinking most men and women capable of making objects of beauty, William Morris privileged the more widely disseminated decorative arts over the fine arts (the latter were too much associated both with mystified notions of artistic genius and the sort of cultural capital, linked with wealth and privilege, later diagnosed by Bourdieu and others).[56] According to Schiller the aesthetic is the common property of us all, because it accords with our human make-up:

---

[52] Cf. Croce (1995) 40: 'Man speaks at every instant like the poet because, like the poet, he expresses his impressions and his feelings in the form called ordinary conversation.'

[53] The Russian is *ostraneniye*. See Lemon and Reis (1965) 12: 'The technique of art is to make objects "unfamiliar", to make forms difficult, to increase the difficulty and length of perception because the process of perception is an aesthetic end in itself and must be prolonged. *Art is a way of experiencing the artfulness of an object; the object is not important.*' Such making strange is indeed characteristic of much poetry but also of effective language use in general (and so cannot of itself be a mark of literariness).

[54] Lyas (1997) 100.

[55] See further Ch. 3, pp. 119, 121 below.

[56] For a fuller discussion see Ch. 3, pp. 118–19 below.

Man, as we know, is neither exclusively matter nor exclusively mind. Beauty, as the consummation of his humanity, can therefore be neither exclusively life nor exclusively form.[57]

For Schiller, as for Morris, all of us are artists, loving the discipline of form:

And as form gradually comes upon him from without—in his dwelling, his household goods, and his apparel—so finally it begins to take possession of him himself, transforming at first only the outer, but ultimately the inner, man too. Uncoordinated leaps of joy turn into dance, the unformed movements of the body into the graceful and harmonious language of gesture; the confused and indistinct cries of feeling become articulate, begin to obey the laws of rhythm, and to take on the contours of song. If the Trojan host storms on to the battlefield with piercing shrieks like a flock of cranes, the Greek army approaches it in silence, with noble and measured tread. In the former case we see only the exuberance of blind forces; in the latter, the triumph of form and the simple majesty of law.[58]

These may be essentializing moves, but, on this occasion, profitably so.

The whole issue of form and content changes complexion if we shift attention from qualities in the work to where, within Kantian aesthetics, it properly belongs, the mind of the receiver. We may then distinguish two modes of reading: the 'transitive' which seeks to extract a content from a piece of writing in a basically utilitarian spirit (as often when we are reading a learned article or a newspaper story) and the 'intransitive' which attends to form as well as content (I borrow these terms from Murray Krieger[59]). Any piece of writing can be read in either way, but if one is reading to make a judgement of taste one must read intransitively. Extreme formalists like Fry may even lose their capacity to do this; Fry talks at times as if he looks at a picture in terms of the form (in his rather restricted sense) in one way, in terms of the content in another.[60] In other words a

---

[57] Schiller (1967) 103. [58] Ibid. 213.

[59] 'My Travels with the Aesthetic' in Clark (2000) 208–36 (p. 212). Krieger wrongly draws the conclusion from his distinction that an aesthetic response is largely to the formal features of a text. Rosenblatt (1981) makes a not dissimilar distinction between 'efferent' and 'aesthetic' reading, the latter focused on what the reader *is living through during the reading event* (p. 22). Any text can be read either way, *King Lear* efferently, a training manual aesthetically. However Rosenblatt prefers the aesthetic as a general model of reading, because language is always 'interpenetrated with life experience' (p. 28).

[60] For attempts by Fry to solve this problem see e.g. 'Retrospect' in *Vision and Design* and two essays in C. Reed (1996) 380–400: 'The Double Nature of Painting' and 'The Meaning of

sort of dissociation seems to have been created in Fry by the continual dogmatic application of his theory of art to his acts of viewing. T. S. Eliot complained that you have to read Milton's verse once for the sense and once for the sound; one may dispute the truth of this particular instance, but most would agree that a sense of such a disjunction would register as a fault.[61] Much commoner is the current tendency to read literature for the content alone. It is odd that this should be the case at a time when a number of theorists are seeking to read texts not normally regarded as 'literary' in an intransitive manner. For example Hayden White's whole project has been about the importance of form as well as content in history-writing; the way historians emplot and trope their material will determine the 'meaning' of their historical narratives.[62] As with poetry, the two terms can be differently conceptualized. White seems to regard unemplotted matter (for example, in a chronicle) as the content, the emplotment and the troping as the form. Taking a slightly broader view we might say that the original context of events is the content (for example, certain data from the fifteenth century), their eventuation (their part in 'the Renaissance') the form. But on any model it remains true that there is, in White's way of putting it, a content of the form.

II

Reading Horace's *Odes* provides a good illustration of many of the points I have been making so far. If we abstract a content from them, it appears that many of the poems are 'about' the 'same'

Pictures 1—Telling a Story'. Fry's practice shows that there can be a third way of reading (perverse as I regard this as being), one attentive to the form alone; a great deal of training is needed to achieve such a mode of reading, which would be even more difficult with literature than with the visual arts.

[61] Kermode (1975a) 263 (from 'Milton 1'). More interesting is Eliot's treatment of Swinburne, whom he regards as living purely in a world of words: 'Compare "Snowdrops that plead for pardon | And pine for fright" with the daffodils that come before the swallow dares. The snowdrop of Swinburne disappears, the daffodil of Shakespeare remains'. This is, for Eliot, a different matter from the bad poet who just cannot get his words and objects to fit ('Swinburne as Poet' in Eliot (1920) 134–6).

[62] Cf. Loesberg (1991) 123 on the ways that 'literary and linguistic structures have made history by making our understanding of it'; for him history, like philosophy, thus flows from the aesthetic.

things (the need for present enjoyment, the joys of friendship and retirement, the changefulness of love, and so forth); that at best they are composed of topoi, the stalest of commonplaces, at worst they subserve the interests of a particular narrow coterie, of patriarchy, and of an unattractive autocracy. On the other hand there is the unusually skilful crafting; Brigid Brophy talks about poems 'held in shape by excellently hard bony forms' by an 'adroit word-tactician'.[63] In them we encounter a style which combines the arty and the prosaic, along with a highly artificial, mannered word-order (constituting what was called by Nietzsche, as we have seen in the first chapter, a verbal mosaic), together with a structural wilfulness which often requires a reader to strain in the attempt, taxing or vain, to apprehend. When I first encountered the *Odes* at school, I was immediately impressed by evocative images, arresting phrases, while often completely baffled by how the various elements fitted together, what the poems as a whole were 'about'. All these characteristics, 'the verbal corrugation',[64] the dance of the structure (involving deliberate disproportion and unpredictable turns), produce poems that achieve a density and originality that has seldom if ever been surpassed. But a purely formalist defence is insufficient, if, as I have been arguing, the judgement of taste is a judgement of form and content together. Clearly, if we judge the *Odes* beautiful, we will be reluctant for their content to be reduced to a paraphrase, a set of commonplaces, an abstracted 'message'.

For the 'structure' of his poems, the way they get from their starting-point to their ending, the order and relative space given to the motifs, Horace had evidently reflected deeply on the way the lyric poets of Archaic and Classical Greece organized their poems. The result is a strange and striking combination of ancient structure with modern content, which may well have made some of Horace's original readers find the poems weirdly experimental. This process of adapting the metres, structures, and procedures of Archaic Greece was something different from (say) Virgil's use of the hexameter, since there had been a continuous tradition of epic writing in Latin since Ennius, and the processes of accommodation were accordingly well advanced. Horace had at least one Latin lyric

---

[63] See Martindale and Hopkins (1993) 23 (quoted from *Arion*, 1970, 128).

[64] So the poet Charles Tomlinson, 'Some Aspects of Horace in the Twentieth Century', in Martindale and Hopkins (1993) 240–57 (quotation, p. 240).

76   *Content, Form, and Frame*

to take as a model, Catullus' Sapphic poem 11, which he imitated in two of the *Odes*:

> Furi et Aureli, comites Catulli,
> sive in extremos penetrabit Indos,
> litus ut longe resonante Eoa
>   tunditur unda,
>
> sive in Hyrcanos Arabasve molles   5
> seu Sacas sagitteriferosve Parthos
> sive quae septemgeminus colorat
>   aequora Nilus,
>
> sive trans altas gradietur Alpes,
> Caesaris visens monimenta magni,   10
> Gallicum Rhenum, horribiles quoque ulti-
>   mosque Britannos,
>
> omnia haec, quaecumque feret voluntas
> caelitum, temptare simul parati,
> pauca nuntiate meae puellae   15
>   non bona dicta:
>
> cum suis vivat valeatque moechis,
> quos simul complexa tenet trecentos,
> nullum amans vere, sed identidem omnium
>   ilia rumpens;   20
>
> nec meum respectet, ut ante, amorem,
> qui illius culpa cecidit veluti prati
> ultimi flos, praetereunte postquam
>   tactus aratro est.

Furius and Aurelius, comrades of Catullus, whether he penetrates to the farthest Indians, where the shore is pounded by the far-echoing eastern wave, or to the Hyrcanians and the effeminate Arabs or the Sacae and the arrow-bearing Parthians, or the levels which the sevenfold Nile colours, or whether he goes beyond the high Alps, visiting the monuments of mighty Caesar, the Gallic Rhine, the horrible and furthest Britons too, ready together to attempt whatever the will of the heavenly ones brings, give as brief message to my girl these not fair words: farewell and long life with her adulterers, whom she holds in her embrace three hundred together, loving none truly, but again and again bursting the belly's arteries of all; and let her not look to my love, as before, which, by her fault, has fallen, like the flower at the meadow's edge, after it has been touched by a passing plough.

Horace could have learned from this poem the use of contrasted registers and tones, the contrived structural asymmetry, the unexpected turns in the argument, the plangent dying fall. Catullus sometimes treats his affair as a kind of marriage, and this poem perhaps makes the renunciation of love into a formal divorce, one form of which was a *repudium per litteras* (cf. *nuntiate* and *moechis*). The opening stanzas are easily read as a humorous, hyperbolical, epicizing, and ebullient tribute to his friends, since a willingness to share an arduous journey was a sign of friendship and part of the military oath (Horace imitated these fantastic hyperboles in *Odes* 1. 22 and 2. 6). The tone changes abruptly with the restrained irony of the litotes *non bona dicta* and the scornful, disgusted sexual language of stanza 5 reinforced by three powerful elisions (the phrase *ilia rumpens* seems not to be obscene, but it is sexually violent). If the poem had ended there, it would have been arresting but it would have fallen short of greatness. However Catullus has another surprise in store for us, in a switch to a more lyrical mode. In epic cut flowers and dead young men are sometimes compared; but the flower motif was doubtless commoner in wedding songs (e.g. Catullus 62. 39 ff.; Sappho, fragment 105). Catullus is presumably ending his lyric in Sapphic metre with an image out of Sappho. Virgil later fused this stanza with a simile in Homer comparing a dead man to a broken poppy for his languorously eroticized picture of the dying Euryalus (*Aeneid* 9. 433–7):

> volvitur Euryalus leto, pulchrosque per artus
> it cruor inque umeros cervix conlapsa recumbit;
> purpureus veluti cum flos succisus aratro
> languescit moriens, lassove papavera collo
> demisere caput pluvia cum forte gravantur.

Euryalus rolls over in death; over his fair limbs the blood goes and his neck collapses and slumps over his shoulders; as when a purple flower cut from below by the plough languishes as it dies, or poppies droop their heads with tired neck when they happen to be weighed down by rain.

It has been suggested that the passage evokes the defloration of a bride with its attendant bleeding. In Catullus it is the man's love which is pathetically 'deflowered', in ironic reversal (the plough is a figure both for the penis and for civilization).[65] The flower at the edge of the field picks up the language of limits of the opening stanzas (*extremos, ultimos*). Virgil's lines are vague, opulent, smooth,

---

[65] Fowler (1987); for this nexus see, most recently, J. D. Reed (1997) 61.

redolent of a certain *fin-de-siècle* decadence. By contrast Catullus describes the flower's destruction in a precise and tactile way; we have the cutting *c* and *t* sounds and the unusual hypermetric elision of *prati* across the line division, suggestive of the cutting. *Tactus* is perfect in sound and sense and in its restraint—a touch is enough. Translations which coarsen the tone ruin the effect (so the Penguin translator, Peter Whigham, has 'slashed' and 'that you, tart, wantonly crushed'). In Catullus all violence of language is drained away in a perfect and perfectly timed diminuendo.

Ode 1.4 to Sestius has a somewhat similar structure; it too might be divided into three asymmetrical sections. The first three of the five stanzas, all three endstopped, describe the coming of spring in contrasting ways but all with excited gaiety: first the change in the weather and the renewal of activity among man and beast; secondly the dancing of Venus and her naked escort under a hanging moon; thirdly a sacrifice to Faunus and the preparations for a party. Then, introduced in bold asyndeton, there is a picture, reinforced by quadruple alliteration, of Death dramatically kicking at the door:

> pallida mors aequo pulsat pede pauperum tabernas
> regumque turres.

pale Death kicks with impartial foot at the huts of the poor and the towers of kings.

Scholars note that a sacrifice to Faunus in the temple on Tiber island was immediately followed by the festival of the dead, the Parentalia.[66] This may help to explain the sensibility that links spring and death, but it does not detract from the effect of sudden interruption (so unexpected that the poet W. S. Landor famously recorded his puzzlement: '*Pallida mors* has nothing to do with the above').[67] Finally, in a single sentence of six and a half lines that cuts across the final stanzas, the poet exhorts rich, happy (*beate*, 14) Sestius to enjoy sex and the symposium. Horace ends by lingering, lovingly and perhaps with a touch of antifeminist wit (the passions of the girls are fainter than the men's), on a vignette of the beautiful Lycidas:

> nec tenerum Lycidan mirabere, quo calet iuventus
> nunc omnis et mox virgines tepebunt.

---

[66] Nisbet and Hubbard (1970) 60, 66–7. [67] West (1995) 20.

nor will you wonder at tender Lycidas, for whom now all the youth is on fire and soon the girls will warm.

This final section takes the form of explicit advice, but the reader must fill out that advice to incorporate the pictures of spring and death that have preceded, to work out the connections between the three parts, to look to implications and associations to make sense of the whole. We could say that it is when we understand how form and content cohere in the poem that we experience beauty, which is also a sense of setting the mind free. There is a similar shift from spring to transience and mortality in *Ode* 4. 7 (*diffugere nives*), but this time smoothly and without the grammatical and tonal disjunctions of 1. 4. As the critic A. D. Nuttall has it, we perhaps find in this transition 'something very strange indeed: the discovery of despair in the very heart of bliss'.[68]

As in the case of *Ode* 2. 5, discussed in Chapter 1, Horace is partly arguing in images, juxtaposing those images without logical connectives. One can contrast the overtly logical structure of Marvell's 'To His Coy Mistress', a poem in other respects usually and rightly seen as 'Horatian'. Like Horace, Marvell blends tones in a way that collapses an easy distinction between light and serious poetry, now grave, now gay, now sardonic, now impatient; the poem combines wit, and even charm, with an erotic urgency that culminates in a violently sexual image.[69] However the form of his poem could be set out as an exercise in logic—if we lived for ever, we could take our time; *however* we all die, *therefore* let us make love while we may:

> Had we but world enough, and time,
> This coyness, lady, were no crime.
> We would sit down, and think which way
> To walk, and pass our long love's day.
> Thou by the Indian Ganges' side
> Shouldst rubies find; I by the tide
> Of Humber would complain. I would

---

[68] A. D. Nuttall, 'Marvell and Horace: Colour and Translucency', in Martindale and Hopkins (1993) 86–102 (quotation, p. 97).
[69] In one respect the poem could be said wittily to play off form against content, since it urges haste at the level of content while employing strong rhymes and numerous monosyllables that together make it majestically unhurried. But one might also see a convergence: the movement of the tetrameters, always shorter than you think, suddenly open out worlds of time, at the poem's climactic turn ('but . . .').

Love you ten years before the flood;
And you should, if you please, refuse
Till the conversion of the Jews.
My vegetable love should grow
Vaster than empires and more slow.
An hundred years should go to praise
Thine eyes, and on thy forehead gaze,
Two hundred to adore each breast,
But thirty thousand to the rest;
An age at least to every part,
And the last age should show your heart—
For, lady, you deserve this state,
Nor would I love at lower rate.

   But at my back I always hear
Time's wingèd chariot hurrying near;
And yonder all before us lie
Deserts of vast eternity.
Thy beauty shall no more be found,
Nor, in thy marble vault, shall sound
My echoing song. Then worms shall try
That long preserved virginity,
And your quaint honour turn to dust,
And into ashes all my lust.
The grave's a fine and private place.
But none, I think, do there embrace.

   Now, therefore, while the youthful glue
Sits on thy skin like morning dew,
And while thy willing soul transpires
At every pore with instant fires,
Now let us sport us while we may,
And now, like amorous birds of prey,
Rather at once our time devour
Than languish in his slow-chapped power.
Let us roll all our strength, and all
Our sweetness, up into one ball;
And tear our pleasures with rough strife
Thorough the iron grates of life.
Thus, though we cannot make our sun
Stand still, yet we will make him run.

Marvell ends too, not with a tangent as Horace so often does, but by pressing home, energetically, the conclusion of his argument; the initially disconcerting enjambment gives special emphasis to the climactic final word. Scholars categorize 'To His Coy Mistress', using a famous Horatian phrase, as a poem of a *carpe diem* type. All such poems can be made to 'mean' much the same, but only by the now familiar process of abstracting a content.

Ode 1. 7 (*Laudabunt alii*) is an even more extreme example of the apparent vagaries of Horatian structure, its unexpected twists and turns. The poem celebrates Tibur (modern Tivoli) and its most famous son, the *nobilis* Lucius Munatius Plancus, who had close connections with the ruling elite. And again it can be divided into three unequal sections. The first (14 lines) is in the form of the priamel, common in early Greek lyric, syntactically straggling: let others write about the famous cities of Greece, I will tell of the beauties of Tibur in Italy. The second section (six and a half lines), introduced without a connective, advises Plancus to take pleasure in wine as solace, whether abroad or at home in Tibur. The third (eleven and a half lines, 21–32), again beginning in asyndeton, tells how Teucer fleeing the anger of his father arranged a party to console himself and his crew before going on with his journey to a new land:

> Teucer Salamina patremque
> cum fugeret, tamen uda Lyaeo
> tempora populea fertur vinxisse corona,
> sic tristes adfatus amicos:
>
> 'quo nos cumque feret melior fortuna parente   25
> ibimus, o socii comitesque.
> nil desperandum Teucro duce et auspice Teucro.
> certus enim promisit Apollo
>
> ambiguam tellure nova Salamina futuram.
> o fortes peioraque passi   30
> mecum saepe viri, nunc vino pellite curas—
> cras ingens iterabimus aequor.'

Teucer, when he fled Salamis and his father, nonetheless is said to have bound his temples wet with wine with a garland of poplar, thus addressing his sad comrades: 'Wherever fortune better than my father bears us, we will go, o friends and comrades. You must not despair with Teucer as leader, and as augur Teucer. For trusty Apollo has promised that there will be a second Salamis in a new land. O brave men and ones who have suffered worse with me often, now drive away cares with wine; tomorrow we will again go over the huge sea.'

The whole is bound together by verbal echoes across the sections and by themes of disavowal and the *carpe diem* philosophy of the lyric *convivium*.⁷⁰ The apparent looseness and difficulty of the structure only encourages us to engage in a free Kantian play that involves various faculties of the mind. Whereas in 'To His Coy Mistress' Marvell's syllogistic logic ties the reader to a particular track through the poem, Horace allows us a greater experience of freedom as we follow verbal hints and implications in our own way—reflecting, it may be, on where we feel at home; or on the relationship between modernity and myth and the role of poetry in either; or on the contrast between the lyric present (*nunc*, 31) and an epic world of time and history (figured, perhaps, by the huge sea of the poem's ending).

Horace is usually seen as a supreme ironist. Irony is a destabilizing trope because it changes meaning but not in an easily quantifiable way (it is rare that a simple inversion of sense takes place). And Horace also likes ironizing, self-deconstructing forms, in particular versions of what scholars have reified into something they call the *recusatio*, the poem of disavowal (supposedly deriving, by way of Virgil's sixth *Eclogue*, from the prologue to Callimachus' *Aetia*). Gregson Davis suggests that what we have here is less disavowal than the equivalent of the rhetorician's *praeteritio*, a figure by which one pretends to pass over something in the very act of mentioning it ('I will not mention X, Y, and Z').⁷¹ In such poems Horace expresses his inability to write in a grand style, frequently assigning the task to others. A typically slippery example is *Ode* 1. 6, where Horace demits the task of praising Augustus' general, Agrippa, in favour of the epic poet Varius, while he confines himself to light themes like the warfare of love:

> Scriberis Vario fortis et hostium
> victor Maeonii carminis alite,
> quam rem cumque ferox navibus aut equis
>   miles te duce gesserit;
>
> nos, Agrippa, neque haec dicere nec gravem   5
> Pelidae stomachum cedere nescii

---

⁷⁰ So Davis (1991) 16–18, 189–99. Thus *undique decerptam olivam* (7) resonates with *populea corona* (23), *carmine perpetuo* (6) with *imbres perpetuo* (16–17), *Tiburni lucus* (13) with *Tiburis umbra tui* (21), *labores molli mero* (18–19) with *vino pellite curas* (31); *uda* (13) echoes *uda* (22), *tristitiam* (18) *tristes* (24). The slippages in the sense are as significant as the repetitions, as we work with language to make sense of an experience of the world.

⁷¹ Davis (1991) ch. 1, 'Modes of Assimilation'; for Davis's discussion of *Ode* 1. 6 see pp. 33–9. I am heavily indebted to this admirable study throughout this whole section.

>   nec cursus duplicis per mare Ulixei
>   nec saevam Pelopis domum
>
> > conamur, tenues grandia, dum pudor
> > imbellisque lyrae Musa potens vetat   10
> > laudes egregii Caesaris et tuas
> >   culpa deterere ingeni.
>
> > quis Martem tunica tectum adamantina
> > digne scripserit aut pulvere Troico
> > nigrum Merionen aut ope Palladis   15
> >   Tydiden superis parem?
>
> > nos convivia, nos proelia virginum
> > sectis in iuvenes unguibus acrium
> > cantamus, vacui sive quid urimur,
> >   non praeter solitum leves.   20

You will be written of by Varius, bird of Homeric song, as brave and victorious over your enemies, whatever achievements, fierce with ships or horses, your soldiery performs under your leadership. I, Agrippa, do not try to speak of these things nor of the weighty bad temper of Peleus' son not knowing how to yield, nor the journeys over sea of duplicitous Ulysses, nor the savage home of Pelops, great themes for a slight person, while modesty and the Muse powerful over the unwarlike lyre forbids me to spoil the praises of excellent Caesar and your own by defect of talent. Who could worthily write of Mars encased in adamantine tunic or Meriones black with Trojan dust or Tydeus' son equal to the gods above by aid of Pallas? I sing parties, I the battles of fierce girls, their nails cut to fight the young men, whether I am free from love or aflame somewhat, light not against my fashion.

I read the irony here as radically destabilizing. Only a grand poem would be worthy of the great man, yet the poem can itself be seen as an effective panegyric (even the name of the addressee, delayed until line 5, may be a surprise substitution for Augustus, patron of Varius). Is the *recusatio* a genuine rejection or, as Davis argues, a form of assimilation; a way of *excluding* epic themes from lyric as an act of generic definition or a way of *including* them? Is decorum maintained or infringed? And what stand does the poem take on the high style, as with the description of Varius as 'a bird of Maeonian song'? When Horace uses reductive phrases in connection with Homeric themes (*stomachum*, *duplicis*), are we dealing with travesty, parody of epic, or with a sign of Horace's incapacity to sustain an epic flight[72] (there is no obvious undercutting of the grand style

---

[72] Pelops is associated with tragedy more than epic, so perhaps Horace cannot even get his genres right.

in stanza 4)? Is the irony critical, elusive, or collusive? Horace exploits vocabulary shared between the two genres (though in 'different' senses) when he uses the love–war trope in stanza 5. Signifiers employable in different discursive arenas are frequently arranged in a hierarchy of value; often one use is termed 'literal', the other 'metaphorical'. Does Horace's use of the trope (a word that itself implies a turn from the 'proper' meaning) accept this hierarchy and the generic hierarchy that goes with it, or does he subvert it? Is he eroticizing epic, or epicizing erotic?[73] Can the poem be read as implying the superiority of lyric as the more inclusive genre? If the *recusatio* is about being true to oneself, is the self a stable or a fleeting thing? When the poet asks 'who could worthily celebrate Agrippa?' a number of answers are possible: 'not me'; 'no-one'; 'Varius'; 'an epic poet like Homer'—or 'me; I have just done it'. Such evasiveness seems typical of Horace in the *Odes*: hence the fondness for negations and negative commands, the deconstructing of the opposition between grand and light lyric, the stress on flux. Even the positioning of some poems can be read ironically. Thus 1. 38 (*Persicos odi*) appears to enact simplicity of life and of the art of the *genus tenue*, giving Horace's moral and aesthetic preferences, as the poet sits privately drinking under an arbour of myrtle (sacred to Venus). But the poem immediately follows a grand public ode about the death of Cleopatra in high Pindaric style and dominated by very different images of drinking.

By the time Horace published his fourth book of *Odes*, he is often supposed to have become more comfortable with the role of court poet, with less need for the ironic evasions of his earlier work. But the book begins with a poem that is a very masterpiece of obliquity (*Intermissa, Venus*). The poem starts with an apotropaic hymn to Venus; aged 50, the poet is too old for love, so Venus is urged to go elsewhere, to the house of the youthful Paulus Maximus, who married into the imperial house and whose marriage the poem may obliquely celebrate (the poem can thus be read, *inter alia*, as an epithalamium for a Roman grandee). The poet has no woman or boy, no inclination for the *convivium*. Why, then, the tears on his cheek, the failure of speech? The poet is after all in love, in his dreams endlessly pursuing the obscure object of desire amid the

---

[73] There is a similar problem with the military language of Marvell's 'Upon Appleton House': is Marvell conjuring the Civil War into his poem, or exorcizing it?

male sports of the Campus Martius. One way of reading this poem is to say it is 'about' the experience of falling in love in the autumn of life. It starts as though it is to be the sort of poem that scholars like to categorize as the *renuntiatio amoris*; and it starts with an instance of self-quotation, intratextuality, from *Ode* 1. 19 (*Mater saeva Cupidinum*), a poem about sexual desire and its imperative demands. An earlier poem of the type is *Ode* 3. 26 (*Vixi puellis*), and this is recalled, together with its surprise ending when Horace asks Venus to grant him one last amour. So Saint Augustine was later to ask God, 'give me chastity, but not yet'. As in these earlier poems Horace raids the language of Roman erotic elegy,[74] and in particular the love–war trope. Paulus will carry 'the standards of Venus' warfare' (*signa militiae tuae*, 16), and, like the poet-lover of elegy, he has a richer rival for his *puella*, one, however, than whom he will prove 'more powerful' (a word with both erotic and political overtones). At line 33 the poem changes direction, from renouncing love to declaring it—the symptoms are there for the poet and us to *read*. And in the final stanza Horace gives himself up to erotic reverie: the tongue-tied lover describes his intense erotic experience in verses which are supremely moving and eloquent, in a beautifully self-deconstructing gesture:

> sed cur heu, Ligurine, cur
>   manat rara meas lacrima per genas?
> cur facunda parum decoro   35
>   inter verba cadit lingua silentio?
>
> nocturnis ego somniis
>   iam captum teneo, iam volucrem sequor
> te per gramina Martii
>   Campi, te per aquas, dure, volubiles.   40

> But why, oh why, my Ligurine,
> Flow my thin tears down these pale cheeks of mine?
>   Or why, my well-graced words among,
> With an uncomely silence fails my tongue?
>
>   Hard-hearted, I dream every night
> I hold thee fast! But fled hence, with the light,
>   Whether in Mars his field thou be,
> Or Tiber's winding streams, I follow thee.   (Ben Jonson)

---

[74] Thus *bella* (2); *regno* (4); *saeva* (5); *mollibus* (6); *blandae preces* (8)—*blandus* is a favourite word of Propertius; *iecur* (12); *teneris* (26); *dure* (40).

Facunda is a particularly brilliant touch—Horace is no inarticulate teenager. On this reading—where Ben Jonson with 'My Picture Left in Scotland' and Marvell with 'Young Love' have been before us—the poem construes itself, under the sign of irony and self-mockery, as an expression of male vacillation, so evident in the erotic sphere; an expression too of youthful arrogance and the sentimental folly of the autumnal *amator*. The phrase 'falling in love' catches something of this, and its potential embarrassments which the poem, on such an account, negotiates so cunningly.

Another way of reading the poem is to say that it is 'about' Horace's decision to resume the writing of lyric, including erotic lyric, after a gap of ten years. Much of the poem's language can then be remapped on to a discourse about writing poetry.[75] First poems readily lend themselves to programmatic readings; this one can be read as offering a sketch of the nature and contents of the whole book—we have the poet growing old, love, praise of a leading figure in Roman society connected with Augustus, all concerns of this collection. The autocitations would then indicate that the poem and the book are the work of the author of *Odes* 1–3. The erotic vocabulary would serve as an intertextual gesture in the direction of another body of writing, its language and motifs. The stress on the appropriateness of love for a young man (Paulus is called a *puer* in line 15) would be the enunciation of a central tenet of Horatian poetics: the principle of decorum. Horace's anxieties about Ligurinus—the combination of compulsion with uncertainty of attainment—would figure such feelings in relation to poetry. A number of key terms in erotic discourse are applicable also to kinds of poetry; thus elegy is 'soft', *mollis* or *tener*, in contrast with 'hard' epic. This slide of the signifier, this traffic of intertextual signifiers between different meanings of key terms, is applicable to a number of words in the poem.[76]

A poem, then, about being too old for love or one about being too old for love poetry? And of course on either reading a duplicitous

---

[75] Thus *idoneum* (literary decorum, 12); *decens* (13); *pede* (metrical foot as well as foot, 27); *novis floribus* (new poetry, poetic garland, 32); *decoro* (35); *volubiles* (of stylistic fluency, voluble as well as rolling, 40).

[76] Cf. *meorum finis amorum* in *Ode* 4. 11. 31–2, which could mean 'last of my love affairs, girlfriends' or 'last of my love lyrics' (which the poem is)—*Amores* can be used as the title of a collection of love poems.

poem, since Horace is writing, and represents himself as desiring. Or should we replace either/or with both/and, arguing that the poem collapses the distinction by its recourse to the mobility of the signifier? Sex is text, at least in a poem. The aporia about love and the aporia about writing would then resolve themselves precisely into an aporia about the lover's discourse. Sex is something you do, love is something you feel, yet there is also no sex without prior text, no experience of love that is not inscription, always already. That paradox might shimmer through the poem's climactic moment of self-revelation: the significance of being tongue-tied in love only registers because of the existence of an eloquent, written discourse of desire within which lovers can situate themselves. Why do I specially value this poem, with which Tom Stoppard, in his play *The Invention of Love*, makes his heartaching Housman catch our hearts?[77] Partly because, as the words dissolve and refigure themselves, it finds a structure of sounds and significations to explore connections between flux and human desire. At all events the complex structure of *Ode* 4. 1 ensures that, whatever the poem 'means', it is no mere concatenation of inert commonplaces.

The following poem, 4. 2 (*Pindarum quisquis*), is constructed out of an analogous disavowal.[78] Horace declares his inability to write a grand Pindaric lyric in praise of Augustus' victory over the Sygambri, and commends the task to Iullus Antonius, son of the triumvir adopted by the *princeps*. But the description of Pindar in stanzas 2–5 is accomplished in a single massive sentence of persuasively Pindaric grandeur, and the image of a bee gathering thyme used to characterize the very different, less inspirational, highly-worked poetry of Horace is taken, paradoxically, from one of Pindar's victory odes. Moreover the collection contains two Pindaric victory poems for the young Caesars, Tiberius and Drusus, heirs of the *princeps*, neither of which appears obviously ironized (*Odes* 4. 4 and 14). Horace writes for Iullus praise in the Pindaric vaunting mode (lines 33–44), which he then contrasts with his own, less ambitious merging of his voice with that of the crowd at the triumph (45–52). At this moment of supposed humility Horace executes a spectacular piece of metrical virtuosity, incorporating within the Sapphic metre of the poem the measure of the old *versus quadratus* that featured in Roman triumphal songs: *O sol | pulcher, o laudande* (46–7), a sort of

[77] Stoppard (1997) 49–51.   [78] For a fine analysis Davis (1991) 133–43.

metrical pun. (Earlier, in line 23, Horace allowed the elision of *que* across the lines, a little liberty in imitation of Pindar's metrical freedom.) Horace ends by describing enticingly and at length, with finely wrought detail, the tiny calf which he is going to sacrifice (symbol of his carefully crafted poetry,[79] and appropriate to his 'little man' pose), in contrast to Iullus' grand hecatombs:

> te decem tauri totidemque vaccae,
> me tener solvet vitulus, relicta
> matre qui largis iuvenescit herbis 55
>   in mea vota,
>
> fronte curvatos imitatus ignes
> tertium lunae referentis ortum,
> qua notam duxit niveus videri,
>   cetera fulvus. 60

You, ten bulls and just as many heifers will release from your promises, me, a tender calf, which leaving its mother grows on the rich pastures to fulfil my vows, imitating with its brow the curved fires of the moon at its third rising, snow white to look at, where it has taken a mark, for the rest tawny.

The poem is one of the longest and grandest of Horace's odes, and involves imitation of both the style and the structure of Pindaric lyric. Is the poem then a Pindaric victory ode, or a mock victory ode, or a mock-mock victory ode? The effects of the ironies ricochet uncontrollably. The poem sets up numerous antitheses—Horace and Pindar, grand and light, swan and bee, large and small, sun and moon—only to unpick them again. Horace then favours, or purports to favour, simplicity, in art as in life, but he does so in a poem which starts by imitating Pindar's grand sweep and which can itself be described as Pindaric in scope and complexity.

Readers have always recognized the importance of transitions within the complex structures of the *Odes*. Writing of the Soracte *Ode* 1. 9 (*Vides ut alta*), the poet J. V. Cunningham observed: 'The meaning lay in the transitions themselves, in a certain balance of sensibility, a nice adjustment between imagery and statement which met the insoluble problems of life with a controlled use of distraction and irrelevance.'[80] In other words we find the play of a textual

---

[79] *Tener* (54) is a word with literary overtones (we recall the sacrificial image and the thin style in Callimachus' *Aetia* prologue); so too *imitatus* (57), which recalls *aemulari* in line 1.

[80] See Martindale and Hopkins (1993) 23 (quoted from *Arion*, 1970, 176 from *The Quest of the Opal*).

'Horace' over the material which establishes its special texture; and this texture transforms what might otherwise seem a set of rather trite topoi into something rich and strange. Another modern poet, Donald Davie, has written a whole poem 'Wombwell on Strike' about Horatian transitions, comparing their effect with that of tunnels on a railway line, an image already used in connection with Horace by Cunningham. Davie suggests that such Horatian procedures may bypass some of life's grittiest problems, like the contest between the miners and the Conservative government of Mrs Thatcher (both Arthur Scargill, the miners' leader, and the poet came from Yorkshire):

> Horace of course is not
> A temporizer, but
> His sudden and smooth transitions
>   (as, into a railway tunnel,
>   then out, to a different landscape)
> it must be admitted elide,
> and necessarily, what
> happens up there on the hill
>   or hill-ridge that the tunnel
>   of syntax so featly slides under.
> I have been reminded of this
> when, gratefully leaving my native
> haunts, the push-and-pull diesel
>   clatters into a tunnel
>   under a wooded escarpment:
> Wentwort Woodhouse, mounded
> or else in high shaws drifted
> over the miners' tramways.
>   Horace's streaming style
>   exhorts me never to pause;
> 'Press on,' he says, and indeed his
> suavities never entirely
> exclude the note of alarm:
>   'Leave the unlikely meaning
>   to eddy, or you are in trouble.'
> Wombwell—'womb well': it is
> foolish and barbarous wordplay,
> though happily I was
>   born of this tormented

>   womb, the taut West Riding.
> Yours was solid advice,
> Horace, and centuries have
> endorsed it; but over this tunnel
>   large policeman grapple
>   the large men my sons have become.[81]

The poem thus appears to criticize Horace for evasion. But, in a manner that seems eminently 'Horatian', it employs a Horatian mode and form (including a complex stanza pattern and elaborate syntax) to do so, thereby, perhaps, partly ironizing or disavowing its claims in the act of making them. In particular the poem's final turn, a picture of embattled miners and policeman, is as moving as it is unexpected, and in a very Horatian way.[82] As with Horace, there is the possibility of a play of irony over the whole ('Horace of course is not'; 'it must be admitted'; 'barbarous' i.e., in this context, non-Latin). The poem does not seem readily to take sides, but rather to acknowledge life's complexities (as over the poet's attitude to being a Yorkshireman: he is 'happy' to be such but the train at least seems 'grateful' to get away). Whatever view one takes of the transitions, they are an essential part of the way Horace's *Odes* mean, and of their beauty and 'virtue', as both Cunningham and Davie, from their seemingly different perspectives, agree.

III

The poem we usually call 'Catullus 64' or 'The Marriage of Peleus and Thetis' (modern acts of framing[83]) has often been criticized as pedantic and precious and lacking in passion. G. P. Goold, for whom Catullus' 'spontaneous and unaffected genius was ill-suited to the learned artificialities of the epyllion', cites a critic for whom Ariadne's description of the Minotaur as her lost brother (150) 'is an

---

[81] Davie (1990) 447–8. The poem is quoted and discussed by Charles Tomlinson in Martindale and Hopkins (1993) 247–50. Davie's 'shaws' may come from Housman's great translation of *Ode* 4. 7.

[82] Richard Thomas ingeniously suggests *per litteras* that the picture of Horace's big classmates, children of big centurions, in *Sat.* 1. 6. 72–3 may be an intertext here: *magni | quo pueri magnis e centurionibus orti*.

[83] In early modern editions the poems are regularly unnumbered but usually are assigned individual titles; for example, the Aldine edition of 1515 has *Argonautica* as the title of 64.

offence to us and ought to have been to Catullus'.[84] By contrast with such modern readers, the poem evidently affected Virgil deeply, for he returned to it often, and not only for his portrait of Dido (indeed the complex handling of time in the *Aeneid* may have been inspired by Catullus 64, with its flashbacks and flashforwards). Epyllion is not an ancient term, and the poem might be otherwise described as an experimental, modernist epic of a type being produced by avant-garde Roman poets in the 50s BC, partly in imitation of Callimachus and other Alexandrian poets. The opening lines of poem 64 with their echoes of Ennius and the rest[85] might have struck an educated reader as both familiar and odd, so that the poem can be said to problematize the whole question of genre, exposing an instability at its heart.

If, with Virgil, we are to adjudge this poem 'beautiful', we will do so, if my argument so far is accepted, on the basis of a response to form and content together, and without a prior concept. Three of the best-known positive readings of the last forty years fall short, to some degree, in that regard. Michael Putnam's account of 1961, an example of biographical criticism, takes the poem to be 'about' Catullus' relationship with Lesbia and his loss of his brother.[86] He tries to establish this by showing similarities in vocabulary, themes, and topoi between poem 64 and other poems in the collection.[87] In other words, his account becomes content driven, as he concentrates on the material, ignoring issues of form. John Bramble's influential reading of 1970 finds the power of the poem in the supposedly ambiguous manner in which Catullus treats his stories.[88] It is clear that Bramble starts from a very specific concept, one of the central doctrines of the 'New Criticism' (a mode of criticism just then migrating from English to Classics), the idea that all good poetry evinces irony, paradox, tension, and ambiguity.[89]

---

[84] Goold (1983) 251–2. A more positive response would be to argue that the reader is jolted by this defamiliarizing touch into remembering Medea; Medea, one of the most potent symbols of male fears about women's sexuality, killed her brother Absyrtus when eloping with Jason, and is a silent presence and absent other, from the very beginning of the poem.

[85] For details see Thomas (1999) 12–29.

[86] Putnam (1961).

[87] It is true that throughout his poetry Catullus has a concern with love, marriage, and betrayal; true too that the subjective, empathetic style of 64 and the constant involvement of the narrator with the events he describes gives the poem a 'personal' quality. But the differences between 64 and the shorter poems are manifold.

[88] Bramble (1970). [89] See e.g. the classic study of 1947 by Brooks (1974).

More sympathetic to me than either is the reading of 1982 by Richard Jenkyns, one to which my own subsequent description will owe much.[90] Jenkyns, rejecting the moralistic accounts of Bramble and others, sees the poem in term's of art for art's sake. Unfortunately he works with a diminished notion of the term, which he wrongly supposes implies a preoccupation with form and style to the detriment of content and a preference for unserious subjects (to constitute what he calls the literature of dandyism). Jenkyns has forgotten that one of Gautier's prime examples of *l'art pour l'art* is Shakespeare's *Othello*, obviously chosen precisely to pre-empt just such a misunderstanding of the phrase. As a result Jenkyns finds mainly display, gorgeous self-indulgence, voluptuousness, and 'sensuous luxury' in Catullus 64 which he sees as 'poetry in which purely aesthetic values are paramount'.[91] So Ariadne's suffering is reduced to mere 'gorgeous pathos'[92] (in sharp contrast to the response of Virgil who used her speech as a basis for Dido's passionate utterances). But the self-conscious stylishness of the poem does not mean that it cannot enrich our sense of experience in more complex ways than Jenkyns's dandyist reading allows. Thus, to give an example that drew the attention of Virgil, Catullus fashioned a vocabulary for exploring female emotion—madness, flame, wound, wave—that later poets, for instance Swinburne, were happy to exploit.

One crucial aspect of the form of Catullus 64 is its narrative structure, the order in which the events of the story (or stories) are organized, the comparative length devoted to its various elements. If one takes the narrative style of Homer's *Iliad*, it could be described as full, leisurely, clear, forward-moving, authoritative, giving, fully, the words of the characters, so as to constitute what Erich Auerbach, with pardonable exaggeration, called a 'perpetual foreground'.[93] The poet derives his authority from without, from the Muse, largely then withdrawing so that the story seems, as it were, to tell itself; there is little sense of a gap between the story and the telling, creating an effect of continual presence, as though we were there. This is the kind of poem, we may well think, that

---

[90] 'Catullus and the Idea of a Masterpiece' in Jenkyns (1982) 85–150.
[91] Jenkyns (1982) 91, 94. A similarly restricted view of what is entailed by claims for art for art's sake mars Lyne (1984) on Ovid and Callimachus.
[92] Jenkyns (1982) 134.   [93] 'Odysseus' Scar' in Auerbach (1973) 3–23.

becomes the basis of a whole culture and its values. By contrast Catullus 64 emphasizes its status as text, as art, and indeed contains an extended account of a work of art, in a narrative that refuses to narrate straightforwardly and which is marked by asymmetry, disproportion, with shifts of manner, now epic, now oratorical, now lyrical, now archaic, now modern. What is this poem about, and what would be a suitable title (to call it 'The Marriage of Peleus and Thetis' is to impose a particular and *premature* closure)? In antiquity poems seem often to have been referred to by their first words, so perhaps *Peliaco quondam* ('From Pelion's [top] once')—the sense of belatedness is potent from the first. What we experience is less closure than deferral of closure, in a series of turns and surprising developments, more characteristic of lyric than of epic.

Catullus 64 begins with a reminiscence of the *Medea* of Euripides in Ennius' version, seeming to promise an *Argonautica*.[94] Soon, however, we are concentrating on a romantic episode, as Peleus, a secondary hero on the voyage, falls for Thetis (first substitute for the unspoken and unspeakable Medea) as the naked Nereids gambol around the ship. The narrative of the marriage that follows is soon interrrupted by another turn, a description of the decorations on the marriage coverlet, constituting more than half the work, 215 lines in studied asymmetry. The coverlet supposedly depicts the deeds of heroes, *heroum virtutes* (51) in proper epic manner, but the signal misleads, since, while Catullus mentions the heroic achievements of Theseus, he concentrates rather on his desertion of Ariadne and the death of his father through his forgetfulness.

The description of the coverlet belongs to the rhetorical tradition of the *ecphrasis*, which goes back to the *Iliad*. But this overspilling *ecphrasis* is out of all proportion to the main narrative, or perhaps constitutes the main narrative (prompting questions about the subject of the poem and the relation between the two stories). The coverlet, it emerges eventually, depicts two scenes, first the deserted Ariadne, secondly the arrival of Bacchus in rescue. But the first scene receives extended description, with numerous 'digressions', while the second is briskly dispatched in merely sixteen lines. Not only is this a major formal asymmetry, it also means that the reader's sense of the coverlet is different from that of the guests. Art

[94] See Thomas (1999) chapter 1.

does not merely describe things, it shapes our sense of them. The coverlet is a work of art with static pictures, much of the poet's description of it is narrative with movement (which increasingly takes us from that work of art to the world it describes), a contrast that forms the basis of Lessing's famous comparison of poetry and painting in the *Laocoön*. The contrast reminds us of two paradoxes. The first is that a painted, or embroidered, or sculpted figure may look lifelike, but it cannot move or speak. The embroidered Ariadne is wild and noisy like a Maenad, yet also silent and still:[95]

> saxea ut effigies bacchantis, prospicit, eheu
> prospicit et magnis curarum fluctuat undis. (61–2)

like the stony statue of a Bacchant she looks forth, alas, she looks forth and seethes with great waves of passion.

Jenkyns rightly compares Keats's 'Ode on a Grecian Urn':[96]

> Heard melodies are sweet, but those unheard
> Are sweeter; therefore, ye soft pipes, play on,
> Not to the sensual ear, but, more endeared,
> Pipe to the spirit ditties of no tone;
> Fair youth, beneath the trees, thou canst not leave
> Thy song, nor ever can those trees be bare;
> Bold lover, never, never canst thou kiss,
> Though winning near the goal—yet, do not grieve;
> She cannot fade, though thou hast not thy bliss,
> For ever wilt thou love, and she be fair![97]

The second paradox is that a narrative may take us into a world that seems for the duration as real as, or more real than, our own; but it is constituted of only words on a page or sounds heard by the ear. Is its authority, then, an illusion?

After the initial description of the abandoned woman and before her soliloquy the poet narrates Theseus' coming to Crete, slaying of the Minotaur, and love for Ariadne. At the end he ostentatiously underlines the digressive character of what he has so carefully planned, in a sort of *praeteritio*: *sed quid ego a primo digressus carmine plura | commemorem* (116–17, 'but why departing from my first

---

[95] The Maenad is also a work of art, a statue, in a sort of *mise en abîme*.
[96] Jenkyns (1982) 126 ; cf. Fitzgerald (1995) 154–5.
[97] We might also compare T. S. Eliot, 'Burnt Norton', 5: 'as a Chinese jar still | Moves perpetually in its stillness'.

theme should I tell of more?'). This self-conscious drawing of our attention to the structure (recalling similar moments in the lyricized narratives of Pindar) breaks the dramatic illusion, introduces the person of the poet, and proffers an extreme of spontaneity while at the same time revealing an extreme of calculation. After the soliloquy there is another 'digression', with the story of Ariadne's curse (echoed by Dido's curse), Theseus' return to Athens, and the death of Aegeus, before we go back, in a ring-composition (also typical of Pindaric lyric), to Ariadne on the shore gazing after Theseus' receding ship. The arrival of Bacchus and his Maenads (subject of the second scene on the coverlet) highlights again the paradoxes of art. Lines full of sound resound noisily with onomatopoeic effects:

> plangebant aliae proceris tympana palmis,
> aut tereti tenues tinnitus aere ciebant;
> multis raucisonos efflabant cornua bombos,
> barbaraque horribili stridebat tibia cantu. (261–4)

some with open hands were beating tambourines, or stirred shrill tinklings on rounded cymbals, for many horns blared booming blasts, and the barbarous reed-pipe screamed with hideous music.

The coverlet, of course, is silent, the sounds are supplied by poet and viewer. And in the final two lines of the *ecphrasis* the narrator 'shuts off' the sounds[98] in a recapitulation (the musical metaphor seems appropriate for this poem) of lines 52–3 (Ariadne on the beach), a ring-composition.

Catullus has not yet finished surprising us. He now resumes the account of the wedding, and has the Fates sing an epithalamium for the bridal pair. Since spinning can be used as a metaphor for composing poetry (in *Eclogue* 6 Virgil, imitating Callimachus, is enjoined by Apollo to write a fine-spun bucolic song, *deductum carmen*), the poet may be playing on the self-referential possibilities of poetry. And the subject of the song is surprising: after the preliminary expected topoi, the career of Achilles, the son-to-be—*heroum virtutes* then at long last, but increasingly darkening into questionable violence and horror. The climax is reached with the sacrifice of Polyxena to appease Achilles' ghost, before the final appeal to the bride and groom to consummate their love is introduced by a powerful and weirdly discordant *quare* (372): Polyxena

---

[98] So Jenkyns (1982) 128.

will be sacrificed, *therefore* enjoy love and produce offspring. The topoi have spun out of control, the marriage song, we may say, deconstructs itself.

Talia quondam (382): so they sang, long ago. With this second, magical *quondam* the poem makes its final turn, in an increasingly grim epilogue that looks back to the times when gods mingled with mortals before human wickedness led them to desert the earth, the light, and men's eyes (*lumine claro* are the last words of the poem). The lines provide a perspective from the modern 'fallen' world on the glamour and vitality of the past, an effect of 'romantic' nostalgia.[99] Even before the epilogue a sense of alterity was strong, the poet often attributing the story to others;[100] now we clearly view the past within the perspective of time and loss. There is a (poetically productive) sense of disjunction between content and form in comparison with their seeming unity in Homer. The sense of distance, of a past recovered (or maybe created) by song, of a dream of a lost world which may never have existed save in imagination and in art, is perhaps stronger in Latin than in Archaic or Classical Greek poetry, and something that makes it more like Romantic or modern poetry. Though less overtly moralizing, the ending of Keats' *Eve of Saint Agnes*, with its sudden change of tense, provides an analogy of sorts:

> And they are gone, aye, ages long ago
> These lovers fled away into the storm.
> That night the baron dreamt of many a woe,
> And all his warrior guests, with shade and form
> Of witch and demon and large coffin-worm,
> Were long be-nightmared. Angela the old
> Died palsy-twitched, with meagre face deform;
> The beadsman after thousand aves told,
> For aye unsought for slept among his ashes cold.

Some critics find some of the writing in the epilogue describing the crimes of the post-heroic world awkward and unexciting (and there

---

[99] For the belatedness of the poem see Fitzgerald (1995) 167: 'The issue that Catullus engages for the spectator/reader is one of the representative adequacy of contemporary art when confronted with the potentially debilitating fact of its belatedness.' In German literature we find a similar sort of post-classicism that laments the passing of the old gods in Goethe, Schiller, Hölderlin, and Heine.

[100] So e.g. *dicuntur* (2); *fertur* (19); *perhibent* (76, 124); *ferunt* (212); the effect is reinforced by the sense of times past in the repeated *quondam* and by *priscis* (50).

are obvious contradictions with the main narrative, since, for example, fratricidal murder occurred in the heroic age). The passage could be read as a falling into naïve, idealistic, moralizing discourse, characteristic of modernity. In other words the epilogue is too elusive to effect a fully effective closure, and the poem perplexes us to the end.

In the *Iliad* there is artistry in plenty, but much of it is discreet, functional, or immediately expressive, and there are numerous periods of relaxation. By contrast, Catullus 64 is (over-)loaded with art, each line exquisitely shaped, keeping us in mind that the poem is a manufactured object, like a costly casket (or coverlet). Furthermore Catullus often selects recherché versions over the familiar (for example, the love at first sight of Peleus and Thetis, the apparently involuntary amnesia of Theseus, the wedding song sung by the Fates rather than by Apollo and the Muses). The obscure learning of the scholar-poet is more than a solemn game; it reminds us, constantly, that the poem is shaped by a strongly individual sensibility.

Under what sign might we read this extraordinary and still (in the wider world at least) underrated poem? Perhaps under that of the labyrinth,[101] which Catullus describes in evocative lines that later caught the imagination of Virgil:

> ne labyrintheis e flexibus egredientem
> tecti frustraretur inobservabilis error. (114–15)

lest, as he emerged from the labyrinth's windings, the building's untraceable wandering baffle him.

Ariadne guides Theseus through the labyrinth by means of a thin thread (*tenui filo*, 113); since *tenuis* can operate as a version of *leptos*, Callimachus' word for his refined style, the phrase is one of a number that encourage us to read the poem metapoetically (others are words of constructing, threading, interweaving[102]). Ariadne's

---

[101] This whole paragraph is heavily indebted to Doob (1990).

[102] e.g. *texta* (10); *politum* (48: cf. Cat. 1. 1 *libellum expolitum*); *plexos* (283); *contexta* (292); *leviter deducens* (312); *contexit* (334). Weaving, like spinning, can figure the writing of poetry, though *textus* in the sense of 'text' seems to be post-Catullan. See Scheid and Svenbro (1996) 106: 'the poem, which interweaves the contrary but complementary themes of nuptial union and disunion, may itself be a "fabric", a metaphorical weaving, in short: a text.' As Scheid and Svenbro show (pp. 95–107), Catullus also exploits the associations of weaving with sex and marriage, and suggest that the poem may be 'the nuptial gift offered a couple celebrating their wedding' (p. 107).

thread might be a guide through the poem's complex interlacements; and the labyrinth a symbol of poetry in general or of Catullus 64, with its plexed windings, in particular. It seems as if Virgil may have read it so, as figuring poetic praxis.[103] Two medieval etymologies of *labyrinthus* are known, and may go back to antiquity:[104] *(e)labor inde*, where *labi* might mean 'move with a smooth motion', or of style 'run smoothly', 'slip', 'fall into error', and *labor intus*, where *labor* can be taken as a noun, 'work', as well as a verb (compare Virgil's gloss *hic labor ille domus*, *Aen.* 6. 27). A labyrinth can thus be construed as a piece of ambiguous figuring, standing for order under chaos, designed chaos, or chaos merely; it is a work of art which can bring bewilderment, confusion, entrapment, or at the other extreme a complex clarity. In terms of the form/content relationship that is the subject of this chapter the labyrinth might figure formed matter, matter available to be formed, or sheer matter. Key words in the poetic descriptions are *anfractus*, *ambages*, *errores*: twists and turns, convoluted processes, evasive speech, and perplexity. And who is in the labyrinth, the poet or the reader, and if the reader, can she find a thread to guide her through its windings? Catullus 64 simultaneously encourages and resists a unified reading, teasing with paradox (thus *Argo* was the first ship, yet Theseus' must have preceded it—or is the coverlet a piece of prophecy?). Readers can play with constructions of likeness or of contrast, since the poem is full of repeated words and related images, echoes, recurrences (like the unexpected visual similarities between Ariadne and the Fates). Are these parts of a grand unity behind apparent chaos, or are there, as some post-structuralists insist, only differences?

Certainly one can find in Catullus what has been termed a 'will to beauty'.[105] Like the aestheticist artists and writers of the nineteenth century Catullus is attracted to all forms of synaesthesia, evoking the fullest possible sensory response. So a remarkable simile likens the crowd leaving the palace to the effect of wind on seawater; light, heat, sound, touch—all are put under contribution:[106]

> hic, qualis flatu placidum mare matutino
> horrificans Zephyrus proclivas incitat undas   270

---

[103] Virgil, *Aen.* 6. 24–30 and cf. 5. 588–95; cf. Ovid, *Met.* 8. 157–68.
[104] So Doob (1990) 95–100.
[105] Fitzgerald (1995) 151.   [106] See Fitzgerald (1995) 160; Jenkyns (1982) 137–8.

> Aurora exoriente vagi sub limina solis,
> quae tarde primum clementi flamine pulsae
> procedunt leviterque sonant plangore cachinni,
> post vento crescente magis magis increbescunt,
> purpureaque procul nantes ab luce refulgent: 275
> sic tum vestibulo linquentes regia tecta
> ad se quisque vago passim pede discedebant.

Hereupon, just as the zephyr, bristling the peaceful sea with morning breeze, rouses the waves to tumble, when dawn rises up to the threshold of the wandering sun; tardily they move forward struck by a gentle breath at first, and softly sound with splashing the guffawing waves, and as the wind strengthens grow bigger and bigger, and floating afar from the gleaming light reflect it back; so then leaving the royal building by the threshold, in all directions they each departed with wandering feet.

But, as we have seen, to find 'beauty' in a poem is not to limit response to style or form. Jenkyns's wallowing, so to say, in gorgeousness occludes too much that makes poem 64 beautiful. The poet has powerful and moving stories to tell, and the various manner of their telling creates a play in the mind over many things: genre and gender; the place of art in the world; the fusion of pain and glory; love and betrayal, sex and violence, just a few among them. All this may provoke the Kantian free play of the imagination, which is part of the value of art:

> we are no longer tied to familiar empirical laws of association. Artistic form does not simply present the world, it represents it, so that it is known and responded to in a new way.[107]

Poem 64 is a poem of origins and lost origins, which continually questions whether events are beginnings or endings. If there has been a fall, is poetry part of that fall? If the wedding is the start of trouble, is it also the start of heroism and the poetry about heroes? The constant shifts of style mean that the work cannot be held to a single account; even the epic sublime is allowed its place, as when Jupiter nods his assent (204–6) or a highly enjambed, long-tailed epicizing simile records the death of the Minotaur (105–11). If we return to the relationship between form and content, we could say that the form of 64 is in one sense belated in relation to the content, but of course the belatedness of the poem is also its content; and this

---

[107] Crowther (1996) 67.

means that the content is unintelligible apart from the form. And for all this the poem was long condemned as frigid, passionless and effete.[108] *O saeclum insipiens et inficetum!*

IV

'Parergon' from *The Truth in Painting* is a classic example of Derrida's deconstructive practice at its best, conducted in a way that is at once witty, elegant, and rigorous. As ever he treats his text—in this case parts of Kant's Third Critique—with the utmost respect, engaging in reading of an almost obsessive closeness, probing passages to reveal, through potential aporias, contradictions, blind-spots, intellectual issues of especial significance and interest. Deconstruction of course is anything but destruction, more a mode of immanent critique necessarily performed from within, so that the reading is always complicit with the systems it is undoing, inescapably. Derrida likes to concentrate on 'marginal' passages that have received less readerly attention; to those who think it more appropriate to go to 'the center and the heart of the matter' he replies: 'The objection presupposes that one already knows what is the center or the heart of the third *Critique*, that one has already located its frame and the limit of its field.'[109]

The passage from Kant from which he takes his title is of this kind, treated as parergal by most commentators but crucial for Derrida's account:

> Even what is called *ornamentation* (*parerga*), i. e. what is only an adjunct, and not an intrinsic constituent in the complete representation of the object, in augmenting the delight of taste does so only by means of its form. Thus it is with the frames of pictures or the drapery on statues, or the colonnades of palaces. But if the ornamentation does not itself enter into the composition of the beautiful form—if it is introduced like a gold frame merely to win approval for the picture by means of its charm—it is then called *finery* and takes away from the genuine beauty.[110]

This paragraph can be related to contemporary discussions about the relationship of ornament to essential form; thus in

---

[108] It is true that most professional Latinists today hold a much more positive view, but then they are now not many in number.

[109] Derrida (1987) 63. Useful discussions include Carroll (1989) 131–54 and Robin Marriner, 'Derrida and the Parergon', in Smith and Wilde (2002) 349–59.

eighteenth-century art theory, such as that of Winckelmann or Reynolds, the human body is regarded as what is essential to a statue. Kant's architectural example is less clear—perhaps the columns are treated as parergal because they constitute the boundary between the inside and the outside of the building. Derrida is also intervening in a post-Kantian debate about the autonomy of art—a notion which, while (on my reading) not to be found in Kant, is both constantly derided and yet in another sense also sanctioned within current art history. As Derrida shows (in a text itself employing a sign of the frame as a regular part of its texture), it is difficult, even impossible, to say where the 'work' ends and the 'world' begins. A picture frame at the very moment when it marks out a special space for the artwork, setting it off to establish a particular relation with the viewer, compromises the work's integrity; for is the frame, the parergon, 'inside' the work or 'outside' or in some in-between, hybrid state? Derrida's analysis draws our attention to 'the necessary and fluid interpenetration of work and border'.[111] This is not to say that, for Derrida, we can readily transcend, or dispense with, the categories:

Deconstruction must neither reframe nor dream of the pure and simple absence of the frame. These two apparently contradictory gestures are the very ones—and they are systematically indissociable—of *what* is here deconstructed.[112]

Derrida also discloses possible contradictions in Kant's theory;[113] in particular it can be argued that a shadowy conceptualization takes place when the judgement of taste ('X is beautiful') is made, since what X is can be seen as a cognitive matter—I shall return to this point in due course.

Derrida, like Kant, is here concerned with the visual arts, but a similar analysis can be, and has been, extended to literature[114] or indeed the world in general. The sociologist Erving Goffman had

---

[110] Kant (1952) 68 §14. [111] Cheetham (2001) 105. [112] Derrida (1987) 73.
[113] 'In the course of the final delimitation (theory of taste as theory of judgment), Kant *applies*, then, an analytic of logical judgments to an analytic of aesthetic judgments at the very moment that he is insisting on the irreducibility of the one kind to the other' (Derrida (1987) 70).
[114] The poet Gerard Manley Hopkins used the image of a frame in connection with metre, as marking out a bounded space for poetry: 'Poetry is speech framed for contemplation of the mind by the way of hearing or speech framed to be heard for its own sake and interest even over and above its interest of meaning.... If not repetition, oftening, over-and-overing, aftering of the inscape must take place in order to detach it to the mind and in this light

already argued that we make sense of events by means of the 'basic frameworks of understanding available in our society'.[115] Similarly we may say that we make sense of poems by framing them in certain ways—those frames can then be seen as neither wholly inside nor wholly outside the work. Or, to put the point differently, it is a problematic issue to say exactly what 'the poem' is. In one sense framing devices help to make poems accessible to us, setting them off from the world, but they also fuel anxieties about boundaries. Moreover, is the poem to be received as an aesthetic thing or as another kind of thing? We might conclude that the pure poem does not really exist. In the words of Barbara Johnson, 'The total inclusion of the frame is both mandatory and impossible'; and she continues, 'the frame thus becomes not the borderline between the inside and the outside, but precisely what subverts the applicability of the inside/outside polarity to the act of interpretation.'[116] Derrida's analysis of the Third Critique points to the difficulty of distinguishing clearly between the extrinsic and the intrinsic, in a poem as much as in a painting, of locating 'the ideal limit—which acts as a frame'.[117] Indeed he applies his method to the Critique itself, read as a work of art:

> The *Critique* presents itself as a work (*ergon*) with several sides, and as such it ought to allow itself to be centered and framed, to have its ground delimited by being marked out, with a frame, against a general background. But this frame is problematical. I do not know what is essential and what is accessory in a work. And above all I do not know what this thing is, that is neither essential nor accessory, neither proper nor improper, and that Kant calls *parergon*, for example the frame. Where does the frame take place? Does it take place? Where does it begin? Where does it end? ... I do not know whether the passage in the third *Critique* where the *parergon* is defined is itself a *parergon*. Before deciding what is parergonal in a text which poses the question of the *parergon*, one has to know what a *parergon* is—at least, if there is any such thing.[118]

As we have seen, the *Iliad* appears comparatively unframed internally—after the poet has appealed to the Muse the story is told 'as it really was' so to say, as though we shared the knowledge of

---

poetry is speech which afters and oftens its inscape, speech couched in a repeating figure.' (quoted Caws (1985) 6, from *The Note-Books and Papers of Gerard Manley Hopkins*, ed. H. House, p. 249).

[115] Goffman (1974) introduction, 10.   [116] B. Johnson (1980) 128.
[117] Derrida (1987) 50.   [118] Ibid. 63.

Content, Form, and Frame

the Muse who authenticates the events. By contrast Catullus 64 contains obvious internal frames, including the epilogue. The presence of such internal frames (while seeming to promise to anchor the discourse) complicates more than it resolves interpretation, according to the Derridean logic of supplementarity. In Simon Goldhill's words, 'The frame... cannot be treated as if it were a figure of clarification, control and order...; rather the frame, as the source and site of difference, is the figure which always already undermines the rigid determination of the boundaries of sense, the sense of boundaries.'[119] Between frame and framed there is always a remainder that escapes any reading. A comparatively little discussed poem in Propertius' first book (16) can easily be read as an allegory of the operations of the frame. The main part of the poem (or is it the main part?) is a lament by the excluded lover at his mistress's door—an instance of the *paraklausithyron*, to use a generic 'frame' employed by modern scholars. This love lament is framed within a speech delivered by the door itself, characterized as a *laudator temporis acti*, who complains about the decadence of the times, the immoral behaviour of the mistress of the house, and the absurd antics of the *exclusus amator* (to use the well-known phrase from Lucretius 4. 1177, from a passage which constitutes one possible external intertextual frame for our poem):

> 'Quae fueram magnis olim patefacta triumphis,
>   ianua Tarpeiae nota pudicitiae,
> cuius inaurati celebrarunt limina currus,
>   captorum lacrimis umida supplicibus,
> nunc ego, nocturnis potorum saucia rixis,   5
>   pulsata indignis saepe queror manibus,
> et mihi non desunt turpes pendere corollae
>   semper et exclusi signa iacere faces.
> nec possum infames dominae defendere noctes,
>   nobilis obscenis tradita carminibus;   10
> nec tamen illa suae revocatur parcere famae,
>   turpior et saecli vivere luxuria.
> has inter gravius cogor deflere querelas
>   supplicis a longis tristior excubiis.
> ille meos numquam patitur requiescere postes,   15
>   arguta referens carmina blanditia:

---

[119] Goldhill (1991) ch. 4, 'Framing, Polyphony and Desire: Theocritus and Hellenistic Poetics', p. 260 (part of an illuminating discussion to which I am much indebted).

"Ianua vel domina penitus crudelior ipsa
    quid mihi tam duris clausa taces foribus?
cur numquam reserata meos admittis amores,
    nescia furtivas reddere mota preces? 20
nullane finis erit nostro concessa dolori,
    turpis et in tepido limine somnus erit?
me mediae noctes, me sidera prona iacentem,
    frigidaque Eoo me dolet aura gelu;
tu sola humanos numquam miserata dolores 25
    respondes tacitis mutua cardinibus.
o utinam traiecta cava mea vocula rima
    percussas dominae vertat in auriculas!
sit licet et saxo patientior illa Sicano,
    sit licet et ferro durior et chalybe, 30
non tamen illa suos poterit compescere ocellos,
    surget et invitis spiritus in lacrimis.
nunc iacet alterius felici nixa lacerto,
    at mea nocturno verba cadunt Zephyro.
sed tu sola mei, tu maxima causa doloris, 35
    victa meis numquam, ianua, muneribus.
te non ulla meae laesit petulantia linguae,
    quae solet irato dicere pota ioco,
ut me tam longa raucum patiare querela
    sollicitas trivio pervigilare moras. 40
at tibi saepe novo deduxi carmina versu,
    osculaque innixus pressa dedi gradibus.
ante tuos quotiens verti me, perfida, postes,
    debitaque occultis vota tuli manibus!"
Haec ille et si quae miseri novistis amantes, 45
    et matutinis obstrepit alitibus.
sic ego nunc dominae vitiis et semper amantis
    fletibus aeterna differor invidia.'

I who of old stood open for great triumphs, a door famous for Tarpeian chastity, whose threshold, wet with the suppliant tears of captives, gilded chariots thronged, now, disfigured by the night-time brawls of drunkards, often make lament, thumped by unworthy hands, and shameful garlands do not fail to hang on me and torches ever to lie around, the signs of the excluded lover. I cannot guard my mistress from nights of scandal, my noble self given over to indecent songs; nor is she called back to spare her reputation, and from living more disgracefully than the immorality of the times. Amid these complaints I am forced to weep more bitterly, made more dismal as a result of the long vigil of a suppliant. He never allows my door-posts to rest, repeating his songs with shrill blandishment: 'Door, crueller by far than your mistress herself, why are you silent, closed to me with your so hard panels? Why are you never unbarred to admit my love, incapable of being moved and delivering my clandestine prayers? Will no end ever be granted my pain, and will there be shameful sleep on a lukewarm threshold? For me as I lie here, midnights, the setting stars, and the cold breeze with frost at dawn are sorry. You alone never pity human pains or respond sympathetically, your hinges silent. O that my poor voice might pass through the open crack and direct its way and strike the dear ears of my mistress! Be she more impassive than Sicilian rock, harder than iron and steel, she will not be able to control her dear eyes, and a sigh will arise amid unwilling tears. Now she lies cradled in the happy arms of another, while my words fall idle with but the night wind to hear them. But you are the only, the greatest cause of my grief, never won over, door, by my gifts. No outburst of my tongue has harmed you, which when drunk is apt to speak in angry jest, that you should allow me hoarse with long complaint to keep tormented vigil at the street corner. No, I have often spun songs for you in modern verse, and kneeling down given pressed kisses to your steps. How often, deceitful door, have I turned in prayer before your door-posts, and with stealthy hands paid the vows due!' With this and anything else you wretched lovers know he drowns out the morning birds. So now through the vices of my mistress and the lover's endless weepings I'm everlastingly slandered in unkind gossip.

We cannot finally determine whether or not the *amator* of this poem is the same as 'Propertius' or the 'I' of the *Monobiblos* as a whole, or a different lover known to the door who narrates the lament. Margaret Hubbard observes that he has a fondness for sentimental and wheedling diminutives that Propertius does not seem to share (*vocula, auriculas*, 27–8)[120]—though the use of *ocellus* is common to both. But the door might be parodying the lover's speech rather than quoting verbatim. Certainly the *amator* has Propertius-like characteristics; in particular he writes new poetry in the thin-spun style of a Roman Callimachean (*novo deduxi carmina versu*, 41), while his manner, like Propertius', can be characterized as *blandus* (16).[121] The door's opening lines attempt to frame our response to the lifestyle of the *domina* and the *amator* within a moral discourse that condemns *luxuria* (12); within this discourse the past is superior to the present, war to love, hardness to softness. But the door is immediately entangled in that slide of the signifier that makes discursive mastery so difficult of achievement. Lines 1 and 4, for example, can easily be reapplied to the erotic sphere—amatory triumphs are encountered everywhere in Roman elegy (e.g. Proper-

[120] Hubbard (1974) 33; but cf. e.g. *lectule* in 2. 15. 2.
[121] So *blandi praecepta Properti* in Ovid, *Tristia* 2. 465.

tius 2. 14), while the same words can describe the tears of captives in war and captives in love (the door's threshold is wet in the present as it was in the past). The door condemns *querelae*, the lover's plaints, but uses a word from the same root as his own utterance: *queror* (6). A *domina* may be the mistress of a house (*domus*) or the mistress of a lover, while *duritia*, the quality of hardness, may characterize sexual *froideur* as well as the panels of a door or martial virtue. The reference to Tarpeian chastity may be a scribal error (Phillimore reasonably emended to *patriciae*) or a reference to something we know nothing about; but it could be an error by the door forgetting that sexual misdemeanours are not confined to the present. The moral discourse of the door, in other words, contends with the lover's discourse over what, and how, particular words are to mean. From the perspective of the lover the door's moralizing may appear merely pompous and facile. Providing a frame does not necessarily give one the last word; and anyway we may choose to reframe poem 16 by the *Monobiblos* as a whole, thereby making the door's voice eccentric rather than central. But of course further reframings which might produce readings more sympathetic to the door's position are always possible, and so on potentially *ad infinitum*. In poem 1. 16 the failure of the door to gain mastery of the discourse by means of framing, and the traffic in signification that occurs between the two discourses across the frame, makes manifest the permeability of all boundaries, the impossibility of achieving complete discursive autonomy. The territorial dispute between the door and the *amator* can never finally be resolved, or resolved only by an exercise of the will to power.

These difficulties about the frame complicate, but they do not dismantle the principal claim of this chapter, that the judgement of taste is a judgement of form and content (however we construe them) together. On this reading the judgement of taste is not a version of the sort of formalism one finds in certain modernist art theories (where the content becomes, one might say, a parergon to the form) or of ideology critique fashionable today (where the form becomes the parergon to the content). Derrida has a point when he claims that Kant may be involved in a contradiction over the role of concepts in aesthetic judgements, but it is not decisive. When the mind marks something off as an X—say a tulip, or, more fuzzily, a landscape—and thus 'frames' it, we could say that there is a shadowy conceptualization at work, since what X is is a cognitive matter;

Content, Form, and Frame 107

but to judge that 'this tulip or this landscape is beautiful' is not to make any specific claim about what sort of a thing a tulip or a landscape is (that would be a matter for the botanist or geographer). To put the point rather barbarously, we could say that the judgement of taste itself constitutes, in the act of judgement, the object as an X that has form and content, as an ergon rather than a parergon, but that it does not *pre*suppose that we have cognition of the X as an X. It thus remains that a judgement of taste is the nearest to a 'free' judgement that human beings can achieve, where the results are not already determined in advance by conceptual considerations; there is instead a free play of the mind. Hermeneutics may involve the imposition of precise frames of interpretation, but the same is not true of the judgement of taste. Clive Cazeaux puts the matter well:

> despite this ingenious display by Derrida of circularity in Kant, it is not the case, as Derrida suggests, that, without its frame, the structure 'collapses forthwith'. For Kant's point is precisely that aesthetic experience is a state of conceptual freeplay, in which *object and concept are not identical* or, in a more Derridean idiom, where there is no clear frame. Aesthetic experience motivates us to find expressions that can begin to describe the experience, and this process is vital to the way in which we assign concepts in our cognitive and moral undertakings. The canvas Kant is working on, I suggest, is broader and more finely woven than Derrida suspects.[122]

In the case of a poem Kant may not anyway have thought that a pure judgement of taste was possible, though that does not prevent us trying to remove from our judgements as much as we can of our normal conceptual apparatus. Within the judgement of taste we do not need to know in advance what is 'work' and what is 'frame'. Instead we may, so to say, experiment with different 'frames', and thereby be enabled to think differently and outside any sort of clear means/end structure. The matter of the frame may also, as we have seen, affect how we construe the content of the work. Pictures change physically through time; poems too change through their reception—views as to what is 'in' a particular poem (or about what constitutes a poem in a particular case[123]) will thus differ. These differences about what is to constitute the content may help to explain why judgements of taste, while universal in terms of their structure and conditions of possibility, are in practice disputed. The disputants are, in effect, judging different objects.

---

[122] Cazeaux (2000) 375; cf. Edmunds (2001) 16–17.
[123] e.g. is 'The Knight's Tale' a poem, or is it only part of *The Canterbury Tales*?

3

Distinguishing the Aesthetic: Politics and Art

CARSON. Was it an ordinary letter?
WILDE. Certainly not.... It was a beautiful letter.
CARSON. Apart from Art?
WILDE. I cannot answer any questions apart from Art.[1]

I

My chapter title alludes to Pierre Bourdieu's *Distinction*, which, as we saw in Chapter 1, attempts to demystify the Kantian concept of taste and to collapse aesthetics into sociology. Whether you prefer Bach's *Well-Tempered Clavier*, or the 'Blue Danube' waltz of Johann Strauss, or a popular song performed by Charles Aznavour is, Bourdieu claims to demonstrate, simply a matter of what class you belong to, through birth and education. It is remarkable that Bourdieu thinks his demonstration of the contingent involvement of class in particular aesthetic preferences (a point most people would readily concede) is sufficient on its own to refute Kant's carefully non-empirical analysis of the conditions of possibility of aesthetic judgement. For a Kantian, who may well not share Bourdieu's (snobbish?) concern with the height of people's brows, all, any, or none of the musical works cited might be deemed 'beautiful', while their arrangement into a hierarchy is no part of the judgement of taste (nor, in my view, of much interest anyway, outside the rebarbative ideological clamours of the culture wars).

As we have also seen, Kant's *Critique of Judgement* does not advance a developed art theory, only a theory of aesthetic judgement. But certainly, in the generations that followed, many laboured to produce art theories that supposedly followed from,

[1] Cited Foldy (1997) 97.

or at any rate were consistent with, Kant's idea of the aesthetic. For Kant there does not appear to be any special class of objects about which a pure judgement of taste could be made, while there is little reason to suppose that he believed in the autonomy of art, and some to cast considerable doubt on any such supposition.[2] It is clear enough that in practice we make all sorts of judgements about the objects we designate works of art (I include literature and music within this term), but it is also reasonable to argue that there are many such objects which, for whatever reason (and these reasons may be mainly cultural, a matter of reception), seem particularly well adapted for the making of aesthetic judgements. One of the first English writers to argue rigorously for art's autonomy is the poet Swinburne, most notably in his study *William Blake* of 1868. Here the notorious phrase 'art for art's sake', designed as the English equivalent of *l'art pour l'art* as championed by Gautier and Baudelaire, makes one of its earliest appearances. Swinburne turns the Kantian distinction between types of judgement into the claim that art belongs to a completely separate sphere from science on the one hand and morality on the other: 'To art, that is best which is most beautiful; to science, that is best which is most accurate; to morality, that is best which is most virtuous.'[3] It follows that art must not deliver, or aim to deliver, a result, while its value is always in the present, not in some putative future effect. It also follows that art can deal with any subject matter it likes, including transgressive or (what would be within another discourse) 'immoral' material: 'Handmaid of religion, exponent of duty, servant of fact, pioneer of morality, she cannot in any way become; she would be none of these things though you were to bray her in a mortar.'[4] If an artist aims to produce a moral effect, the result is likely to be non-art: 'Art for art's sake first of all, and afterwards we may suppose all the rest shall be added to her . . .; but from the man who falls to artistic work with a moral purpose, shall be taken away even that which he has—whatever of capacity for doing well in

---

[2] §51 and particularly the note mentioning 'simple aesthetic painting' is the nearest that he comes to such a position (Kant (1952) 187).

[3] Swinburne (1868) 98.

[4] Ibid. 90. Cf. p. 93: 'Philistia had far better (always providing it be possible) crush art at once, hang or burn it out of the way, than think of plucking out its eyes and setting it to grind moral corn in the Philistine mills; which it is certain not to do at all well.'

either way he may have at starting.'[5] (I would argue that Swinburne would have better not made the argument in precisely this form; the motives of artists are unusually opaque, so it is wiser to concentrate on reception than production.)

Swinburne is fully alive to the implications of his view, and, in 1868 at least, willing to accept them. It means that he cannot value his beloved Victor Hugo for the political radicalism that he himself admired and shared, at least in a form abstracted from the artistic whole. In a footnote he spells this out to us, and to himself:

> the work—all the work—of Victor Hugo is in its essence artistic, in its accident alone philanthropic or moral. I call this the sole exception, not being aware that the written work of Dante or Shelley did ever tend to alter the material face of things; though they may have desired that it should, and though their unwritten work may have done so. Accidentally of course a poet's work may tend towards some moral or actual result; that is beside the question.[6]

But already by 1872, in an essay on Hugo for the *Fortnightly Review*, Swinburne was equivocating on the subject. Closely reworking the arguments from his earlier treatment, he tries to have it both ways, again with Dante and Shelley as further examples. He continues to insist that 'the worth of a poem has properly nothing to do with its moral meaning', that 'art can never be a "handmaid" of any "lord"', but he also refuses 'to admit that art of the highest kind may not ally itself with moral or religious passion, with the ethics or the politics of a nation or an age'.[7] Thus, in his attempt to steer between the Scylla of 'art for art's sake' and the Charybdis of moralism, he is forced to rely on an unconvincing distinction between art being the 'handmaid' of morality (bad) and art 'allying itself' with morality (good). While we may agree with Swinburne that we want an art theory which will allow for all types of poets including those who write 'with the faith and the fervour of Dante',[8] the rigour has disappeared from his argument, leaving only the flabbily permissive thought that the artist must write as he will—the problem of the relationship between art and morality remains unresolved. It will not be the last time we see a theorist abandoning the high ground of art's non-instrumentality for an easy, or uneasy, compromise. Indeed we may say that Kant himself

---

[5] Swinburne (1868) 91.   [6] Ibid. 93.   [7] Swinburne (1872) 258.
[8] Ibid. 259.

pointed the way when, perhaps in a (misguided) attempt to connect the various parts of his scheme, he suggested that beauty could be regarded as a symbol of morality.[9] It is as though the separation of judgement presupposed by the aesthetic always in the end proves just too disconcerting, or dangerous, to be strictly adhered to.

Two celebrity libel cases later in the nineteenth century served to reveal some of the tensions between art for art's sake and the wider concerns of society. In 1877 John Ruskin denounced, with characteristic intemperance, Whistler's painting *Nocturne in Black and Gold (The Falling Rocket)*, exhibited at Sir Coutts Lindsay's Grosvenor Gallery, a venue for what was regarded as progressive art:

Lastly, the mannerisms and errors of these pictures [by Burne-Jones], whatever may be their extent, are never affected or indolent. The work is natural to the painter, however strange to us; and it is wrought with utmost conscience of care, however far, to his own or our desire, the result may yet be incomplete. Scarcely so much can be said for any other pictures of the modern schools: their eccentricities are almost always in some degree forced; and their imperfections gratuitously, if not impertinently, indulged. For Mr Whistler's own sake, no less than for the protection of the purchaser, Sir Coutts Lindsay ought not to have admitted works into the gallery in which the ill-educated conceit of the artist so nearly approached the aspect of wilful imposture. I have seen, and heard, much of Cockney impudence before now; but never expected to hear a coxcomb ask two hundred guineas for flinging a pot of paint in the public's face.[10]

Whistler, equally if differently cantankerous, decided to sue. The trial is often interpreted as a conflict between the avant-garde artist and the philistine, bourgeois public. Certainly the defence team tried to play on philistine prejudices against aestheticism. But matters were far more complicated. Ruskin was the greatest art critic of the age, by no means merely a defender of conventional middle-class views. Artists associated with art for art's sake appeared on both sides of the argument—Burne-Jones for Ruskin, Albert Moore for Whistler (Frederic Leighton would have done likewise, had he not been summoned to Windsor to be knighted on the very day of the trial). Many of the issues both about and within

---

[9] In a sense the 'Analytic of the Sublime' already involves some infection of the aesthetic by morality; certainly it lacks the radical clarity of the 'Analytic of the Beautiful'.

[10] Merrill (1992) 135–6. This monograph contains a complete reconstruction of the trial. For this interpretation of the trial I am indebted to Liz Prettejohn.

art for art's sake received an airing. Who had the right to judge the artistic quality of a work of art, the public or the artist alone? Was the meaning of a painting something the painter had to make unambiguously plain, or was it up to the viewer to make of the artwork what he could?[11] How sketchy could a painting be and still be regarded as a finished work of art (an issue likewise with the French Impressionists)? In what respects, and to what degree, need a painting be mimetic (there was no clear concept yet of abstract art, and Whistler's painting ostensibly represented a view of the Cremorne pleasure-gardens by night with a firework display)? Should art be valued for its representational accuracy, or should it be more about the creation of mood and of harmony? Could art rely on design, or form, alone, or would that render it inertly passionless (Burne-Jones wittily described a painting supposedly by Titian, brought into court by way of contrast to Whistler's, as 'an arrangement in flesh and blood'[12])? Was the value of art connected with the amount of time spent on its physical making? This last issue occasioned a dramatic exchange between one of the defence counsels and Whistler:

> SIR JOHN HOLKER. The labor of two days is that for which you ask two hundred guineas?
> WHISTLER. No. I ask it for the knowledge I have gained in the work of a lifetime. (*Applause*)[13]

Whistler was able to set out aspects of his aestheticist credo, which I looked at in the last chapter:

> By using the word 'nocturne' I wished to indicate an artistic interest alone, divesting the picture of any outside anecdotal interest which might have been otherwise attached to it. A nocturne is an arrangement of line, form, and color first. The picture is throughout a problem that I attempt to solve. I make use of any means, any incident or object in nature, that will bring about this symmetrical result.[14]

In the event the jury decided that a libel had been committed but awarded Whistler only a farthing in damages. No-one can tell which

---

[11] As Whistler put it, 'As to what the picture represents, that depends upon who looks at it' (Merrill (1992) 151).
[12] Merrill (1992) 174.   [13] Ibid. 148.
[14] Ibid. 144. The judge, in his summing up, showed a good understanding of some of the aesthetic issues: 'Mr. Whistler did not say he was painting Cremorne Gardens or Battersea Bridge. What he said was that he had an effect in his mind that he was attempting to produce on canvas' (p. 191).

of the many possible factors, and prejudices, most influenced the jury's decision; but the implication was clear that, in its view, the case should never have been brought. *Whistler v. Ruskin* was hardly a practical victory for the improvident Whistler, who had invested considerable funds in the trial. But it could, after all, be seen as something of a victory for art. For it had been decided that the value of art was not an issue that could be resolved in a court of law; art, it might be inferred, had its own nature, its own province, its own laws. It could not be judged in accordance with the quotidian operations of means–ends rationality. The trial aroused considerable interest in both British and French avant-garde circles, and became one of the founding events of artistic modernity.

The second round, in 1895, was to be altogether more malign. The Marquess of Queensberry had been harassing Wilde, sending him a card probably inscribed 'To Oscar Wilde posing as Somdomite'.[15] Wilde decided to sue for libel; aestheticism was likely to be again on trial. Wilde had taken up, with gusto, the role of a new Whistler (somewhat to Whistler's annoyance). No doubt Wilde had *Whistler v. Ruskin* in mind, and in the event, at least on occasion, he surpassed his master, most notably when defending himself in the second trial with his moving speech on Platonic love, which was applauded in court. Edward Carson, the defence counsel in the first trial, appeared initially to play ball. Although Carson had gathered damning evidence about Wilde's sexual activities, he started not with that but by interrogating Wilde on his views about the relationship between art and morality. The exchanges between the two men are somewhat reminiscent of those between Pentheus and Dionysus in Euripides' *Bacchae*, or Christ and Pilate in St John's Gospel. This is because in all three cases the interlocutors are employing different—and incompatible—discourses, which produces a lack of fit between point and counter point, the opposite of a meeting of minds, as in the following exchanges:

> I don't myself believe that any book or work of art ever produces any effect on conduct at all. I don't believe it.
> But am I right in saying that you do not consider that when you come to write these things, you do not consider the effect in creating morality or immorality?—
> Certainly not.

---

[15] See Ellmann (1987) 412. For a full reconstruction of the three trials see Hyde (1973); Holland (2003).

I think I may take it that so far as your works are concerned, you pose as not being concerned about morality or immorality?—I do not know whether you use the word 'pose' in any particular sense.

'Pose' is a favourite word of yours, I think?—Is it? I have no 'pose' in this matter. I do my own work in writing a plot, a book, anything. I am concerned entirely with literature, that is with art. The aim is not to do good or to do evil, but to try and make a thing that will have some quality of beauty that is to be attained or in the form of beauty and of wit and of emotion.

Listen, sir. Here is one of the 'Phrases and Philosophies for the Use of the Young': 'Wickedness is a myth invented by good people to account for the curious attractiveness of others'. Do you think that is true?—I rarely think that anything I write is true. [*Laughter*] . . .

This is in your introduction to *Dorian Gray*: 'There is no such thing as a moral or an immoral book? Books are all well written or badly written?' That expresses your view?—My view of art, yes.

May I take it that no matter how immoral a book was, if it was well written it would be a good book?—If it were well written it would produce a sense of beauty, which is the highest feeling man is capable of. If it was badly written it would produce a sense of disgust . . .

A well-written book putting forth sodomitical views might be a good book?— No work of art ever puts forward views. Views belong to people who are not artists. There are no views in a work of art.

We will say a sodomitical novel might be a good book according to you.—I don't know what you mean by a sodomitical novel.

Dorian Gray. Is that open to the interpretation of being a sodomitical book?— Only to brutes—only to the illiterate; perhaps I should say brutes and the illiterate.

An illiterate person reading *Dorian Gray* might consider it a sodomitical book?—The views of the Philistine on art could not be counted: they are incalculably stupid. You cannot ask me what misinterpretation of my work the ignorant, the illiterate, the foolish may put on it. It doesn't concern me. What concerns me in my art is my view and my feeling and why I made it; I don't care twopence what other people think about it. . . .

The affection and the love that is pictured of the artist towards Dorian Gray in this book of yours might lead an ordinary individual to believe that it had a sodomitical tendency, might it not?—I have no knowledge of the ordinary individual.[16]

Wilde was sentenced to two years' hard labour, two trials later, not for writing *Dorian Gray*, but for 'indecent' homosexual acts. We cannot know for certain what led Carson to commence his cross-examination by trying to undermine Wilde's artistic views, with the

---

[16] Holland (2003); Ellmann (1970) 436–8; Hyde (1973) 107–10. For a good discussion of this aspect of the trial see Foldy (1997) ch. 5.

risk that Wilde would have the opportunity of getting the better of the argument; but there was obvious advantage in seeking to establish a connection between those views and his sexual acts. Certainly the press was not slow to make such an equation. 'The aesthetic cult, in the nasty form, is over', one paper trumpeted.[17] The *National Observer* even suggested that Wilde, a bacillus invading decent English life, commit suicide:

> There is not a man or woman in the English-speaking world possessed of the treasure of a wholesome mind who is not under a deep debt of gratitude to the Marquess of Queensberry for destroying the High Priest of the Decadents. The obscene imposter, whose prominence has been a social outrage ever since he transferred from Trinity Dublin to Oxford his vices, his follies, and his vanities, has been exposed, and that thoroughly at last.[18]

No less severe was the *Daily Telegraph*, which identified the 'tendency' of aestheticism as being the breakdown of family values: 'The superfine Art which admits no moral duty and laughs at the established phrases of right and wrong is the visible enemy of those ties and bonds of society—the natural affections, the domestic joys, the sanctity and sweetness of the home....'[19] Alan Sinfield has argued that it was only after the trials that effeminacy was fully elided with homosexuality, and the stereotype of the gay aesthete firmly established, to dire effect.[20] Certainly the trial was an immediate disaster both for gay men and for aestheticism, which even today often arouses an occluded, or not so occluded, homophobic response.[21] However, we should perhaps also remember Zhou Enlai's often quoted assessment of the results of the French Revolution: 'It's too early to tell'. In the long run it may be conceded that many of the views for which Wilde stood and for which he suffered have prevailed.

---

[17] *News of the World*, 26 May 1895 (quoted Ellmann (1987) 450). For the reception of the trial in the press see Foldy (1997) ch. 3.

[18] Quoted Hyde (1973) 156; Foldy (1997) 55.   [19] Quoted Foldy (1997) 54.

[20] Sinfield (1994). Sinfield simplifies considerably—for example, there are representations of the gay aesthete in literature before the trials—but in general his view that the event was pivotal is surely indisputable. The 1890s saw other signs of illiberalism, perhaps to be connected with the increasing power of the popular press, something Wilde himself deplored in 'The Soul of Man Under Socialism'.

[21] A good example would be critical reaction to the Royal Academy's Leighton Exhibition of 1996; see Barringer and Prettejohn (1999) pp. xiv–xvi.

Wilde's defence of art's autonomy should not be taken to imply that the two spheres of 'art' and 'life' never, in practice, impact on each other. For example, the philistine reads a work of literature as though it were everyday moral discourse, with inevitable consequences. Rather, Wilde is calling us to rethink and, if necessary, reconfigure, the two terms. Thus Wilde likes to suggest that, rather than art imitating life in good Platonic fashion, life imitates art. Thus it is painters like Turner, Whistler, and Monet who have created the current weather:

> Where, if not from the Impressionists, do we get those wonderful brown fogs that come creeping down our streets, blurring the gas-lamps and changing the houses into monstrous shadows? To whom, if not to them and their master [i.e. Whistler], do we owe the lovely silver mists that brood over our river, and turn to faint forms of fading grace curved bridge and swaying barge? The extraordinary change that has taken place in the climate of London during the last ten years is entirely due to this particular school of Art.... At present, people see fogs, not because there are fogs, but because poets and painters have taught them the mysterious loveliness of such effects. There may have been fogs for centuries in London. I dare say there were. But no one saw them, and so we do not know anything about them. They did not exist till Art had invented them. Now, it must be admitted, fogs are carried to excess.[22]

In one elegant witticism Wilde anticipates, though without rancour, one of the central concerns of students of Orientalism: 'The actual people who live in Japan are not unlike the general run of English people: that is to say, they are extremely commonplace, and have nothing curious or extraordinary about them. In fact the whole of Japan is a pure invention.'[23] The Wildean paradox characteristically reverses a hierarchy, or the tenor of an argument. At its worst the result can be facile or plain silly, but at its best such paradox may provoke the reader to an act of transvaluation, enabling her to break out of the tired categories of 'common sense'.[24]

Above all, Wilde's aestheticism is about every individual's self-realization. In what is perhaps his greatest essay, 'The Soul of Man under Socialism' (1891), Wilde gives his support to the abolition of private property and a fair distribution of resources, so that each

---

[22] Ellmann (1970) 312 (from 'The Decay of Lying', *Intentions*).   [23] Ibid. 315.
[24] See Dollimore (1991) ch. 1 and *passim*. An example from the exchange with Carson cited above is Wilde's transvaluation of the discourse of classism. 'Brutes and the illiterate' become, paradoxically, not members of the lower classes but middle and upper class philistines, readers like Carson himself. As usual Carson misses, or affects to miss, the point.

individual can be free from want and thus become most fully himself. On the other hand he is alive to the dangers of authoritarian collectivism and its 'economic tyranny'. Bernard Shaw and his Fabian friends used to scoff, we are told, at a passage like the following: 'It is to be regretted that a proportion of our community should be practically in slavery, but to propose to solve the problem by enslaving the entire community is childish.'[25] But it was the impractical aesthete whose analysis accords better with subsequent experience. As the judgement of taste is concerned with particulars, so the aesthetic polity revolves around the individual. We saw in the last chapter how Pater conscripted Plato as a fellow lover and aesthete. Wilde makes a still bolder conscription: Christ as aesthete. This is explicit in *De Profundis* where Wilde's experience of prison led him to reflect on the significance of suffering. Christ here 'ranks with the poets' and 'his entire life also is the most wonderful of poems'.[26] But the idea is already operative in 'The Soul of Man', suggesting perhaps a long meditated sense of identity. In Wilde's Utopia[27] everyone would be an artist, though not necessarily in the sense in which that word is normally understood:

And so he who would lead a Christlike life is he who is perfectly and absolutely himself. He may be a great poet, or a great man of science, or a young student at a University, or one who watches sheep upon a moor; or a maker of dramas, like Shakespeare, or a thinker about God, like Spinoza; or a child who plays in a garden, or a fisherman who throws his net into the sea.[28]

For Wilde his own life was a work of art, and who is to say that he was wrong in regarding it as his finest one?[29]

---

[25] Wilde (1986) 24; cf. p. 21: 'if there are Governments armed with economic power as they are now with political power; if, in a word, we are to have Industrial Tyrannies, then the last state of man will be worse than the first.' This is not of course to endorse liberal economics—Wilde has already called for the abolition of private property.

[26] Wilde (1986) 166; cf. p. 165: 'there was nothing that either Plato or Christ had said that could not be transferred immediately into the sphere of Art and there find its complete fulfilment.'

[27] 'A map of the world that does not include Utopia is not worth even glancing at, for it leaves out the one country at which Humanity is always landing.... Progress is the realization of Utopias' (Wilde (1986) 34).

[28] Wilde (1986) 30.

[29] On one famous occasion Wilde told Gide that he put only his talent into his works, his genius into his life (Hyde (1973) 75). Compare Foucault who, during an interview in 1983, observed that the 'transformation of one's self by one's own knowledge is... something rather close to the aesthetic experience' (quoted Bowie (1990) 13).

Oscar Wilde was a socialist of an attractive but distinctly idiosyncratic kind. William Morris, another artist associated with the Aesthetic Movement, espoused a more readily recognizable form of socialism. But there was no conflict between his political beliefs and his commitment to beauty. '*Have nothing in your houses that you do not know to be useful, or believe to be beautiful,*' Morris told the Birmingham Society of Arts and School of Design in 1880 (the careful distinction between 'know' and 'believe' is properly Kantian).[30] But Morris also wanted art to be freed from the effects of the inequalities of wealth, something that may help to explain his preference for the 'decorative' over the 'fine' arts. In a lecture to the Trades Guild of Learning in 1877 he declared that he would rather give up art altogether than see its survival wholly dependent on such inequalities:

Sirs, I believe that art has such sympathy with cheerful freedom, open-heartedness and reality, so much she sickens under selfishness and luxury, that she will not live thus isolated and exclusive. I will go further than this and say that on such terms I do not wish her to live. I protest that it would be a shame to an honest artist to enjoy what he had huddled up to himself of such art, as it would be for a rich man to sit and eat dainty food amongst starving soldiers in a beleaguered fort.

I do not want art for a few, any more than education for a few, or freedom for a few.[31]

News From Nowhere (1890) is Morris's version of a socialist utopia, one that has arisen in England after a period of revolution. It is also an aesthetic utopia, dedicated to beauty as well as fairness. Art has now lost its name 'because it has become a necessary part of the labour of every man who produces'.[32] Morris looks to a time when the distinction between artist and craftsman is no longer made, and in his utopia of makers there is also no conflict between utility and beauty (a mill in the new world, we are told, is as beautiful in its way as a Gothic cathedral).[33] Probably there is no room in such a society for great works of high art (Morris has not been the only person to

---

[30] Morris (1994) 76 (from 'The Beauty of Life'). This was one of two slogans in this lecture; the other was '*an art made by the people and for the people as a joy for the maker and the user*'.
[31] Morris (1998) 253 (from 'The Lesser Arts').
[32] Ibid. 160.
[33] Ibid. 215; cf. p. 238 (from 'The Lesser Arts').

be suspicious of the notion of genius as elitist[34]); but if so, the price is well worth paying. For Morris aesthetic excellence and social equality can, perhaps indeed must, coexist. A similarly democratic view of the aesthetic, 'prefigured in the very process of living and inscribed in the body',[35] was later taken up by the pragmatist philosopher John Dewey, for whom again we are all, at least potentially, artists. We can see the basis of the aesthetic when we notice 'the delight of the housewife in tending her plants, and the intent interest of her goodman [i.e. husband] in tending the patch of green in front of the house'.[36] Isobel Armstrong, who quotes this sentence from *Art as Experience*, does so with some evident embarrassment ('his aestheticization of the ordinary is often bald'). Admittedly Dewey is not as effective a stylist as Morris, but if we feel any distaste, we might wonder whether its sources are not largely snobbish or condescending.

We saw in the first chapter how widespread is the current belief that the aesthetic is essentially a reactionary or traditional category, a category used to cloak withdrawal from political engagement and evade, or mystify, the workings of ideology. One objection to such belief is the way that it freezes, essentializes all the terms involved. The oddity that can result has been amusingly characterized by David Bromwich:

To want to make, as Benjamin did in his *Arcades* study, a direct inference from the duty on wine to Baudelaire's 'L'Ame du Vin', without adducing any intermediate chain of evidence, is a *left* position. To say of such a procedure what Adorno said of an early draft of the study, that it is 'located at the crossroads of magic and positivism', is a *right* position.[37]

---

[34] Tolstoy in *What Is Art?* likewise espouses a democratic view of human creativity as 'a means of union among men', to secure the brotherhood of man, which leads him to condemn works of high art (which would include most of his own greatest works); see Feagin and Maynard (1997) 170–1.

[35] See I. Armstrong (2000) 162–70 for a discussion (the quotation is from p. 162). For Dewey the aesthetic is thus 'the clarified and intensified development of traits that belong to every normally complete experience' (from Feagin and Maynard (1997) 53).

[36] I. Armstrong (2000) 162.

[37] Bromwich (1989) 280. Barthes (1990) 22 writes, complainingly: 'An entire minor mythology would have us believe that pleasure (and singularly the pleasure of the text) is a rightist notion', concluding 'It is obvious that the pleasure of the text is scandalous: not because it is immoral but because it is *atopic*' (p. 23).

Within particular contingencies the aesthetic can be, and has been, used for a variety of ends describable in a variety of ways. The current orthodoxy is also quite at odds with the history of aesthetics during the period of modernity, as we have already seen in connection with Victorian Britain. If we want to work with this particular terminology, there are both left-wing and right-wing versions of aesthetics, both 'right' and 'left' objections to aesthetics. One of the unfortunate results of the current consensus is that the discourse of aesthetics has been largely abandoned to the right.[38] Another is that we are presented with a stark choice between aesthetics and politics, in a way likely to do damage to both.[39] Moreover, by imposing quasi-necessary determinants on art, Bourdieu and those who think like him create a stifling view of culture in which change is virtually beyond conceptualization; by contrast the aesthetic allows for shock and surprise, for the unconditioned.

The blanket hostility to the aesthetic from the left is perhaps odd, given the distinguished history of Marxist aesthetics.[40] Marx himself allowed a measure at least of autonomy to art, and believed that in a socialist society the potential of sensory response would be increased with 'the complete *emancipation* of all human senses and attributes': 'The man who is burdened with worries and needs has no *sense* for the finest of plays; the dealer in minerals sees only the commercial value, and not the beauty and peculiar nature of the

---

[38] So Eagleton (1990) 60–1; I. Armstrong (2000) *passim*.

[39] The experience reported in Carroll (1989) p. xii will be a familiar one to many: 'A few years ago, I gave a graduate seminar on the critical role of a certain notion of art and literature in the work of Jacques Derrida. After the first class, in which I attempted to describe what I felt was the complexity of the questions of "the aesthetic" and "the literary" in his work, as well as what their radical theoretical implications might be, a first-year student approached me with a discouraged look on his face. He felt very uneasy listening to me, he said, because what I seemed to be saying went against everything he believed and everything he had been taught to believe in his undergraduate classes on literature and theory. He could not conceive of the possibility that any approach to "aesthetics" could, even under the best of conditions, have *critical* rather than idealist or aestheticist effects. Because he claimed he had always been taught to be "suspicious" of all forms of aesthetics, the choice of how to deal with art and literature was for him stark and uncompromising: either one treated art and literature from an historical-political perspective or one approached it with formalist-aesthetic categories. In the first case, one was a critical thinker; in the second, an idealist or an aestheticist. It was as simple as that.'

[40] For a useful introduction see Cazeaux (2000) pt. 3, 'Marxism and Critical Theory', with excerpts from Marx, Lukács, Adorno, Marcuse, Habermas, and Jameson; also David Craven, 'Marxism and Critical Art History', in Smith and Wilde (2002) 267–85.

minerals'.[41] On this view the aesthetic is part of what Marxists, following the master, like to call our 'species-being' ('human nature' being a term rather thoroughly compromised by repressive ideologies). Marx, of course, had been brought up on German Romantic aesthetics; one recalls that A. W. Schlegel regarded language as a collective poetic act, the 'great, not yet accomplished poem in which human nature represents itself', which in effect makes poets of all of us, as contributors to language development.[42] There is, unsurprisingly, a strong utopian element in the Marxist aesthetic tradition. Ernst Bloch, for example, regards art as the potential site of 'the not-yet-conscious', 'the not-yet-become'; for him a key idea is hope, and a key term *Vor-Schein*, which his translators render 'anticipatory illumination'.[43] One contemporary classicist who has recently appealed to this way of thinking is Edith Hall:

Athenian tragedy is... a supreme instantiation of what Marxists call art's 'utopian tendency'; this expression denotes art's potential for and inclination towards transcending in fictive unreality the social limitations and historical conditions of its own production. To put it more simply: Greek tragedy does its thinking in a form which is vastly more politically advanced than the society which produced Greek tragedy.... Tragedy's multivocal form and socially heterogeneous casts suggest an implicit egalitarian vision whose implementation in the actual society which produced it was absolutely inconceivable.[44]

One could evoke Kant's notion of the 'aesthetic idea' or Derrida's 'iterability', the potential for new readings contained within the text. But it is significant that this paragraph comes from a chapter on Athenian society in a book which is mainly concerned with Greek tragedy as an expression of the ideology of the *polis* (the current consensus); aesthetic issues feature far less than would have been the case thirty years ago.

Some of the liveliest debates about aesthetics still take place within Marxist, or Marxisant, circles. For Terry Eagleton there is both a good and a bad side to claims about the autonomy of art (the

---

[41] Cazeaux (2000) 214–15 (from the fragment 'Private Property and Communism').
[42] Quoted in M. P. Clark (2000) 81.
[43] Bloch (1988) pp. xv, xxxv–xxxvi, 16, and *passim*. Eagleton (1990) 350 quotes Adorno: 'even in the most sublimated work of art there is a hidden "it should be otherwise"... as eminently constructed and produced objects... point to a practice from which they abstain: the creation of a just life.'
[44] Hall (1997) 125. Note how this formulation both reifies Greek tragedy and, paradoxically (from a Marxist perspective), separates it from the social world of ancient Athens.

good includes the hostility to narrow instrumentalism), and the aesthetic is both emancipatory and repressive (not least in the association of art with commodity fetishism).[45] By contrast Tony Bennett argues that materialism is *necessarily* at odds with the aesthetic, and thus that the aesthetic as a category has no use for Marxists today.[46] He is suspicious of the Schillerian view that art has a special role in the transformation of the subject (*Bildung*) or in removing misrecognitions of the ideological.[47] Bennett's position is that literature is simply one cultural practice among numerous others, and should be treated as such. The problem here, as often, is the movement of reification. 'Literature' (however we conceive it) can indeed be treated like any other cultural practice, and particular contingent analytic advantages may come from so doing. But there are other contexts where we may want, again for good reason, to distinguish a great poem from a routine newspaper report or a typical speech in parliament, even if the idea of literature is today defunct (though it is worth insisting again that such deliberations have nothing to do with the Kantian judgement of taste).[48] Closing down whole discourses, other than as a temporary provocation, seems unlikely to increase human understanding.

The objections to the notion of aesthetic autonomy are so familiar today that I need hardly rehearse them in detail. Among the arts 'literature' (itself an historically variable category) is often said to be among the more impure, and certainly it is bound up, in complex ways, with most of the discourses and practices that comprise a culture. Quite obviously it does not occupy a separate space wholly unaffected or uncontaminated by the political.[49] It is unlikely that

---

[45] Eagleton (1990) 9, 28, and *passim*.

[46] Bennett (1990) 144, 175, 186-90, and *passim*; although I disagree with most of its conclusions, this book is a thought-provoking one and avoids many of the pitfalls of vulgar Marxism. There is, however, something depressingly technocratic about Bennett's vision of education.

[47] For the argument that literature can help resist the dominant ideology because of what Murray Krieger calls its 'duplicitous' character see M. P. Clark (2000) 225, 11; also Levine (1994) 15-17.

[48] So Bromwich (1989) 17-19.

[49] Barthes (himself something of an aesthete) has a particularly felicitous formulation (Barthes (1990) 32): 'There are those who want a text (an art, a painting) without a shadow, without the "dominant ideology"; but this is to want a text without fecundity, without productivity, a sterile text (see the myth of the Woman without a Shadow). The text needs its shadow: this shadow is *a bit* of ideology, *a bit* of representation, *a bit* of subject: ghosts, pockets, traces, necessary clouds: subversion must produce its own chiaroscuro.'

Shakespeare, perhaps the central figure in the Western canon, would have achieved this status had not English—like Latin— become a hegemonic world language as a result of British imperialism. Indeed a sense of the politics of language can bestow a special and valued sharpness. Duncan Kennedy gives an instructive example from Roman love poetry. When Propertius (2. 1. 47) writes *laus in amore mori*, the utterance gains power and point if we recall the socio-political resonances of the word *laus* that aesthetically minded critics can ignore: 'I get my glory from dying in love'[50] (though that does not make the poem instrumentalist in the manner of a political manifesto). Politics and the interpretation of texts are linked, contingently and historically, in myriad ways. In practice discourses are seldom if ever neutral in respect of power[51] (though this is different from saying that they *never* could be, that such a discourse is *unthinkable*). Such points are the *communes loci* of all those for whom the literary canon is something exclusionary and oppressive.[52] And it is difficult to deny the limitations and injustices that the canonical enacts and helps, in some measure, to perpetuate. Anne Elliot, in Jane Austen's *Persuasion*, responds to Captain Harville's observation, 'I do not think I ever opened a book in my life which had not something to say upon woman's inconstancy,' with the quiet but firm reply: 'Men have had every advantage of us in telling their own story.' But John Guillory is right in his insistence that a critique of the canon and a critique of the aesthetic should not simply be elided. Indeed the point can be made more strongly: the canon and its politics has nothing to do with the Kantian aesthetic. Guillory argues that the ideological work done by the canonical is anyway a matter of its institutional use, and the cultural and linguistic capital bestowed within particular institutional settings, rather than of some essential ideological content in canonical works; these are reactionary or progressive less in themselves than in their reception and dissemination in specific contexts (as we shall see in connection with the *Eclogues* later in this chapter).[53] Hence, for example, the politics of particular New Critics are a very different

---

[50] Kennedy (1989) 141–2. [51] See e.g. Bennett (1990) 134.
[52] For some reflections on the canon, and a bibliography, see Martindale (1996a).
[53] Guillory (1993) p. ix, 21–3; cf. p. 43: 'a text tradition is not sufficient in itself either to constitute or to transmit a culture.' For example, Virgil's *Georgics* could be put to both militaristic and anti-militaristic uses: see Richard F. Thomas, 'The *Georgics* of Resistance: From Virgil to Heaney', in Farrell (2001) 117–47.

matter from the cultural effects of the New Criticism as a movement within schools and universities.[54] Ironically the critique of the canon may actually have helped to create and sustain belief in a unitary Western culture (something that in historical terms is largely mythical), thereby inadvertently playing into the hands of cultural conservatives. Guillory himself calls, not for an attempt to abolish those judgements of value that a canon supposedly reflects or embodies, but for a reformation of the conditions under which they are made: 'Socializing the means of production and consumption would be the condition of an aestheticism unbound, not its overcoming' (though that, as he admits, 'is only a thought experiment').[55]

All this is by no means the only objection to much of what I have been calling 'ideology criticism' as widely practised today. Another is the way that the individual work tends to disappear into an often reified context. We look 'through' the work, as it were, to something else, as someone might look through the pictorial complexities of a painting by Whistler to see 'devotion, pity, love, patriotism'. That perhaps is the implication of Helen Vendler's belief that 'one cannot write properly, or even meaningfully, on an art work to which one has not responded aesthetically'.[56] In his book *Who Needs Greek?*, in which he argues for a new interdisciplinary model for reception allied with 'cultural studies', Simon Goldhill offers a richly 'thick description' of the first English performance of Strauss's opera *Electra* as an act of cultural negotiation; in a chapter of seventy pages, it is only at the very end that he has anything to say about the music, and then only to describe a comparatively uninteresting—at least from a strictly musical point of view—debate between Bernard Shaw (who initially hadn't even heard the opera) and the critic Ernest Newman. And yet, arguably, it is the quality of that music that makes the discussion worth having in the first place. Such siren calls to a dominant culturalism, however learned and sophisticated, hardly offer us a viable future, if the works discussed do not command our attention. Moreover such discussions are often themselves ideological in a negative sense (as diagnosed, for example, by Roland Barthes in *Mythologies*) in that they conceal the aesthetic value system that continues to operate, all the more powerfully because it is unacknowledged (as Goldhill simply takes for granted

---

[54] Guillory (1993) pp. xi–xii, ch. 3.   [55] Ibid. 340.   [56] Vendler (1988) 5.

the excellence of Strauss's *Electra*). At all events there seems a limitation to Goldhill's culturalist methodology if, in an analysis of an opera, it is only really the libretto that is discussed. *Who Needs Greek?* is ideology criticism at something near its best. At its worst such criticism often combines a crude version of Marx's base–superstructure model (history or context operating as base, the work as superstructure[57]) with a naïve representational realism, in order to condemn the work as patriarchal, racist, imperialist, elitist, and all that. In such cases immanent ideology simply replaces the older immanent authorial intention as the master-key to meaning. As a result 'much of what passes for political analysis of historically canonical works is nothing more than the passing of moral judgment on them'.[58] In its methodology (if not in its moral/political commitments) this is not unlike the way neo-classical critics condemned the Homeric poems for 'lowness' of both style and subject. The present consensus within ideology criticism (positivistic historicism in uneasy alliance with a politicized poetics of suspicion) will hardly do as a total explanation of the phenomenon of art; it leaves out of account too many factors in the reception of artworks, assumes immunity from (or an unprecedented capacity to see through) the false consciousness that has affected art-lovers for centuries, and fails to account for phenomena associated with the reception of art during those centuries other than by denial or dismissal. In seeing through it fails to see. We need to avoid the circularity that dogs discussions of art objects, in which the presupposition of a determinate relationship between the object and something identified, with more or less sophistication, as social or cultural 'reality' renders the enquiry incapable of finding anything except what was proposed at the outset.[59] These discussions are too collusive with the current, late-capitalist order, with its relentless pursuit of aims and objectives, and its obsession with matching

---

[57] Bennett (1990) ch. 3 is good on this. The base–superstructure model is anyway only found in Marx's *Critique of Political Economy*.

[58] Guillory (1993) 25.

[59] Cf. Thomas Docherty, 'Aesthetic Education and the Demise of Experience' in Joughin and Malpas (2003) 29: 'My contention here is that the premature politicisation—"realisation"—of the text or of the aesthetic encounter is *always* barbaric and anathema to culture; for it actively denies the experience of the present moment, refuses the encounter with death that is at the centre of all art, an encounter that is actually a moment of transgression, a moment of engagement, an "event" or an adventure whose outcome cannot be given in advance.'

'products', including artistic products, to the 'cultures' that consume them.

Moreover the resolute foregrounding of political factors can lead, on occasion, to some very unconvincing readings. We saw in the first chapter how Yun Lee Too is determined to present Aristotle's *Poetics* as having nothing to do with literary aesthetics as a post-Kantian might understand them, but rather as being wholly concerned with the formation of an elite citizen body. Of course it is possible to find a political subtext in particular passages. For example, when Aristotle argues that tragedy, unlike comedy, is a 'serious' genre dealing with people who are 'good' and 'noble' (i.e. kings and heroes), one could posit a social as well as a literary agenda. But to interpret the whole of the *Poetics* in this way would require considerable ingenuity. For example, most people would see a remarkable *literary* insight in Aristotle's analysis of the superiority of the plots of the Homeric poems to those of the numerous Thebaids and Heracleids: where most epic poets tell episodes from the story of a single hero, Homer gives unity of action to the *Iliad* by recounting the wrath of Achilles and its effects, not his whole life (the poem is the story of Troy, not of Achilles). Now a political reading of this passage might just be possible (though Too does not offer one): thus one might argue that the elite male citizen requires an ability to extrapolate an organic unity out of a mass of data (John Barrell does something rather similar with Joshua Reynolds's theory of painting[60]). But such an interpretation seems unduly strained. Interestingly Too's monocular vision (which again and again causes her to close down interpretation) leads her to share Plato's view that we need to decide between those texts and discourses we can accept into our city and those we cannot. Thus she is sympathetic to the view of certain feminists that degrading images of women should be banned, not because of any results they may cause but because they embody the debased valuation of women within patriarchy, not then for what they do (always a problematic issue) but for what they are. This is a bold if illiberal view, but who is to decide which images are indeed demeaning? Any such idea of censorship implies an essentializing view of the 'text' presumed to have inherent meaning (as we have seen in the exchanges between Wilde and Carson); to a student of reception one objection to this is

[60] Barrell (1986).

that it precludes texts from yielding new meanings which might also prove politically and ethically beneficial. In practice ideology criticism almost always tests the work against criteria that are already known. As an alternative to this one can argue for an aesthetic way of knowing, which involves risking the unknown. Peter de Bolla gives his sense of those risks thus: 'The risks I have in mind concern our ability or willingness to open ourselves to a text... that is, to acknowledge that the text might know what we, as yet, do not (or could not), and that knowing *this* (acknowledging it) is bound to be either beneficial or potentially harmful to us (or indeed at different times both).'[61]

The thesis of this chapter is a modest one, that *an aesthetic judgement of a work of art can be as legitimate as a political one* (I use the word political to cover a full range of non-aesthetic categories including the economic, the ethical, the social, and so on); moreover *such a judgement does not have to be merely a political judgement in disguise* (though, of course, in any particular case it may be, or may be interpreted as such). I leave until the end of the chapter whether a stronger claim might be made, whether *the aesthetic is in some sense a prior or privileged category*, at least in respect of art objects. In his posthumously published *Aesthetic Theory* Adorno puts the case for the double character of art—'its autonomy and *fait social*', with the inevitable dependencies and conflicts that result.[62] Of course Adorno is fully aware that there is no universal concept of art, and that the idea of art's autonomy is the product of history and subject to historicization. But the fact that an idea has a history is no argument against the value of using it, in clearly defined ways, in the present. Adorno's sense of art's doubleness has much in common with the position of Lyotard in *Discours, figure*.[63] For Lyotard the tense of art (as opposed to conceptual knowledge) is the future perfect: what will have

---

[61] de Bolla (2001) 97. This particular formulation is not quite Kantian; one might say rather that the subject's encounter with the object is not bound by prior clear concepts—hence the results are not known in advance. Isobel Armstrong (2000) 256–7 also emphasizes the value of the aesthetic for new forms of experience and 'knowledge'.

[62] Adorno (1997) 225–61 (quotation, p. 229); this a substantially revised version of Adorno's text from that originally published in 1970. Beech and Roberts (1996) 105 observe that for Adorno 'it is only art which is capable of providing an immanent critique of instrumental reason'.

[63] I follow the account given by Carroll (1989) 30–52 (quotation, p. 31).

been.[64] And he distinguishes the realm of discourse from that of visual forms and colours; the first is largely closed, the latter is 'the realm of movement, difference, reversal, transgression'. Within 'literature', as well as visual art, we can find the disruptions of figure, outside the determinations of discourse; as a result poetry, when it paints with words, can exceed language while working with it.

I am myself pretty relaxed about the question of what is art; as far as I am concerned art can be anything anyone likes so long as she can argue effectively for the object being described as such. So I have no problems with the notion which David Carroll calls 'paraesthetics', and which he defines thus:

> *Paraesthetics* indicates something like an aesthetics turned against itself or pushed beyond or beside itself, a faulty, irregular, disordered, improper aesthetics—one not content to remain within the area defined by the aesthetic. Paraesthetics describes a critical approach to aesthetics for which art is a question not a given, an aesthetics in which art does not have a determined place or a fixed definition.[65]

It is just that this is consistent with one possible reading of the Third Critique. In my view autonomy should be located, so to say, not in art's production but in its reception. And I think a case can be made that, for an object to be worth calling art, it must have a capacity for being autonomous, that is for being something about which the judgement of taste can be made, without reference to specific ends. I also think that this is a compelling way to approach, or try to approach, a poem.[66] Likewise a jug made for a particular ritual or practical use or a play designed to promote a particular cause (and which may have served those purposes admirably) may be judged beautiful, and thus be *to that extent* autonomous. In such ways experience of an artwork as an autonomous object can result in an extension of my being, without a moral result, without, that is, my becoming a better person.[67] It is perhaps such things that are sometimes evoked in claims about art's 'transcendence' (another bugaboo of the ideology critic). Of course great works of art are

---

[64] Carroll (1989) 156. The future perfect is also the tense of knowledge in anti-realist accounts.

[65] Ibid. p. xiv.

[66] So, in a powerful passage, Donoghue (1995) 328–9.

[67] Compare Croce (1995) 11: 'Our practical interests, with their correlative pleasures and pains, are blended, become confused now and then, and disquiet our aesthetic interest, but never become *united* with it.'

produced within specific historical contexts and material circumstances; but, in de Bolla's words, 'the sense of their transcendence, of their capacity to arouse such strong affective responses no matter what context they are placed in, whether or not the viewer is trained or comes from a similar cultural context, is often very intense'. And he is right to conclude that this is 'something we should acknowledge and investigate rather than feel awkward or embarrassed about'.[68] But of course we might have this affective response to something that, for moral or political reasons, we may want to reject. Ideology critics regularly cite Walter Benjamin's dictum that Fascism aestheticized politics, while Communism politicized art.[69] Certainly there is something seductive but terrifying about the passage from one of Marinetti's manifestos that Benjamin quotes:

> War is beautiful because it initiates the dreamt-of metallization of the human body. War is beautiful because it enriches a flowering meadow with the fiery orchids of machine guns. War is beautiful because it combines the gunfire, the cannonades, the cease-fire, the scents, and the stench of putrefaction into a symphony.

But those who cite Benjamin rarely draw what might seem one obvious conclusion, that there is surely great virtue in keeping, with Kant, the two categories—politics and aesthetics—apart.

II

It is high time to explore some of these issues through an example. In *Ode* 2. 7 Horace welcomes home an old friend:[70]

> O saepe mecum tempus in ultimum
> deducte Bruto militiae duce,
>   quis te redonavit Quiritem
>   dis patriis Italoque caelo,

---

[68] de Bolla (2001) 27–8. Of course the notion of transcendence can be used in a multiplicity of different ways; in ideology criticism its pejorative use is often little more than an unthinking act of self-positioning. It would help debate if those who use words like 'transcendence', 'idealist', 'materialist', etc. made clear what precise meaning they were assigning them.

[69] Benjamin (1992) 234–5 (from 'The Work of Art in the Age of Mechanical Reproduction').

[70] For this ode see the commentaries of Nisbet and Hubbard (1978) and West (1998); also Davis (1991) 89–98; O'Gorman (2002). In what follows I have made extensive use of all these accounts.

Pompei, meorum prime sodalium, 5
cum quo morantem saepe diem mero
    fregi coronatus nitentes
      malobathro Syrio capillos?

tecum Philippos et celerem fugam
sensi relicta non bene parmula, 10
    cum fracta virtus et minaces
      turpe solum tetigere mento.

sed me per hostes Mercurius celer
denso paventem sustulit aere,
    te rursus in bellum resorbens 15
      unda fretis tulit aestuosis.

ergo obligatam redde Iovi dapem
longaque fessum militia latus
    depone sub lauru mea, nec
      parce cadis tibi destinatis. 20

oblivioso levia Massico
ciboria exple, funde capacibus
    unguenta de conchis. quis udo
      deproperare apio coronas

curatve myrto? quem Venus arbitrum 25
dicet bibendi? non ego sanius
    bacchabor Edonis—recepto
      dulce mihi furere est amico.

O you that with me have often been led to supreme crisis when Brutus was leader of our warfare, who has given you back as a Roman citizen to gods of the fathers and the Italian sky, O Pompey, first of my comrades, with whom I often broke up the lagging day with neat wine, shining hair crowned with Syrian malobathrum? With you I experienced Philippi and swift flight, leaving my little shield behind not with honour, when valour was broken, and threatening warriors touched the base ground with their chins. But me swift Mercury carried up in my fear through the enemy in a thick mist, while you the wave sucking back into war again bore on seething waters. Therefore give back to Jupiter the feast owed him and lay down your limbs weary with warfare under my laurel, and don't spare the casks reserved for you. Fill up the burnished cups with the Massic of oblivion, pour ointments from full shells. Whose care is it to hurry to complete garlands of moist celery or myrtle? Whom will Venus declare master of drinking? I will go bacchic not more soberly than the Edonians—it is sweet for me to rave having got back my friend.

On 23 September, 1937, in an address at the opening of the Mostra Augustea della Romanità, an exhibition devoted to the achievements of Rome and Augustus, the organizer, Professor Giglioli, praised Mussolini as the Emperor's modern successor, citing the opening of Horace's *Epistle* 2. 1 on the burdens sustained by the head of state.[71] This kind of information is today sometimes brought forward with a definite hint that there is something nastily totalitarian about Horace's poetry. The objection to such an imputation is not that it is anachronistic but that it is essentializing; Horace's poetry was appropriable by Fascists, but it does not follow that it *is* fascistic (it has been appropriated for many other political positions over the last 2000 years).[72] There has indeed been something of a political turn in Horatian studies since the 1960s and 1970s (which were the glory days for New Critical practice among Latinists); this turn has brought new insights, but it has not been accomplished without cost. To deny ourselves the pleasures that the *Odes* might offer because we disapprove, if we do, of some of the ideological implications we ascribe to them would be to act like those early Christians who believed that classical literature should be rejected root and branch because of the evils of paganism. At its worst such puritanism can spill over into a form of Pharisaism:

the poetry's [the *Satires*] attacks on the unbalanced, immoderate excesses of its characters draw on the symbolic capital of its plebeian posture precisely in order to raise itself above the herd, and speak to the world of the civilized, namely the powerful in their role as the cultured. The poems, then, interweave counter-sublimation with sublimation so as to establish the right to belong to *the* 'in-group' of the community, the circle of Maecenas, and to speak in its name, to speak its claim to represent the community at large, to inter-articulate elite with populace.... And classical scholarship has welcomed this disarming representation as a package.[73]

---

[71] The date was chosen because it was Augustus' birthday, and the address was printed in the catalogue; I am grateful to Dr Catharine Edwards for these details.

[72] For some reflections on these matters see the introduction to Martindale and Hopkins (1993) 18–22, while for a particularly acute discussion of general issues about ideology and its operations see Kennedy (1992).

[73] Henderson (1999) 185. Of course I am attacking 'Henderson' rather than Henderson (who has done more than most to reinvigorate the study of Latin poetry). One might argue that Henderson knows exactly what he is doing here, but any resulting irony in the writing can be still read as offensively collusive.

Writing of this kind almost inevitably invites a retort of *tu quoque*. Academic classicists, who virtually all teach in elite institutions complicit with existing inequalities of power and wealth, should think hard before casting the first stone. Have any of us earned the right to criticize Horace like that? Isn't such discourse both self-congratulatory and sentimental? Politicizing accounts of Horace's *Odes* stress their role both in helping to create and sustain Augustan ideology and in promoting the advancement of the author as an elite Roman male, on the principle that 'literature is politics by other means'[74] (the influence of New Historicism is particularly evident here). It is worth insisting that what we are dealing with in such claims is a mode of reading, of interpretation, not something that can be regarded as in any sense 'factual': the problems of intentionalism are well known, while there is nothing worth calling 'evidence' to demonstrate any *actual* effects Horace's poems may have had in promoting the Augustan settlement. And one defect of this way of reading is that it tends to homogenize the poems, to make them all do the same kind of work.

'This is a political poem': so begins, breezily, David West's discussion of *Ode* 2. 7. By this West presumably means that this poem relates to significant 'public' issues and events, in this case the Philippi campaign (where Horace and Pompeius both fought on the 'wrong', losing side) and the *clementia* Augustus showed towards former opponents which allowed for a general amnesty in 30 BC (an event mentioned by the historians Velleius Paterculus and Dio). But many have sought to redefine the categories involved, since, it can be argued, the promotion of consensus and the status quo can be just as 'political' as a concern with constitutional programmes, conflicts, and change.[75] Thus Horace's stance of rural quietude and devotion to the golden mean, in poems which West would presumably describe as 'personal' or 'private', were, on this view, positions

---

[74] Habinek (1998) 13; cf. p. 101: 'he [Horace] did manage to legitimize literature...and to make it available as one means of social differentiation and cultural unification.'

[75] Typical radical slogans of the 1960s were 'The personal is the political' and 'Everything is political', slogans designed as provocations encouraging us to reconfigure our categories. West's second paragraph begins: 'This is not only a political poem. It is also warmly personal.' West's rhetoric presents the categories as unproblematic, naturalizing them as matters of common sense. One can argue against this that the boundaries of all such categories are labile, being continually relocated, renegotiated, discursively in a process that could itself be termed 'political'.

best calculated to promote harmony and thus help cement the position of the *princeps*. However that may be, a politicizing reading of our ode would treat it as an important document of the Augustan Age and a celebration of the Augustan settlement. The question 'Who has restored you to Roman citizenship?' becomes, then, not an open question expressing a delighted surprise, but a question expecting the answer 'Augustus'. The name of Horace's old friend itself has obvious civil war resonances (perhaps he owed his name to the family of Pompey the Great if Horace did not simply invent him). Horace represents himself as rescued from the battle of Philippi by Mercury, a god with whom he has a specially close affinity. Perhaps in this detail too he was imitating the Archaic Greek poet Archilochus, who, in one surviving fragment (5 West[76]), which Horace is recalling, describes how he abandoned (*kallipon*, cf. Horace's *relicta*) his shield in order to make his escape from his Thracian adversaries. But we recall too that Horace closely associated Mercury and the youthful Octavian at the close of *Ode* 1. 2 (Augustus may also lurk behind Jupiter in line 17). Horace's self-deprecating description of his Falstaffian behaviour at Philippi can be read as a tactful way of negotiating his relationship with the *princeps*.[77] At the party the two friends will run wild on 'forgetful Massic wine' (*oblivioso Massico*); wine traditionally frees human beings from care, but here the forgetfulness brought by a specifically Italian wine may be, more precisely, forgetfulness of civil war. In the final sentence the word *furere* describes the Bacchic excesses of the symposium (Maenads, like the civil war battles, are associated with Thrace), pointedly replacing a very different kind of fury, the madness of civil war, now laid to rest by the victory of Augustus. Of course one can make something rather different, and slightly more subversive, of this set of possible resonances. If the wine brings forgetfulness, the poem perhaps does not—after all Brutus is mentioned by name, two whole stanzas are devoted to the account of Philippi, even the *ciboria* (22) suggest Egypt and the final stages of civil war ('The *ciborium* is properly the cup-shaped

---

[76] 'One of the Saioi rejoices in the shield, which by a bush I left behind, not willingly, in perfect condition. But I saved myself. What does that shield matter to me? Let it go. By and by I shall get another one no worse.' Alcaeus also threw away his shield, so the gesture may become generic.

[77] Nisbet and Hubbard (1978) 108: 'Horace's poem is a masterpiece of tact.'

seed-box of the *colocasium* or "Egyptian bean"'[78]). The act of forgetting is also, necessarily, an enactment of memory; the poem can be made more devious than it looks.[79]

Using most of the same data, Gregson Davis offers a very different, and much more 'literary' reading of the poem, by putting it within the frame not of Augustan politics but of genre and literary tradition. Lyric for Davis centres on the celebration of the *convivium* in the present, not, like epic, on the memorialization of the past and of history. The *convivium* with which our poem ends involves, as expected, wine (*cadis, oblivioso Massico, arbitrum bibendi, bacchabor*), sex (suggested by *myrto*, the plant of Venus, and *Venus*, referring to the top throw of the dice), and communality. Lyric is a version of the *genus tenue*, so that *deducte* in line 2 may refer not only to Brutus' leadership (with the play on *duce*) but, punningly, to the *deductum carmen*, the thin-spun song, that takes as one point of departure the poetics of Callimachus' *Aetia* prologue. Pompeius is invited to forget the epic world of battle and take refuge under Horace's laurel (*sub lauru mea*), which Davis takes as a figure for Horatian lyric poetry. The poem thus becomes the enactment of the *imbellis lyra*, negotiating the rhetorical polarities of *bellum* and *convivium*. There may also be a pun on the name of Horace's old commander-in-chief, since the word *brutus* can on occasion operate as a near synonym for *gravis*, a word regularly used in connection with high poetry, tragedy, and epic. For Davis Horace's self-representation at Philippi is not a conciliatory gesture, a way of massaging the potential embarrassments of his shift of political allegiance, but part of his self-construction and self-validation as a lyric poet, a 'mode of authentication' in which, by means of a 'mythologized *bios*', the poet's 'lyric vocation is sanctioned and vindicated'.[80] Horace follows in the footsteps of the *lyrici* Alcaeus and Anacreon, who had likewise thrown away their shields. He is also, as we have seen, recalling a passage of Archilochus, which Davis, accepting the interpretation of Hermann Fränkel, sees as

---

[78] Nisbet and Hubbard (1978) note ad loc.; they add that the Egyptian bean is 'in reality a gigantic water-lily ten feet high, "Nelumpium speciosum"'.

[79] Compare the reading of 3. 14 in Oliensis (1998) 148.

[80] Davis (1991) 90; cf. p. 93: 'the Philippi debacle is recast in the mold of an emblematic "lyric" event.'

expressing a specifically anti-Homeric and anti-epic viewpoint, in an 'authoritative redefinition of values'.[81]

Davis's approach is pretty relentlessly formalistic, and, like some political readings, tends to make all Horace's odes sound rather alike. The aesthetic critic may wish not only to differentiate Horace from other Latin poets, but also to differentiate a particular ode from the rest—what is *this* poem *to me*? The ode's last word is *amico*, and the ode may prompt thoughts about friendship. Pronouns—'I', 'you', 'we'—are important in friendship ('Because it was he, because it was I'[82]), and the structure of 2. 7 is articulated in part through its pronouns (in order *mecum, te, cum quo, tecum, me, te, tibi, ego, mihi*), though we never have *nos* (the friends have been divided since Philippi). Pompeius is 'first' of Horace's friends, which may mean 'first in time', or 'first in importance', or both; certainly the friendship belongs to Horace's youth, youth being a time when friendships can be most intense, and there have been long years of separation—a kind of death. In lines 6–7 (*morantem saepe diem mero | fregi*) Horace characterizes that friendship by means of an echo of Callimachus' second epigram where the poet mourns a dead friend, of which there is a famous translation in English by William Cory:

> They told me, Heraclitus, they told me you were dead;[83]
> They brought me bitter news to hear and bitter tears to shed.
> I wept as I remembered how often you and I
> Had tired the sun with talking and sent him down the sky.
>
> And now that thou art lying, my dear old Carian guest,
> A handful of grey ashes, long, long ago at rest,
> Still are thy pleasant voices, thy nightingales, awake,
> For Death, he taketh all away, but them he cannot take.

If we read the opening question as an expression of amazement, Pompeius' reappearance has indeed something of the flavour of resurrection (*recepto amico*). Relationships are one way of measuring out a sense of one's life history, and the ode may also prompt reflections on life's vicissitudes, and how they can be incorporated

---

[81] Ibid. 91.
[82] Montaigne, book 1, 28 ('On Friendship').
[83] The plangent repetition in this line does not feature in the Greek; perhaps Cory is recalling the analogous repetition in the opening line of the Postumus *Ode* (2. 14): *Eheu fugaces, Postume, Postume.*

into a coherent or satisfactory story. Horace's account of Philippi involves 'wit', in the sense made famous by T. S. Eliot: 'It involves, probably, a recognition, implicit in the expression of every experience, of other kinds of experience which are possible.'[84] And of course any reflections of this or other kind cannot be separated from the pleasure one takes in the way the words are slotted, with a sense of inevitability, and in intricate and complex combination[85], into the elaborate movement of the Alcaic metre. Repetitions, or near repetitions, of words, frequent in this poem (*saepe* 1 and 6, *militiae/ militia, fregi/fracta, celerem/celer, sustulit/tulit*), again challenge the reader to make them a part of her reading, in the free play of imagination and judgement, without any necessary determinate result. As I argued in detail in the last chapter, aesthetic response is a response to form and content together.

We get different readings, clearly, depending on whether we foreground the political or the aesthetic. Neither type of reading can simply be ruled out *a priori*. These readings may be reconcilable in a particular case, or we may have to choose between them, at least in any given encounter with a text.[86] Moreover, it can be argued, a particular version of poetics may be in tension with a particular version of politics. Don Fowler suggests that Horace's Callimacheanism and Epicurean commitment to the simple life make it impossible for him to write effective grand poetry in praise of the regime:

If we start to think of the deeds of the Great and the Good in aesthetic terms, as rival artists, then poetics have a potentially political import. Caesar thunders on the Euphrates: but isn't that bad art, combining thunderous bombast with the tumid Assyrian river? Isn't Greatness itself suspect? The polite tones of the *recusatio* ... conceal a poetic manifesto in which the small-scale genres are actually *preferred* to

---

[84] Kermode (1975*b*) 170.

[85] A particularly striking instance is the interwoven *quis udo | deproperare apio coronas | curatve myrto?*, where the grandiose and archaic *deproperare* is combined with less recherché vocabulary.

[86] Cf. O'Gorman (2002) 85: 'How can we (or Horace, for that matter) claim in the same breath that the proper context of this lyric is Augustan Rome and the Greek lyric canon?'. She goes on to argue for a form of aesthetic historicism. For an example of how the application of different frames to an ode of Horace produces incompatible readings see Martindale (1993*a*) 11–12. One might also ask how far art, or some art, strives to be art, strives, that is, to force open a gap which enables it both to be at least partially autonomous and also to be read by future readers as such. Horace is after all much concerned with the afterlife of his poems.

sublimity on aesthetic grounds: where does that leave the artistic achievement of the Great Leader?[87]

However, as we saw in connection with *Ode* 4. 2 in the last chapter, matters may not be quite so simple. Fowler himself concedes that we might be able to find in Horace 'a "Bacchic poetics" in which sublimity and inspired excess transfigure the tropes of Callimacheanism and the *furor* of the inspired poet in a guilty will to power';[88] in other words Horace's politics might be used to deconstruct his poetics as much as vice versa. One might further ask if Callimacheanism might not be part of the political settlement, whether the *pax Augusta* should be construed as an aesthetic or a political event.[89] In other words one could argue that the tension between 'aesthetics' and 'politics' is already inscribed within the *Odes*, where there is a tussle between quietism and laureatism, Callimachus and Pindar, withdrawal and engagement. Thus *Ode* 4. 2 encodes the public/private dichotomy within generic distinctions between grand and humble lyric. In other words the categories aesthetic and political can be seen as feeding off each other, in a movement of mutual complicity. Each discourse may contain traces of a repressed other, which can always be re-invoked, so that poeticization can be criticised for occluding politicization, and vice versa. But in turn such re-invocations might be said to involve imperialistic pretensions. The critic will have to negotiate such binds as best she may.

III

Issues about canonicity, as we have seen, are not aesthetic, in any Kantian sense; rather they have to do with the politics of reading,

---

[87] D. Fowler (1995) 254. The point might be extended to cover the wider dispute between political and aesthetic criticism. The aesthete is accused of triviality and a frivolous withdrawal from the world; she replies that her opponent is strutting, self-important.

[88] D. Fowler (1995) 266. For Fowler, as for many in our post-colonial ideological world, 'greatness' is above all *politically* suspect. See my later discussion of the *Aeneid*, pp. 139–40. The difficulties of disentangling political (whose politics?) and aesthetic readings are considerable. The Kantian aesthetic should involve no presuppositions about whose politics you might explore.

[89] In *Ode* 2. 9 Horace praises the way Augustus makes the river of the Medes roll smaller eddies, while the Geloni ride within bounds (*intra praescriptum*) on narrow plains (*exiguis campis*). The language fuses imperialism with the poetics of Callimachus.

with institutions and education (though obviously they involve, or at any rate invoke, judgements of artistic value). Hostility to the canon does not of itself entail hostility to aesthetics. But inevitably any student of Latin literature and the discipline of Classics (whose very name expresses its canonical preoccupations) cannot situate himself 'outside' the operations of the canon. In his book *In Search of the Classic*, a plea for a return to 'humanist' values, Steven Shankman offers his definition of a literary 'classic' as follows: 'in terms of what I call the classical position, a work of literature is a compelling, formally coherent, and rationally defensible representation that resists being reduced either to the mere recording of material reality, on the one hand, or to the bare exemplification of an abstract philosophical precept, on the other.'[90] There are a number of respects in which this formulation seems to me to be vulnerable. First, it is remarkably unhelpful: for example, if one wanted to draw up a list of classic works, it would not enable one to distinguish usefully between a 'great' play by Shakespeare and a decent play by one of his better contemporaries. Secondly, it is curiously negative, as one checks off to see if a work does, or does not, fall short in being overly mimetic, or propagandistic, or whatever; a more productive approach would be to enquire into the sources of power (in all likelihood, different in each case) that cause particular pieces of writing to engross, move, astonish, delight, or overwhelm us in various ways. Thirdly, it is highly idiosyncratic, as Shankman brushes aside familiar usages (the classic as canonical text and so on)—*pace* Humpty-Dumpty, words will not simply mean what we say they mean regardless of history and use. Shankman would have done better to imitate Frank Kermode and investigate past usages of the term, including its revival by T. S. Eliot (most notably in 'What is a Classic?', his Presidential address to the Virgil Society in 1944), before asking whether and how it might still serve for us.[91] One of the virtues of Kermode is that, while his commitment to 'literature' is as large as any of the traditionalists, he is—or at least was—far more alive to the institutional bases of reading and interpretation than they; the institution both acts as gatekeeper to legitimate exegesis and assists in the process of rendering modern the canonical work by accommodating it to the needs of the present, by allegorizing if you will. Allegory, reception,

[90] Shankman (1994) p. xiii. [91] Kermode (1975a).

accommodation, appropriation—these are not keywords for Shankman, though the effects of their operations are everywhere to be discerned within his own writing.[92]

Shankman's further insistence that a classic is not reducible either to pure form or pure ideology is convincing enough. However, his discussion of these difficult issues skates over some pretty thin ice. Take the case of Virgil, about whom Shankman evidently feels not a little discomfort. If one looks at the matter 'historically', it is hard not to agree with Eliot that Virgil is 'the classic of all Europe',[93] as the author who was at the centre of the Western literary canon for 1800 years, longer than any other so far. A theory of the classic that excludes Virgil is unlikely to be entirely persuasive. But it is clear that the *Aeneid* has very often been read as, in some senses, endorsing the *imperium Romanum* and the Augustan principate (according to Servius, Virgil's 'intention' was 'to praise Augustus through his ancestors'). More than this, the poem is implicated, or so it can easily be argued, in the whole history of Western imperialism, a history that was once an object of congratulation but which has now become an embarrassment to many.[94] Accordingly, Shankman espouses the common, indeed orthodox 'liberal' view that Virgil's support for Rome and Augustus is qualified, undercut, or even undermined, by the poem's emphasis on suffering and uncertainty (there are both left- and right-wing versions of this interpretation): it is thus 'the extreme qualification of its own ideological message' that makes the *Aeneid* a classic. The earlier view ('from the Middle Ages through the nineteenth century') is characterized as 'prejudiced' since readers 'tended to interpret the poem in ways that confirmed their own beliefs and aspirations' (the lack of self-awareness would be remarkable were it not so characteristic of academic critics).[95] There is considerable over-simplification of the reception here, but, if we leave that aside, the idea that Dante, Milton, and innumerable other intelligent readers for a thousand years got it 'wrong'—whereas modern

---

[92] See Martindale (1998).
[93] Eliot (1957) 70. See also Michèle Lowrie, 'Literature is a Latin Word', in Farrell (2001) 29–38.
[94] For a fuller discussion of the politics of the *Aeneid* in relation to the poem's reception see Martindale (1993*b*).
[95] Shankman (1994) 219, 223.

scholars have finally offered a true account—is as patronizing to the past as it is patently absurd of the present. Moreover, we should recall Hans-Georg Gadamer's justified insistence that 'prejudices' should not be regarded as a barrier to good reading but as an essential precondition of it.[96] We read from where we are, or we do not read at all (though where we are may be difficult to determine, and may shift). Moved perhaps by similar embarrassments Gordon Williams attempts to distinguish 'ideas' from 'ideology', with ideas characterizing the *Aeneid* and ideology Augustus' *Res Gestae*.[97] Of course one can argue that the *Aeneid* is a richer, more complex and multi-faceted text than the *Res Gestae*, but that of itself does not show that the poem is not saturated in ideology. Indeed, one could argue that texts like the *Aeneid*, just because of their complexity, can underpin ideological positions with particular success. The *Aeneid*, instantly a school text, may have done more than the *Res Gestae* to perpetuate what might be called an Augustan world-view and Augustan values.

Shankman's treatment of the issue of pure or autonomous art is hardly more satisfactory. Here Virgil is involved again, this time as the poet of the *Eclogues*. Shankman is suspicious of pastoral on the grounds that it 'encouraged the isolation of the quality of formal beauty from ethical and cognitive concerns'; he finds the genre 'precious and self-enclosed', comparing it to 'that other late-to-emerge...equally decadent genre, literary criticism', and endorsing Dr Johnson's famous (or infamous) critique of Milton's *Lycidas*.[98] Once again Shankman can be said to be flying in the face of history: E. R. Curtius wrote of *Eclogue* 1 that 'it is not too much to say that anyone unfamiliar with that short poem lacks one key to the literary tradition of Europe'.[99] It would seem more consonant with his traditionalism for Shankman to have explored the possible reasons for the widespread appeal of pastoral in the West. If he had done so, it would have become clear that political and ethical readings of the *Eclogues* are everywhere to be found. Far from treating pastoral as self-contained, Renaissance theorists, following

---

[96] Gadamer (1975).   [97] G. Williams (1983) 233–4.

[98] Shankman (1994) 187, 196, 191. Of course assigning a work to a genre is a purely conceptual matter and not part of the judgement of taste. Pastoral is a category, and as such could be a political category.

[99] Curtius (1953) 190.

Servius, saw it as a usefully oblique mode of addressing a variety of social, political, and intellectual concerns. Modern scholars have also read the poems politically. For example, *Eclogue* 1 involves issues of exile and dispossession as well as ideals of community, and the shadows of its ending have been read as bringing either comfort or threat. It is commonplace to say that, in comparison with Theocritus, Virgil politicizes pastoral space by admitting elements of the wider world, including the world of high politics, into his green one. More than this, the poems can be seen as political through and through, as constituting in fact a potent ideological vehicle. Indeed, the modern environmental movement, with its prescriptions for the good life designed to counter ever-encroaching urbanism and the rape of nature, might be construed as a modern version of pastoral. Significantly the allegorizations of the *Eclogues* favoured by modern scholarship include some of a rather evidently environmentalist hue; so according to A. J. Boyle the poems investigate 'the psychological chaos and spiritual impoverishment which Virgil sees as the city's legacy and *the corollary of technological growth*' (italics mine).[100] And in general, at least since Schiller's *On Naïve and Sentimental Poetry*, Virgil's green places have been constituted as a privileged site of the harmonious co-operation between Man and Nature.[101]

The relationship between the political and the aesthetic can be said to figure both within the *Eclogues* themselves and within writing about them (indeed my contention would be that, because of the importance of reception in the making of meanings, this distinction between text and commentary can, and should, be partially collapsed). The poetry of third-century BC Alexandria to which Theocritus' *Idylls* belong is often seen as comparatively 'pure', at least in comparison with the earlier 'political' poetry of Classical Athens, the poetry of the *polis*. There is an obvious paradox here. Callimachus, the most important and innovative writer of the period, worked under the ruling Ptolemies and composed poems in their praise. Artists—in this at least like academics—have some complicity with the political systems they work under, whatever claims to purity they may make or have made for them. The *Eclogues* likewise are often presented as inhabiting a charmed enclosure. When Paul Veyne argues that Roman love

---

[100] Boyle (1986) 15.   [101] See Halperin (1983) 42–9.

elegy is a kind of literary game bearing little relation to any social realities he calls it pastoral in city clothes; elegy for him takes place 'outside the world, just like bucolic poetry'.[102] The *Eclogues* in other words are an *unproblematic* instance of evidently aesthetic play; whereas many have been misled by elegy, 'such pastoral fiction never fooled anyone'. In what is perhaps the most influential account of the *Eclogues* written by a classicist in the twentieth century, 'Arcadia: the Discovery of a Spiritual Landscape', Bruno Snell argued that they are set, not in any actual Mediterranean countryside but in 'a far-away land overlaid with the golden haze of unreality'[103]. Although Virgil allowed political matters to intrude into his Arcadia, in this departing from Theocritean precedent, he converted them into myth, being indeed 'always careful not to get involved in the slippery problems of political action; in fact one may presume that they never even penetrated to his dreaming ear'. And, like Veyne, Snell stresses the poetic autonomy of the *Eclogues*, which 'represent the first serious attempt in literature to mould the Greek motifs into self-contained forms of beauty whose reality lies within themselves'; as a result, for the first time, 'art became "symbol"'. The New Historicist Louis Montrose has observed how theories of pastoral have a way of becoming theories of literature, and certainly many of those who have been drawn to pastoral seem anxious to clear a space for the aesthetic uncontaminated by more banausic discourses in what can itself be seen as 'an exemplary pastoral process'; in Montrose's words, 'to write *about* pastoral may be a way of displacing and simplifying the discontents of the latter-day humanist in an increasingly technocratic academy and society.'[104] The pastoral world can readily function as an emblem for the academic world (as previously for the monastic world).

It is easy to find elements in the *Eclogues* to support such an aestheticizing reading. Pastoral is, in general, unusually self-conscious about its own status as art, to the extent that critics sometimes claim that this is what the genre is fundamentally 'about'; for example the literary theorist Wolfgang Iser finds in

---

[102] Veyne (1988) 101. For a critique of Veyne's general approach see Kennedy (1993) 95–100.
[103] Snell (1953) 282; the two subsequent quotations are from pp. 294 and 308.
[104] Montrose (1983) 415.

Politics and Art 143

the invented world of the *Eclogues* not so much Snell's landscape of the mind as 'a work of art that thematizes art itself',[105] one indeed that largely frees itself from the traditional referential function of poetry as *mimesis* articulated by Plato and Aristotle. For Paul de Man, following William Empson, 'the pastoral theme is, in fact, the only poetic theme, ... it is poetry itself':

> What is the pastoral convention, then, if not the eternal separation between the mind that distinguishes, negates, legislates, and the originary simplicity of the natural? A separation that may be lived, as in Homer's epic poetry..., or it may be thought in full consciousness of itself as in Marvell's poem ['The Garden'].

In de Man's view we must strive to avoid falling into the trap of all 'impatient "pastoral" thought: formalism, false historicism, and utopianism'.[106]

Certainly *Eclogue* 6 is now normally read metapoetically, as a poem about poem-making, one that constitutes a poetics relevant to Virgil's whole project. Significantly, although the piece has some bucolic colour, its principal matter is mythology, not the rustic world. It opens with a *recusatio*, a refusal enjoined by Apollo to write about kings and battles, which is a close imitation, seemingly the first in Latin, of a passage from the *Aetia* prologue where Callimachus answers his critics and defends his poetic practice. Virgil justifies writing Theocritean bucolic poetry by appealing to Callimachus' aesthetic credo, his championing of stylistic refinement, *leptotēs* (as Theocritus himself had already done in *Idyll* 7).[107] Apollo had told Callimachus, 'poet, feed your offering as fat as possible, but keep the muse lean (*leptaleēn*)'. With witty appropriateness Virgil gives the Callimachean imagery a more specifically pastoral turn. Tityrus is instructed to feed his sheep fat, but the song of the Theocritean poet, troped as a shepherd, is to be fine-spun (*deductum carmen*).[108] Virgil's muse will display *tenuitas* (*tenuis* is used of the shepherd's reed-pipe both literally and

---

[105] Iser (1993) 34.
[106] de Man (1983) 239, 241 (from 'The Dead-End of Formalist Criticism').
[107] For Callimachus' text and a list of Latin texts derived from it see Hopkinson (1988). Cameron (1995) has recently challenged many of the orthodoxies about Callimachus, particularly the view that the *Aetia* prologue is an attack on traditional narrative epic. If his views are accepted, Latin literary history will need to be modified accordingly.
[108] *Deductus* may also on occasion have political connotations (*deducere* can mean 'found a colony'); see Virgil, *Georgic* 3. 11.

with reference to the poetry associated with it), and will be a species of play, *lusus*, far from the gloom of traditional martial themes (*tristia bella*).

The song of Silenus which follows, a catalogue of mythological tales, might almost be a blueprint for Ovid's *Metamorphoses*, the work that in so many ways can be seen as the climax of Roman Alexandrianism. It begins with a tiny cosmology, in the style of Hesiod (a poet also evoked by Callimachus in the *Aetia* prologue[109]) and with Lucretian echoes, and continues with abbreviated narrations of various myths, several of them involving metamorphosis or love or both. At its centre is a mini-epyllion, a miniaturization of the miniature epic that Catullus and his fellow modernists favoured. It tells, obliquely and with a sort of hyper-refined lyricism, of Pasiphae's perverse desire for the bull, and it even includes, in the manner of some other epyllia including Catullus 64, an inset-narrative (the story of the Proetides who imagined they had become cows). The writer projects himself empathetically into his story, and consoles (*solatur*) the victim for her pathological condition. This is the sort of writing that, in both content and preciosity of style, traditionalists, ancient and modern, might stigmatize as 'decadent' (Jasper Griffin compares it to Wilde's *Salome*[110]). Contemporary translators have enormous difficulty in finding any convincing equivalent for this kind of writing, so we have to go back to Dryden to find a satisfactory version:

> Then mourns the madness of the Cretan queen—
> Happy for her if herds had never been!
> What fury, wretched woman, seized thy breast?
> The maids of Argos, though, with rage possessed,
> Their imitated lowings filled the grove,
> Yet shunned the guilt of thy preposterous love,
> Nor sought the youthful husband of the herd,
> Though tender and untried the yoke he feared,
> Though soft and white as flakes of falling snow,
> And scarce his budding horns had adorned his brow.
> Ah, wretched queen, you range the pathless wood,
> While on a flowery bank he chews the cud,
> Or sleeps in shades, or through the forest roves,
> And roars with anguish for his absent loves.
> 'Ye nymphs, with toils his forest-walk surround,

---

[109] But see now Cameron (1995) ch. 13 'Hesiodic Elegy'. [110] Griffin (1986) 32.

And trace his wandering footsteps on the ground.
But, ah, perhaps my passion he disdains,
And courts the milky mothers of the plains.
We search the ungrateful fugitive abroad,
While they at home sustain his happy load.'

Silenus' song also compliments a second-generation neoteric, Virgil's friend Gaius Cornelius Gallus, who composes a poem in imitation of Euphorion, another Alexandrian of ostentatious obscurity, and becomes Hesiod's successor, receiving the pipes with which, like Orpheus, Hesiod used to bring down (*deducere*) the trees from the mountains. And in all this we have both a poetics of eros and an erotics of poetry (Silenus recalls songs Apollo sang by the river Eurotas after killing his lover, the beautiful and beautifully named boy Hyacinthus), together with a heralding of the Orphic and Apollonian powers of poetry; poets create the world of myth, create, that is, their own kind of reality, one far from the tedium and *tristitia* of high politics, and one in which they are sovereign. From a different perspective, of course, one could call this escapism.

Veyne's conception of aesthetic play is consonant both with the importance of singing contests in Theocritus and Virgil and with the characterization of the *Eclogues* by one of their most intelligent early readers. The poet Horace contrasts the martial poetry of 'fierce' Varius with what may be rendered 'the sensitive and witty *epos* that the Italian Muses who rejoice in the countryside have bestowed on Virgil': *(epos) molle atque facetum | Vergilio adnuerunt gaudentes rure Camenae (Satire* 1. 10. 44–5).[111] The sophisticated, at times whimsical, wit of the *Eclogues* is something that much modern criticism (eager to stress the 'serious', even dark, side of the poems, in an understandable anxiety to free them from any imputations of triviality) frequently underplays. The tenth *Eclogue*, for example, is one of which rather heavy critical weather has been made; the poem is widely read as acknowledging the failure of pastoral (already threatened in *Eclogue* 9 by the inruptions of politics and war), since the world of the shepherds proves impotent to assuage the passional dolours of Gallus who, in a concretization of a common erotic trope, is literally dying of love (*amore peribat*, 10). The poem

---

[111] I follow here the interpretation of Halperin (1983) 213–14; editors usually take the adjectives adverbially. Pastoral was not at this date formally separated as a genre; Horace, like Quintilian, sees the hexameter *Eclogues* as a form of 'epic'.

is seen as staging a debate about literary modes, the deficiencies and limitations of pastoral leading in the end to its abandonment by Virgil. Certainly *Eclogue* 10 explicitly presents itself as closural, the last of the collection (*extremum laborem*, 1), and the shadows of evening fall across its close:

> Haec sat erit, divae, vestrum cecinisse poetam,   70
> dum sedet et gracili fiscellam texit hibisco
>
> . . . .
>
> surgamus: solet esse gravis cantantibus umbra,   75
> iuniperi gravis umbra; nocent et frugibus umbrae.
> ite domum saturae, venit Hesperus, ite capellae.
>
> To have sung these things, goddesses, while he sat and wove
> A frail of thin hibiscus, will suffice your poet
>
> . . . .
>
> Let us arise: for singers heavy is the shade,
> Heavy the shade of juniper; and shade harms fruit.
> Go, little she-goats, Hesper comes, go home replete.   (Guy Lee)

Umbra, shade, is readily taken as a figure for bucolic writing (the beginning of the first *Eclogue* saw Tityrus reclining *lentus in umbra*), while *surgamus* might imply, allegorically, that the writer will proceed to other, perhaps 'higher' poetic forms (already in the fourth *Eclogue* he had assayed *paulo maiora*, a slightly grander, panegyrical theme[112]). Virgil tropes himself as an inhabitant of his bucolic world, himself sitting at ease while Gallus pours forth his passionate complaint, and weaving his slender hibiscus basket (which could stand for the poem itself and its stylistic *gracilitas* or for the whole now-completed eclogue book—as we saw in the last chapter, weaving had been used as a metaphor for writing poetry by Catullus and others); this passage evidently elides being a shepherd and writing Theocritean verse. There is a sense of completion: the poet has sung enough (*sat*), the flocks are fed full (*saturae*)—the sheep are fat, though the bucolic muse must remain lean. The lines thus constitute a sort of *sphragis* or seal for the entire collection (designed as an artistically satisfying whole), which introduces, or reintroduces, its author. The poem fuses with wit and virtuosity material from two literary models, themselves both probably indebted to Callimachus' thin-spun verse, Theocritus (especially

---

[112] For some possible resonances of *maiora* see Cameron (1995) 470–1.

the first *Idyll* in which the shepherd hero Daphnis dies) and Gallus, where the object of imitation was in a different metre (elegiac couplets). Since, according to Servius, *Amores* was the title Gallus gave his elegies, *sollicitos Galli dicamus amores* (6) could be translated either 'let me describe Gallus' troubled feelings of love/love affair', or 'let me speak of Gallus' poems the *Amores* with their depiction of troubled love' (further the genitive here could mean poems by Gallus or poems for Gallus); the line punningly collapses the distinction between love as an emotion and its literary expression in a text. Although Gallus' love poetry is lost, except for a fragment recovered some years ago in Egypt,[113] there are pretty clearly reminiscences of it in his lament, which constitutes a song within a song (the performance element is strong here as throughout the *Eclogues*). But this does not mean that Virgil is solemnly debating the merits and demerits of different genres, let alone acknowledging the failure of his own bucolic art, including its failure to deal with the vicissitudes of erotic passion (there is anyway no clear distinction between bucolic and elegiac love which share many of the same tropes). Virgil has to compose verses to honour or to help his friend for Lycoris herself to read. We could say that Virgil is expressing poetic and erotic solidarity with Gallus, with consummate art is helping him court his *docta puella*, his learned mistress.[114] Virgil himself is a lover of Gallus (73), so is perhaps humorously presenting himself as Lycoris' rival in erotics. There is an undertow of (often pleasing) melancholy about much pastoral writing, but it is easier to read this comparatively sprightly, poised poem as primarily an exercise in wit, *facetiae* (Horace, as we have seen, found the *Eclogues* 'sensitive and witty'). Veyne is quite insistent:

I do not for an instant believe that... Virgil meant to deliver a 'message' to us, to draw melancholy conclusions about 'the final failure of poetry, unable to purge the passions'. What reader would think of taking a poetic fiction for some moralist's guidebook, drawing such a clear lesson from it? This epilogue merely signifies that, the pastiche being ended, the two poets again become what eternity will change

---

[113] For the text see Anderson *et al.* (1979) 138 ff. For Gallus and Virgil see in particular Ross (1975), esp. ch. 5.

[114] *Pauca meo Gallo, sed quae legat ipsa Lycoris, | carmina sunt dicenda* (2–3—from the new fragment we now know that these lines too echo Gallus: *carmina... | quae possem domina dicere digna mea*).

them into.... The confusion of genres was only a momentary game, the flock can reenter its fold.[115]

One may contrast the stress on poetic autonomy we encounter in Veyne or Snell with some of the uses the *Eclogues* were put to in the last century. In 1917 John H. Finley, commissioner of education for New York State and president of the State University, in his poem 'Virgil's First Eclogue Remembered' appropriated the piece to argue for US intervention in the First World War. In 'Build Soil: A Political Pastoral' the conservative Robert Frost used the same poem to criticize Roosevelt's liberal agricultural policies, while in Latin America, from a different point in the political spectrum, *Eclogues* 1 and 9 could serve to provide oblique support for land reform.[116] In the Renaissance, when the fashion for pastoral poetry on the Virgilian model was at its height, critics underlined the political subtexts of the *Eclogues*. Thus Sidney wrote in his *Apology for Poetry* (published 1595), 'Is the poor pipe [i.e. pastoral poetry] disdained, which sometimes out of Meliboeus' mouth can show the misery of people under hard lords or ravening soldiers, and again, by Tityrus, what blessedness is derived to them that lie lowest from the goodness of them that sit highest?'; while George Puttenham in *The Art of English Poetry* (1589) sees the eclogue as a late and oblique form of poetry devised 'not of purpose to counterfeit or represent the rustical manner of loves and communication, but under the veil of homely persons and in rude speeches to insinuate and glance at greater matters, and such as perchance had not been safe to have been disclosed in any other sort, which may be perceived by the *Eclogues* of Virgil, in which are treated by figure matters of greater importance than the loves of Tityrus and Corydon'.[117] Renaissance texts of the *Eclogues* often featured the ancient commentary of Servius, which presented the poems as intermittently allegorical (Puttenham's 'by figure'), in contrast to Theocritus' *Idylls*, supposedly written on one level (*simpliciter*); Donatus had been of the same opinion, stating that there is a certain amount of figurative allegorical discourse 'neither nowhere nor everywhere' (*neque nusquam neque ubique aliquid figurate dici, hoc est per allegoriam*). Such scraps of evidence as we

---

[115] Veyne (1988) 103–4; see too Conte (1986) 120–1.
[116] See for these details Ziolkowski (1993) 156–63, 21–2.
[117] Loughrey (1984) 33–4 (texts modernized).

possess might suggest that the *Eclogues* were read allegorically throughout antiquity. Quintilian (8. 6. 46), citing lines from *Eclogue* 9 to illustrate a particular type of allegory, assumes that Menalcas in this poem is to be understood as Virgil. Apuleius (*Apology* 10) tells that through the masks of Corydon and Alexis Virgil is expressing his love for a slave boy of Pollio's. Despite their continual appeals to the supposed responses of ancient readers, modern scholars reject the story (while for the most part accepting Apuleius' identifications in the same passage of the various women in love elegy), although something like it seems already assumed in one of Martial's epigrams (8. 56) and elsewhere; it might suggest a possible reading of *Eclogue* 2 as a witty coterie piece. As a result of the influential second *Eclogue* in particular, pastoral can be given, as by Gide or John Addington Symonds, a homoerotic reading (which could be political), as well as a 'green' political and/or a 'pure art' reading.

'Where he [Servius] goes most astray is in allegorizing the *Eclogues*'; Richard Jenkyns's comment is typical enough of modern scholarship.[118] By contrast, Annabel Patterson argues that such hostility to what she calls 'the Servian hermeneutic' can be seen as an occlusive attempt to depoliticize the *Eclogues*, to represent them as comparatively pure art untainted by ideology, whereas to both Servius and those poets influenced by the Servian tradition they were the loci of social and political concerns as much as of artistic ones. As Patterson puts it (thereby herself becoming a modern shepherd-scholar):

Among the competing ideologies proleptically displayed in the *Eclogues* are Roman republicanism, the classic statement of the claims of the many to equal consideration; the counter-claim of the privileged few to special treatment on the grounds of special talent; the hegemonic needs of the holders of power for cultural authentication; the responsibility of the intellectual for providing that authentication, in the interests of stability; the value of political or social stability in nurturing the arts; the responsibility of the intellectual for telling the whole truth, in the interests of social justice; the intellectual's claim to personal autonomy.[119]

Classicists, in a way that can be related to romantic and post-romantic aesthetic preferences, are happier with symbolism, a mode of fusion which implies wholeness, than with allegory

---

[118] Jenkyns (1992) 155. [119] Patterson (1988) 8.

which works by fragmentation and discontinuity. Thus it is frequently argued that Tityrus in *Eclogue* 1 cannot stand for Virgil, because he is an elderly man and an ex-slave; but it is *because* Tityrus is different from Virgil (or Daphnis in *Eclogue* 5 from Julius Caesar) that he can be (as Servius supposed) an allegory of him— allegory is precisely a figure of disjunction. Significantly it is only with *poetic* allegory that modern criticism seems at all comfortable; the poems are acknowledged to be self-reflexive, allegorizing their own writing. We have seen how commentators are happy to discuss the possibility that the end of *Eclogue* 10 is a farewell to pastoral, with *umbra* figuring bucolic poetry, whereas they would not even think to cite Servius Danielis' gloss on *in umbra* in *Eclogue* 1 'under Augustus' protection' *allegorice sub tutela Imperatoris Augusti* (though a glance at the dictionary will show the political connotations of 'shade'). Jasper Griffin comments that if Virgil did lose his farm, or have one restored to him, 'this series of transactions...was...inherently unpoetical';[120] while he regards *Eclogue* 4 as not so much 'a response to a political settlement' (the poem may be a celebration of the peace of Brundisium and a sort of epithalamium for the marriage of Antony and Octavia) as a poetic fantasy. Yet *Eclogue* 4 has continually been evoked in precise political circumstance; Dryden, for example, echoes it in connection with the Restoration of Charles II in *Astraea Redux*. The poem, of course, became the subject of the most famous of all allegorizations of the *Eclogues*, and one whose resonance has lasted well into the modern period, as being 'about' the birth of Christ. In *Purgatorio* 22, in a notable piece of fiction making, Dante has Statius tell 'the poet of the bucolic songs' that he was first drawn to Christianity by reading the fourth *Eclogue*; this is not mere historical naïvety (Dante knows perfectly well that the *virgo* of line 6 is the goddess Astraea, not the Virgin Mary), but rather a matter of different reading habits. Recently Seamus Heaney has turned to Virgilian pastoral as one way of responding to the Irish 'troubles'. His 'Bann Valley Eclogue' (included in *Electric Light*, 2001) is a modern version of Virgil's fourth *Eclogue*, and takes the form of a dialogue between Poet and Virgil (his 'hedge-schoolmaster'). Heaney stresses the political resonances of his model:

---

[120] Griffin (1986) 24; the subsequent quotation is from p. 29.

> Here are my words you'll have to find a place for:
> *Carmen, ordo, nascitur, saeculum, gens.*
> Their gist in your tongue and province should be clear
> Even at this stage. Poetry, order, the times,
> The nation, wrong and renewal, then an infant birth
> And a flooding away of all the old miasma.

To readers after the Good Friday Agreement this poem can give something of the power *Eclogue* 4 might have had for its original war-weary Roman readers.

Politicizing accounts of the *Eclogues* may take both admiring and hostile forms. The poems may be praised for articulating a desire for simplicity (though always from the perspective of the sophisticated), and constituting a protest, sometimes overt, more often implied, against the evils of the city, even an implicit pacifism. Thus Servius claims that *Eclogue* 1 not only thanks Octavian for restoring the poet's farm, but also criticizes him over the sufferings of the dispossessed. Or they may be criticized for concealing the realities and oppressions of rural life, in a way that serves the interests of the ruling class. Thus the editors of *The Penguin Book of English Pastoral*, writing in the Marxizing tradition of Raymond Williams's *The Country and the City*, argue that the genre is 'a way of *not* looking at the countryside': 'For the pastoral vision is, at base, a false vision positing a simplistic, unhistorical relationship between the ruling, landowning class—the poet's patrons and often the poet himself—and the workers on the land; as such its function is to mystify and to obscure the harshness of actual social and economic organization.'[121] One response to such criticism is to say that it rests on a naïve representational realism. There is no unmediated way of representing the countryside (and mediated ways of looking can be ways of looking, not of feigning). Any representation is, in the words of Simon Schama, 'the product of culture's craving and culture's framing' (his *Landscape and Memory* argues that 'landscapes are culture before they are nature; constructs of the imagination projected onto wood and water and rock', texts 'on which generations write their recurring obsessions').[122] Or one could say that no reader anyway ever mistook

---

[121] Barrell and Bull (1974) 4. On this extraordinary, essentializing view pastoral is not readable as oppositional. Barrell's views have had a huge influence on the interpretation of British landscape painting of the 18th and 19th centuries.

[122] Schama (1995) 7, 61, 12.

the pastoral world for the real countryside, while there are, in C. S. Lewis's words, 'many causes (reasons too) that have led humanity to symbolise by rural scenes a region in the mind which does exist and which should be visited often'.[123] But the argument that pastoral never fooled anyone sits uneasily, perhaps, with the memory of Marie Antoinette and her courtiers playing at shepherds as the poor starved and the old order began to crumble. Certainly anti-pastoralists like the poet George Crabbe found the Virgilian tradition an oppressive one: 'From Truth and Nature shall we widely stray | Where fancy leads, or Virgil led the way' (*The Village*, 1783).[124]

At the very least one must recognize that Virgil's green spaces are somewhat 'lordly possessions'.[125] Indeed we could say that this is what gives Virgilian pastoral part of its appeal, the glow of a loved beauty (inevitably selective) that is often tinged with the pathos of distance. There is both the strength of a remembered rural simplicity and the poignancy deriving from a sophisticated separation from that simplicity. Virgil shapes his rustic world into a form that allows him and his friends and patrons to make their own appearance there without embarrassment alongside the shepherds. Corydon in *Eclogue* 2 is said to produce artless verses (*incondita*); but his song is decked out with obtruded artistry (what Crabbe would call 'the tinsel trappings of poetic pride'), including the notorious line *Amphion Dircaeus in Actaeo Aracyntho* (24), mannered, allusive, Graecizing (it can be turned into a Greek hexameter with the lightest of adjustments). For all the supposed rusticity of the bucolic style, its 'lowness', the *Eclogues* belong rather evidently to 'high' culture; as one feminist scholar puts it, 'access to the pastoral speaking postion is determined by cultural possessions—of specific educational, class, gender, and racial identities', while 'the lowly are not assigned a subjectivity of their own'.[126] To Montrose and his fellow New Historicists the question is not what pastoral is, but what it does[127]; and what it does is to mediate social relations and cultural exchanges among the elite. Such

---

[123] Loughrey (1984) 142 (from *The Allegory of Love*, 1936, ch. 7).

[124] See Raymond Williams in Loughrey (1984) 155–7; Dr Johnson persuaded Crabbe to emend the second line to 'Where Virgil, not where Fancy, leads the way'.

[125] Schama (1995) 546.

[126] S. Smith (1993) 170–1.   [127] So Montrose (1983) 416.

Politics and Art

'demystifying' ('remystifying'?) political readings tend to become exact mirror images of the mystified aesthetic readings they seek to displace. A recent critic of pastoral makes the point well: 'What is occurring here is a kind of aesthetic scapegoating: the creation of a stable category of pure, "empty", idyllic formalism allows for the simultaneous creation of a category of pure, "full" political meaning, of an unmediated real uncontaminated by "the mirror of art".'[128]

The argument partly revolves round both *what* the *Eclogues* represent (if indeed they are referential) and *how* they represent. Iser insists that they are not mimetic in any traditional sense; in his view the tendency to treat them as such vitiates Snell's account, in which the pastoral world serves to represent an internal landscape, as much as any other. The green cabinet is a cabinet of tropes, but there is no straightforwardly 'proper' sense to which those tropes can be reduced (this is a familiar post-structuralist position about textuality in general). Signified and signifier float free, so that the signs 'no longer denote given positions or substances; instead, they insinuate links, unfold directions, and adumbrate realizations in order to reveal what cannot be denoted'.[129] The poems do not imitate politics, instead politics are inscribed within poetry that has become its own concern.[130] This is a subtle reading, not least because it respects the self-imitation of the eclogue world without making that self-imitation autonomous, but it still assumes that the text is subject to a single account. However, one could argue for an intermittent mimetic element in the *Eclogues*; in antiquity some of the poems (which indeed are indebted to mime and display some interest in characterization) were performed on stage as miniature dramas. Perhaps then, just as the *Eclogues* may be discontinuously allegorical (Servius comments that Tityrus should be understood as Virgil, but not everywhere, only where reason requires, *ubi exigit ratio*), so they are discontinuously mimetic. This fits well enough with the landscape setting, which critics so frequently describe as Arcadian and idealized. It is true that the depiction (like any representation of nature) involves selection but what seems most distinctive is not the element of idealization (one should not forget the bare rock and bog that surround Tityrus' farm in 1. 48–9) but

---

[128] Haber (1994) 5.   [129] Iser (1993) 31.   [130] Ibid. 34.

again the discontinuity and disjunction. The landscape is a composite of Theocritus' Sicily and various Italian scenes and indeed Arcadia (perhaps out of Gallus' poetry[131]); but one element in this mix is a precision of visualization which involves a form of *mimesis*, like the picture of the goats Meliboeus used to watch hang (*pendere*) on the hills around his farm (1. 76) that Wordsworth greatly admired.[132]

In general the modern critical stress on the structural unity of the collection may serve to conceal the considerable variousness of its contents—*Eclogues*, 'Selections', the title the book was in all probability given by later editors (Virgil's was *Bucolica*), serves to suggest that, certainly in comparison with the *Georgics* or *Aeneid*, it is fragmented as much as unified, composed at it were of chips from the writer's block. Indeed *Eclogue* 9 operates with what might be termed a poetics of fragmentation as, amid the chaos brought by the land confiscations, the two farmers on their way to town recall snatches of the songs of Menalcas (as we have seen taken in antiquity to be a mask for Virgil himself); these Virgilian bucolic fragments, two closely imitated from Theocritus, two recalling Roman political life (Caesar's comet, the land confiscations), are in turn framed by a bucolic dialogue which imitates and inverts Theocritus' celebratory *Idyll* 7, proclaiming, in lines that particularly caught the imagination of Renaissance readers, the impotence of poetry amid the weapons of war (11–13). We could say that what is shown here is precisely the impossibility of creating an enclosed self-sustaining aesthetic domain, but to take this as the final 'message' of the whole book would be to privilege this poem at the expense of, say, *Eclogue* 6.[133]

'Alternate singing is proper to a Pastoral' (so Rapin, the leading neo-classical theorist of the genre, in 1659).[134] One can imagine a pastoral dialogue debating the issue of aesthetics versus politics (Renaissance writers used the mode to stage religious debates as

---

[131] So Kennedy (1987*a*).

[132] For the reference see the note of Clausen (1994) ad loc. For the politics of landscape in the *Eclogues* see Joy Connolly, 'Picture Arcadia: The Politics of Representation in Vergil's *Eclogues*', in Farrell (2001) 89–116.

[133] On *Eclogue* 9 see Christine Perkell, 'Vergil Reading his Twentieth-Century Readers: A Study of *Eclogue* 9', in Farrell (2001) 64–88.

[134] Loughrey (1984) 41 (Thomas Creech's translation of 1684).

well as to explore the role of the intellectual in society).[135] The two singing contests, *Eclogues* 3 and 7, provide different models of dialogue, one ending in compromise and harmony, the other in victory for one party, both agonistic, competitive, the second more abrasively so. Such *amoebean* poems (as they are called) rarely involve any substantive engagement at the level of content—engagement is rather primarily formal, in terms of rhetorical organization and sentence structure.[136] In an analogous way the two kinds of critic treated in this chapter seem often to be talking past each other. Yet, as we saw earlier, aesthetics and politics can be thought of as differential terms rather than ontological entities, on which view each term is necessarily present within the other, at however occluded a level. And more pragmatically we can say that we need both discourses, and the *Eclogues* seem to acknowledge that need. Seamus Heaney, in a series of essays that compose yet another apology for poetry, observes that we want poems to be 'a source of truth and at the same time a vehicle for harmony'.[137] Heaney seeks himself 'to affirm that within our individual selves we can reconcile two orders of knowledge which we might call the practical and the poetic; to affirm also that each form of knowledge redresses the other and that the frontier between them is there for the crossing.' Heaney's 'liberal' approach to these matters has its considerable attractions, though, as we have seen, aesthetics and politics do not necessarily sit comfortably or harmoniously together, either in the *Eclogues* or elsewhere.

The *Eclogues*, then, can be read aesthetically, or politically, or both, in various different ways, many of them incompatible. Like most traditionalists, Shankman displays a dislike of this scandal of interpretation, of the messiness that accompanies contingency and change and 'democratic' interpretative freedom. He quotes with approval Socrates' remarks in the *Phaedrus*: 'Once a thing gets put into writing, the composition, whatever it may be, drifts all over the place, getting into the hands not only of those who understand it, but equally of those who have no business with it.'[138] Hence the

---

[135] Auden's distinction between the Arcadian and the Utopian has a bearing on this dispute; see Loughrey (1984) 90–2 (from *The Dyer's Hand and Other Essays*, 1962) and the poem 'Vespers' from *The Shield of Achilles*.

[136] For an interesting reading of the amoebean third *Eclogue* see Henderson (1999) ch. 6.

[137] Heaney (1995) 193, 203.   [138] Shankman (1994) 310 n. 17 (from *Phaedrus* 275e).

appeal of the 'timeless' classic; as Shankman puts it (begging all the important questions), 'if Plato's work is truly classic, then it will be perpetually relevant'.[139] One can sympathize with such desire, analogous to our fear of death—love is not love which alters when it alteration finds. One thinks of Shakespeare's Troilus for whom the change in Cressida's feelings undermines his grasp of self and world: 'this is, and is not, Cressid.' But even Sir Joshua Reynolds, while arguing in his 'Fourth Discourse' that for paintings in the grand style 'there must be something either in the action, or in the object, in which men are universally concerned', concedes the role of custom, tradition, and education in the establishment of such 'universals':

> Strictly speaking, indeed, no subject can be of universal, hardly can it be of general, concern; but there are events and characters so popularly known in those countries where our Art is in request, that they may be considered as sufficiently general for all our purposes. Such are the great events of Greek and Roman fable and history, which early education, and the usual course of reading, have made familiar and interesting to all Europe, without being degraded by the vulgarism of ordinary life in any country. Such too are the capital subjects of scripture history, which, besides their general notoriety, become venerable by their connection with our religion.[140]

A history of the canon confirms the temporal fluctuations of value—Michelangelo and Shakespeare are among the very small number of creative artists whose position within it has not so far shifted over the centuries. And even in such cases different works are valued and for different reasons; contestation is a part of the reception of any text, and to freeze the interpretation of a 'classic' would not be to ensure its continued life.

Is the idea of the classic of any use to us today other than as part of a historical enquiry? The term can conveniently be applied to any work that has been a reference point for a significant number of readers over a reasonable length of time; in that sense *The Waste Land* could be called a classic of Modernism, whatever value any individual reader assigns to it and however much institutional factors have operated in assuring its success. It is certainly worth looking into the possible reasons why certain episodes, sections, or scenes from canonical texts have exercised a fascination on so many

---

[139] Shankman (1994) 63.   [140] Reynolds (1975) 57–8.

readers—the Hector–Andromache scene in the *Iliad*, Aeneas' visit to the Underworld, the Falstaff scenes in the *Henry Fourth* plays, particular characters in Dickens's novels, and so forth.[141] Unfortunately, since Eliot, espousal of the classic has (to its detriment) usually been associated with a reactionary political agenda. Kermode was surely right to sense a connection between classic and empire, each claiming *imperium sine fine* in both time and space. Classic and empire constitute, for Eliot, the interface between the aspect of time and the aspect of the timeless, enabling us to grasp, or at least experience in practice, their co-inherence. The classic thus has metaphysical as well as political entailments. Kermode seeks to secularize such a conception for a pluralistic age. The classic for him becomes a text which possesses 'a surplus of signifier'; 'the work...stands there, in all its native plurality, liberated not extinguished by death, the death of writer and reader, unaffected by time yet offering itself to be read under our particular temporal disposition.'[142] This is an attractive formulation, in line with the last century's commitment to heterogeneity, ambivalence, polysemy, undecidability; it is also one advantageous to the contemporary academy with its constant, market-driven need for fresh interpretation. Nonetheless, I think Kermode gets the point back to front. Any text (good or bad) that has been around for a long time as an object of exegetical attention will have been assigned a plurality of interpretations (though how far these interpretations tell us about how and why the text has been enjoyed is an open question). A classic (in the sense of a work to whose value one is committed) is not such in virtue of its capacity for multiple interpretations; rather these interpretations are the result of its

---

[141] A 'traditionalist' might say that it is hard to see what these reasons could be other than that such scenes present us with compelling representations of important human possibilities—what Dr Johnson would have called instances of 'general nature'—in language that is memorable and/or of expressive power, or at any rate adequate to its purpose. (Most 'radical' responses to this point are, to my thinking, unsatisfactory.) For Johnson's view of 'nature' see Clingham (2002), esp. ch. 2. Nature for Johnson is not the same as the sort of 'realism' which he and we especially associate with the modern novel. For Johnson the two great poets of nature were Homer and above all Shakespeare: 'Johnson...emphasizes the transformational aspect of Shakespeare's drama that "approximates the remote and familiarizes the wonderful"...that has the power to shape the mind, and to give readers or viewers a direct feeling for life that, paradoxically, goes beyond and deeper than the immediate, the empirical, or the realistic' (Clingham (2002) 38–9).

[142] Kermode (1975a) 140–1.

being inscribed institutionally as a classic. The notion of the classic both embodies and also to an extent occludes the issue of literary quality.

IV

So far my argument has been that aesthetic accounts of works of art are one among many possible legitimate modes of analysis of those works. This is the position taken by Peter de Bolla:

> This does not mean that all encounters with art are *aesthetic*; nor does it imply that *aesthetic* encounters are necessarily better, more valuable, useful, or pleasurable than any others. Responses to a painting, say, may be political or economic; aspects of its presentation—say, its depiction of a narrative or its social meanings—may be exclusively attended to.[143]

In the final section of this chapter I want to look briefly at two highly seductive accounts that accord a more privileged role to the aesthetic in relation to other discourses, both accounts, as it happens, by distinguished classicists (Classics once played a leading role in such discussions, and perhaps might do so again). Both develop Kantian ideas in ways which are consonant with the arguments of the *Critique of Judgement*, but which are not necessarily entailed by them. For Friedrich Schiller the aesthetic is the indispensable propaideutic for a transformed polity, for Walter Pater it is foundational for all enquiry. And both writers give a key role in human affairs to art, Schiller for its power to create the conditions of possibility for a more harmonious existence, Pater as the way of most profitably filling the interval until 'our place knows us no more': 'Some spend this interval in listlessness, some in high passions, the wisest, at least among "the children of this world," in art and song.'[144] While both have much to teach us, both to an extent blur the distinction between judgements of taste and judgements of practical reason in a way that perhaps compromises the radical purity of Kant's system, at least as set out in its most cogent form in the 'Analytic of the Beautiful'.

---

[143] de Bolla (2001) 13; this formulation implies, though, that non-aesthetic qualities can be 'extracted' from the artistic whole without difficulty.

[144] Pater (1980) 190.

In his work of 1795 *On the Aesthetic Education of Man*, often referred to as his *Aesthetic Letters*, Schiller shows himself an attentive and highly intelligent reader of Kant. But he also sought ways of presenting speculative ideas that were not those of analytic philosophy, ways that could give imaginative vividness to what in Kant is highly abstract. Schiller's adoption of an epistolary form means that we are presented with one half of a dialogue with the other half implied, so that response on the part of the reader is always required. Schiller is defending the aesthetic as theorized by Kant against the utilitarian opponent of beauty who argues that it deflects us from 'serious and strenuous effort', leading us to 'neglect reality':[145] even if it does no harm (which it may), what could be the positive value of art? Schiller remains true to the Kantian insistence that the beautiful has no determinate purpose:

> we must allow that those people are entirely right who declare beauty, and the mood it induces in us, to be completely indifferent and unfruitful as regards either *knowledge* or *character*. They are entirely right; for beauty produces no particular result whatsoever, neither for the understanding nor for the will. It accomplishes no particular purpose, neither intellectual nor moral; it discovers no individual truth, helps us to perform no individual duty and is, in short, as unfitted to provide a firm basis for character as to enlighten the understanding.[146]

However, Schiller argues that experience of beauty, particularly in art, is nonetheless valuable for two principal reasons, first, because it has the capacity to harmonize discordant aspects of a human personality and thereby create the conditions for realizing our full potential humanity and secondly, because it offers us an experience of freedom precisely because of its indeterminate nature ('it is only through Beauty that man makes his way to Freedom'[147]). Schiller calls this experience of freedom 'a state of pure determinability'.[148] It is a condition not, as its critics sometimes claim, of contentlessness but rather of infinite potential in which the mind is opened to

---

[145] Schiller (1967) 65–7; cf. p. 7: '*Utility* is the great idol of our age, to which all powers are in thrall and to which all talent must pay homage. Weighed in this crude balance, the insubstantial merits of Art scarce tip the scale, and, bereft of all encouragement, she shuns the noisy market-place of our century.' Schiller, thou shouldst be living at this hour!

[146] Schiller (1967) 147, a passage that enraged Ruskin.

[147] Ibid. 9; cf. p. 215: '*To bestow freedom by means of freedom* is the fundamental law of this kingdom.'

[148] Schiller (1967) 141.

innumerable possibilities: 'The scales of the balance stand level when they are empty; but they also stand level when they contain equal weights.'[149] As a result 'the aesthetic state' becomes 'the most fruitful of all in respect of knowledge and morality'.[150] If someone were to read, say, the *Aeneid* and immediately wish to go out and found a city, one could be sure from his response that the experience had not been a properly aesthetic one.[151] Rather the aesthetic leaves us as it were in suspense, with many possibilities available but none already determined: 'we are at such a moment master in equal degree of our passive and of our active powers, and we shall with equal ease turn to seriousness or to play, to repose or to movement, to compliance or to resistance, to the discursions of abstract thought or to the direct contemplation of phenomena.'[152] This notion of aesthetic determinability—an ideal state that may not often be realized in practice—allows the radical Schiller (who, like Kant, initially supported the French Revolution) to theorize the possibility of change (political, social, artistic) in all human affairs. Thus, given that our natures are to a high degree determined, how—particularly in a world in which the divine has been so to say largely bracketed off—can human communities become radically different? The answer to this conundrum turns out to lie precisely in the aesthetic. Moreover, the artist has the potential to produce something radically new. Schiller believed that the artist would do well to turn away from the conformities of the present and find inspiration in antiquity for a revolutionary art: 'Then, when he has become a man, let him return, a stranger, to his own century; not, however, to gladden it by his appearance, but rather, terrible like Agamemnon's son, to cleanse and to purify it.'[153] One could say that Horace did something similar by imitating the lyric poets of Archaic Greece, Sappho, Alcaeus, and Pindar.

Schiller's emphasis on the freedom involved in aesthetic experience is a convincing development of key ideas in the *Critique of Judgement*.[154] Less obviously Kantian (though still not necessarily

---

[149] Schiller (1967) 141. [150] Ibid. 151—from the crucial 22nd letter.
[151] See Schiller (1967) 153–5. [152] Ibid. 153. [153] Schiller (1967) 57.
[154] So Guyer (1993). Indeed Guyer can be said to read Kant through Schiller. See, for example, p. 18: 'the heart of Kant's connection between aesthetics and morality is the view that it is only by preserving its freedom from direct constraint by concepts, even didactic concepts of morality itself, that the experience of beauty can serve the purpose of giving us a palpable experience of freedom, which is its deepest service to the needs of morality'; cf. pp. 22, 96, 105.

inconsistent with some versions of Kantianism) is Schiller's stress on the power of art to harmonize and unify different elements in human personality, corresponding roughly to the sensual and intellectual sides of our nature, and thereby help to harmonize and unify society. Art thus provides a solution to what Marxists would later call Alienation.[155] To this end Schiller distinguishes what he calls the 'sense-drive', which is concerned with direct apprehension of the world in time and to which 'the whole of man's phenomenal existence is ultimately tied', from the 'form-drive', whose concern is organization and law free of the flux of temporality: 'If the first drive furnishes only *cases*, this second one gives *laws*—laws for every judgement, where it is a question of knowledge, laws for every will, where it is a question of action.'[156] These two drives are mediated by the 'play-drive' of which experience of art constitutes the paradigm case. And play is in no sense a pejorative term, rather the play-drive is quintessentially human:

> But how can we speak of *mere* play, when we know that it is precisely play and play *alone*, which of all man's states and conditions is the one which makes him whole and unfolds both sides of his nature at once? ... I, therefore, would prefer to put it exactly the opposite way round and say: the agreeable, the good, the perfect, with these man is *merely* in earnest; but with beauty he plays.[157]

Different kinds of beauty in art can be particularly beneficial for particular types of human being. Thus 'melting' beauty (the beauty as it might be of the *Eclogues*) is good for someone in whom the form-drive is dominant so that he is tensed, 'tensing' or 'energizing' beauty (the beauty of the *De Rerum Natura*, say) for someone who is relaxed.[158] As often in Schiller, these formulations have a double valence: for a history of the world, or at any rate a fable about the history of the world (in earlier times there was no such division

---

[155] Schiller (1967) 35: 'Everlastingly chained to a single little fragment of the Whole, man himself develops into nothing but a fragment; everlastingly in his ear the monotonous sound of the wheel that he turns, he never develops the harmony of his being, and instead of putting the stamp of humanity upon his own nature, he becomes nothing more than the imprint of his occupation or of his specialized knowledge.'

[156] Schiller (1967) 81. For a suggestive account of the usefulness of Schiller's categories in thinking about the value of art see J. Armstrong (2000) 151–68.

[157] Schiller (1967) 105–7; cf. p. 107: 'For, to mince matters no longer, man only plays when he is in the fullest sense of the word a human being, and *he is only fully a human being when he plays.*'

[158] For the two types of beauty see Schiller (1967) 111–15.

between intellect and sense[159]), and for the individual and his self-development and educational growth. It is probably wrong to see these drives as versions of Freud's deep psychology; rather, they are best regarded as heuristic categories, figurative ways of describing human beings, according to which everything that happens shows a dialectical movement, the drives coexisting and acting upon each other rather like supply and demand in the economic theory of Adam Smith. Moreover a formulation in language requires a narrative order for things that are fused in practice (another example would be intuition and cognition within Kant's system, processes which are simultaneous, not successive in their actual operations).

In a letter of 1793 Schiller offered 'a well-executed English dance' as his image of 'the ideal of a beautiful society', 'symbol of one's own individually asserted freedom as well as of one's respect for the freedom of the other'.[160] Paul de Man, who quotes this passage, is suspicious, as we saw in the last chapter, of this Romantic stress on unity, fusion, harmony, which ignores, among other things, the deconstructive operations of textuality. For de Man all this is an instance of ontological bad faith, a clear case of aesthetic ideology. 'Aesthetic education', he writes, 'by no means fails; it succeeds all too well, to the point of hiding the violence that makes it possible.'[161] Art, in his view, should not be asked to provide a reconciliation of conflict: 'The idea of innocence recovered at the far side and by way of experience, of paradise consciously regained after the fall into consciousness...is, of course, one of the most seductive, powerful, and deluded topoi of the idealist and romantic period.'[162] In Schiller's defence, one can point out that the harmonization of the drives is an ideal more than an achieved actuality, and anyway not a goal, only a starting-point. Schiller is certainly not describing an instrumentalist method of acculturation to a dominant ideology; on the contrary any 'result' of aesthetic experience cannot be known in advance. But we may agree with de Man that, in the moral and political significance assigned to

---

[159] Schiller (1967) 31: 'At that first fair awakening of the powers of the mind, sense and intellect did not as yet rule over strictly separate domains.'
[160] de Man (1984) 263.   [161] de Man (1984) 289; cf. Hamilton (2003).
[162] de Man (1984) 267.

art, Schiller blurs types of judgement that Kant had carefully picked apart, and which perhaps are better kept apart.[163]

Pater's privileging of the aesthetic takes a rather different form. One obvious criterion for the superiority of a particular paradigm is its comprehensiveness: if you can tell a story which can incorporate your rivals' stories, whereas they cannot tell one to incorporate yours, then your story might justly be said to prevail. In the eloquent 'Conclusion' to *The Renaissance* Pater gives his justification for the primacy of the aesthetic. Within Pater's project, it can be argued, aesthetics is foundational in that it offers the starting-point for an understanding of history and ideology and so on; as a result politics becomes not the 'other' of aesthetics but more its extension.[164] Within this system art, which 'comes to you proposing frankly to give nothing but the highest quality to your moments as they pass, and simply for those moments' sake',[165] assumes a central importance. For Pater, as Jonathan Loesberg shows, whereas science, philosophy, moral, religious, and ethical commitments are kinds of perception leading to other goals, by contrast art is perception that is self-directed.[166] The beginning of the 'Conclusion' weaves together ideas from (among other sources) Heraclitus, the Atomists, the English empiricist tradition (especially the sceptical Hume), and contemporary science to suggest that we live in a world of unending flux in which energy and matter, both phenomena without and (at an even greater rate) the human mind within, are always forming and re-forming themselves:

> To such a tremulous wisp constantly re-forming itself on the stream, to a single sharp impression, with a sense in it, a relic more or less fleeting, of such moments gone by, what is real in our life fines itself down. It is with this movement, with the passage and dissolution of impressions, images, sensations, that analysis leaves off—that continual vanishing away, that strange, perpetual, weaving and unweaving of ourselves.[167]

---

[163] On this see also Christopher Norris, 'Deconstructing Genius: Paul de Man and the Critique of Romantic Ideology', in Murray (1989), 141–65.

[164] This is the argument of Loesberg (1991), for whom Pater 'construes aestheticism as a mode of historical and social interpretation' (p. 8). For my view of Pater I am greatly indebted to this outstanding study.

[165] Pater (1980) 190.

[166] Loesberg (1991) 15: 'art is perception leading to perception itself.' For a different view see C. Williams (1989).

[167] Pater (1980) 188. For some of Pater's intellectual affiliations see McGrath (1986).

All we can fully know are changing mental impressions of a shifting external 'reality'. These impressions gain their sharpness and specificity through changes in our physical life, through contrast and difference—Pater instances 'the moment... of delicious recoil from the flood of water in summer heat'.[168] It is thus with perception, with the aesthetic, that all ladders start. And thus the judgement of taste is the only sort of knowledge of which we can be absolutely certain: 'every moment some form grows perfect in hand or face; some tone on the hills or the sea is choicer than the rest.'[169] Accordingly it advantages us to try and fit as many 'pulsations', as many quickened aesthetic responses, as possible into our life, not as a flight from reality but as a particularly intense engagement with it:[170]

> In a sense it might even be said that our failure is to form habits: for, after all, habit is relative to a stereotyped world, and meantime it is only the roughness of the eye that makes any two persons, things, situations, seem alike. While all melts under our feet, we may well grasp at any exquisite passion, or any contribution to knowledge that seems by a lifted horizon to set the spirit free for a moment, or any stirring of the senses, strange dyes, strange colours, and curious odours, or work of the artist's hands, or the face of one's friend. Not to discriminate every moment some passionate attitude in those about us, and in the very brilliancy of their gifts some tragic dividing of forces on their ways, is, on this short day of frost and sun, to sleep before evening. With this sense of the splendour of our experience, and of its awful brevity, gathering all we are into one desperate effort to see and touch, we shall hardly have time to make theories about the things we see and touch.[171]

It should be noticed that the aesthetic, the experience of the beautiful, here encompasses not art and nature alone but also human beings, 'the face of one's friend'.[172] The bitter-sweet timbre of the passage acknowledges not only the glory of such aesthetic

---

[168] Pater (1980) 186.
[169] Ibid. 188; cf. Kirwan (1999) 5: 'Beauty is the one thing we do "know" absolutely, its being is to be perceived, and thus it guarantees its own reality.'
[170] Loesberg (1991) 26.   [171] Pater (1980) 189.
[172] Cf. 'Preface' p. xx, where 'the engaging personality in life or in a book' is included in Pater's idiosyncratic list of objects of aesthetic attention. For Schiller too a human being can be experienced aesthetically, if 'without our taking into consideration in judging him any law or any purpose' he 'please us simply as we contemplate him and by the sheer manner of his being' (Schiller (1967) 143). The face of the friend has also since become the location of the ethical encounter *par excellence*, as in the interpersonal ethics of Levinas.

knowing but also its limitations, even in relation to those we love. But with such limitations we must, necessarily, be content.

Pater has been accused, by T. S. Eliot among others, of an incapacity for sustained thought. Certainly even less than Schiller does Pater argue in the manner of an analytic philosopher. Rather he fuses thought and feeling as had Donne, at least in Eliot's admiring account of him. The 'Conclusion' is thus both a remarkable exercise of the rational mind and, in a strict aestheticist sense, a work of art, indeed one of the most perfect that we have.[173] Eliot's essay on Pater is a remarkably peevish and disagreeable production; his real quarrel with Pater is over religion. In a much quoted phrase Eliot accuses Pater's artistic views of having been 'not wholly irresponsible for some untidy lives'[174]—was Eliot's own life so tidy, we might ask, that he had earned the right to make that particular criticism? But in one respect we may feel that Eliot comes close at least to hitting his target, and that is when he slyly asserts that, in the 'Conclusion' and elsewhere, Pater, by recommending a particular way of living, makes ethics predominate over aesthetics: 'Pater is always primarily the moralist.'[175] Aesthetic theories often turn out to be, at least in part, moral theories in disguise. Certainly the 'Conclusion' presents an argument about how we should choose to live. And, as we have repeatedly seen, there are real gains in trying to keep morality and the aesthetic apart.

So, in the final analysis, I would not want the Kantian aesthetic quite to go in the direction taken, in their very different ways, by both Schiller and Pater. Kant's judgement of taste is always particular, and is thus radically unhierarchical. Therein lies much of its value. To bring hierarchy in by the back door, however gracefully it is done, is thus, to my thinking, a mistake of a fundamental kind. But certainly both Schiller and Pater make persuasive claims for the aesthetic. By contrast, to claim, as do so many today, that there is no such thing as a purely aesthetic judgement is to claim that all judgements must be determinate (that is to say, must

---

[173] See Elizabeth Prettejohn, 'Walter Pater and Aesthetic Painting' in Prettejohn (1999) 36–58.

[174] Eliot (1930) 105. The essay, originally entitled 'The Place of Pater', was subsequently reprinted in *Selected Essays* as 'Arnold and Pater'.

[175] Eliot (1930) 101.

involve subsuming a particular under a rule or a universal, relating the object to what we already know). But if the idea of human freedom is to have meaning, it is vital that some judgements are non-determinate, that we have other models before us than means–end rationality. Otherwise all we can do is act out, on Bourdieu's model, our predetermined self-interest and the interest of the class or group to which we belong, assimilating everything to the already-known. Kant and those, not least the artists, he inspired thought nobly of the soul and no way approved this opinion. For the aestheticist to accept, in however nuanced a form, the assumptions of the ideology critic is to have been already defeated. The aesthetic must be loved, if it is to be loved, not because it is superior to something else, but simply for its own sake.

4

The Aesthetic Turn: Latin Poetry and Aesthetic Criticism

The aesthetic critic needs always to be on his guard against the confusion of mere curiosity or antiquity with beauty in art.[1]

I

The title of this chapter signals its concerns by means of a pun. 'The aesthetic turn' is modelled on such phrases as 'the linguistic turn' or 'the cultural turn', which embodied, and promoted, claims that a particular paradigm shift in interpretation had occurred in the humanities and social sciences. At the same time it suggests that, in a scholarly world still dominated by the new culturalism and by ideology critique (most conspicuously so, perhaps, in post-colonial studies), it is high time that aesthetics had, as we say, its turn. Accordingly I want to go back to the issue I touched upon at the end of the first chapter. If the arguments put forward so far have any validity, what consequences, if any, do they have for the student of Latin, or indeed any other, poetry? What sort of criticism do I want Latinists, or at least some of them, to write in future? We are particularly fortunate in Britain to have a distinctive tradition of 'aesthetic criticism' which could be traced from Ruskin through Pater to Adrian Stokes in the last century[2], a tradition which, if not providing models to copy (an unaesthetic procedure according to

---

[1] Pater (1894) 210.
[2] See the introduction to Carrier (1997). For Stokes, in relation to Ruskin and Pater, see Read (2003); for a bravura example of Stokes's version of aesthetic criticism see his account of 'Verrocchio's Lavabo' in *The Quattro Cento* (Stokes (2002) 58–67). Other critics who, at least on occasion, might be claimed for this tradition include Swinburne (an important influence on Pater), Henry James, R. A. M. Stevenson, Charles Ricketts, G. K. Chesterton, Herbert Horne, William Empson.

Kant), can at any rate serve as exemplars of the kind of thing we might essay. And indeed Pater's essays, in particular, will dominate the explorations of this final chapter.

Aesthetics has traditionally taken the visual as the model for talking about art. Both Plato and Kant make prominent use of visual examples to expound their theories. Socrates in *Republic* 10 famously uses a painting of a bed to show that an artwork is at two removes from reality (the painting is a copy of a bed in the sensible world which in turn is a copy of Zeus' bed, or the form of the bed). Kant, as we have seen, cites such things as flowers and birds of paradise as instances of pure beauty. This is no doubt partly because the visual makes it easy to present the argument in a particularly perspicuous form—it is quite obvious that to judge the beauty of a tulip you have to look at it. The stress on the visual can be linked to a preference—of which there is a particularly influential statement in Aristotle—for sight and hearing (which have a greater distance so to say from the object of perception) over the other senses, touch and taste in particular being common to all living things and therefore, in Aristotle's terms, 'lower'.[3] Also with poetry aesthetic issues seem to become more complicated. A poem, as something about which to make the judgement of taste, seems less like a fixed 'object' than does a work of visual art, more like a process.

Yet, after all, in the *Republic* Plato is obviously far more interested in the poetry of Homer (which provided the powerful alternative to philosophy in Greek culture) than in paintings of beds (indeed the implausibility of the example suggests that he is not wholly in earnest). Kant is quite clear that poetry has the position of primacy among the arts, since it allows for the greatest experience of freedom generated through aesthetic ideas:

Poetry (which owes its origin almost entirely to genius and is least willing to be led by precepts or example) holds the first rank among all the arts. It expands the mind by giving freedom to the imagination and by offering, from among the boundless multiplicity of possible forms accordant with a given concept, to whose bounds it is restricted, that one which couples with the presentation of the concept a wealth of

---

[3] See e.g. Stewart (2002) 20–1 (Stewart's book is a powerful plea for a return to the centrality of the senses in the experience of poetry). Pater does not seem to share this bias, speaking in the 'Conclusion' of the way that 'each object is loosed into a group of impressions—colour, odour, texture—in the mind of the observer' (Pater (1980) 187).

thought to which no verbal expression is completely adequate, and by thus rising aesthetically to ideas. It invigorates the mind by letting it feel its faculty—free, spontaneous, and independent of determination by nature—of regarding and estimating nature as phenomenon in the light of aspects which nature of itself does not afford us in experience, either for sense or understanding...[4]

Moreover a painting, like a poem, requires time for any adequate encounter, so that viewing it, like reading a poem, can be figured as a process rather than as a matter of instantaneous, panoptic vision. For Pater 'seeing' is certainly a word of power, whose efficacy is by no means confined to works of visual art: 'A counted number of pulses only is given to us of a variegated, dramatic life. How may we see in them all that is to be seen in them by the finest senses?'[5] As Elizabeth Prettejohn puts it, 'here "seeing" is more than a casual expression; blending receptivity with discrimination, seeing is the model for the aesthetic critic's approach to both art and life.'[6] This patient, slow, attentive seeing is necessary for aesthetic response. Wilde makes of this a memorable epigram: 'To look at a thing is very different from seeing a thing. One does not see anything until one sees its beauty.'[7] Throughout his writings Ruskin stresses the value of this attentiveness, and in *Praeterita* gives a particularly memorable example of its application. Eschewing more sensational sights, Ruskin discovers, 'lying on the bank of a cart-road in the sand', the beauty of a little aspen tree against the blue sky, 'more than Gothic tracery, more than Greek vase-imagery, more than the daintiest embroiderers of the East could embroider, or the artfullest painters of the West could limn':

Languidly, but not idly, I began to draw it; and as I drew, the languor passed away: the beautiful lines insisted on being traced,—without weariness. More and more beautiful they became, as each rose out of the rest, and took its place in the air. With wonder increasing every instant, I saw that they 'composed' themselves, by

---

[4] Kant (1952) 191–2 §53.
[5] Pater (1980) 188 (from the 'Conclusion'). For Pater language for the writer was analogous to marble for the sculptor (Pater (1973) 65, from 'Style'). Similarly for Proust style was a matter less of technique than of 'vision' (Nehamas (2002) 67). Likewise it makes sense to say that words 'come to appearance' in any memorable utterance wherever they 'become striking in their audibly and visually perceptible arrangement': Seel (2003a) 23. Seel cites in illustration the response of a character in a novel by Philip Roth to Shakespeare's 'And thus the whirligig of time brings in his revenges'.
[6] Prettejohn (1999) 1.   [7] Ellmann (1970) 312 (from 'The Decay of Lying').

finer laws than any known of men. At last, the tree was there, and everything I had thought before about trees, nowhere.[8]

A lack of such careful 'seeing' can produce only stale or lazy aesthetic judgements, whether we are dealing with a painting or a poem. Jeannette Winterson well describes what can result from such inattention:

> She went to look at paintings. She looked at them until she could see them, see the object in itself as it really is, although often this took months. Her own ideas, her own fears, her own limitations, slipped in between. Often, when she liked a picture, she found she was liking some part of herself, some part of her that was in accord with the picture. She shied away from what she couldn't understand, and at first, disliked those colours, lines, arrangements, that challenged what she thought she knew, what she thought had to be true.[9]

Winterson here gives us her version of Kantian disinterest; we are urged to put aside aspects of the self that would impede us from making a pure judgement of taste. 'The object in itself as it really is' is a famous Arnoldian phrase to which we shall shortly be returning. Aesthetic judgement in the Kantian view results from a necessarily subjective encounter with a thing, but the power of disciplined, attentive seeing that Pater advocates means it need not be merely 'subjective' in the negative sense in which the word is so often used today.

Pater gives his fullest account of the character of aesthetic criticism in the 'Preface' to *The Renaissance*. He starts with an elegant reformulation of the radical particularity of aesthetic judgement as described by Kant: 'To define beauty, not in the most abstract but in the most concrete terms possible, to find, not its universal formula, but the formula which expresses most adequately this or that special manifestation of it, is the aim of the true student of aesthetics.'[10] In *Marius the Epicurean* (significantly subtitled *His Sensations and Ideas*) Pater exhibits his hero undergoing 'this life of

---

[8] Ruskin (1907) ii. 111–12 (*Praeterita*, vol. 2, ch. 4, §77). It was his first sight of the Alps at Schaffhausen that was for Ruskin 'the revelation of the beauty of the earth' and a 'blessed entrance into life', the beginning of his career as an aesthete and art critic (Ruskin (1907) i. 164–5 (ibid., vol. 1, ch. 6, §134–5).

[9] Winterson (1995) 39.

[10] Pater (1980) p. xix. Compare Wilde: 'like Goethe after he had read Kant, we desire the concrete, and nothing but the concrete can satisfy us' (Ellmann (1970) 382; from 'The Critic as Artist').

realized consciousness in the present' which constitutes what may be called an aesthetic education—'an education partly negative, as ascertaining the true limits of man's capacities, but for the most part positive, and directed especially to the expansion and refinement of the power of reception; of those powers, above all, which are immediately relative to fleeting phenomena, the powers of emotion and sense'.[11] In that sense Pater's criticism, though it involves 'the flow of mind among phenomena',[12] is far from being 'idealist' in the usual modern sense, being wholly grounded in the concrete and particular of the here and now. Pater is not among those who 'would change the colour or curve of a roseleaf for that *ousia achrōmatos, aschēmatistos, anaphēs*' of Platonic metaphysics.[13]

It follows that the aim of the aesthetic critic is to isolate the 'virtue' (as of 'a herb, a wine, a gem'[14]) of each artwork, the special quality that for her makes it what it is and not something else. For example, on Pater's account, the virtue of Wordsworth, unequally distributed in his works, is 'that strange, mystical sense of a life in natural things, and of man's life as a part of nature, drawing strength and colour and character from local influences, from the hills and streams, and from natural sights and sounds'.[15] Pater's own criticism is often described as 'impressionistic'—this is true only if the word 'impression' is used in the rigorous sense of Pater's 'Preface', that is the impression the critic has of the object by means of his or her sensory and perceptual equipment. Pater's criticism may not be like that of the more plodding modern academic, but it aims at, and achieves, a peculiar *precision*.[16] Moreover much modern criticism merely subsumes its object under some existing

---

[11] Pater (1986) 84–5 (from ch. 9, 'New Cyrenaicism'). Pater presents such aesthetic education as a new form of the contemplative life; in part he is clarifying the doctrines of the 'Conclusion' to *The Renaissance* which, found shocking by some, was omitted from the 2nd edition, though subsequently reinstated 'with some slight changes' (Pater (1980) 186, n.1).

[12] Donoghue (1995) 53.

[13] Pater (1973) 2 (from 'Coleridge's Writings'; the Greek, from Plato's *Phaedrus* 247c, translates as 'being without colour, without form, not to be touched'). The passage is picked up by Wilde (Ellmann (1970) 382, from 'The Critic as Artist').

[14] Pater (1980) p. xx.

[15] Ibid. p. xxii; cf. his remarks in his essay 'Wordsworth' (Pater (1973) 104–5).

[16] Among his aims is 'to use words like beauty, excellence, art, poetry, with a more precise meaning than they would otherwise have' (Pater (1980) p. xix).

concept. The work of art is made to 'illustrate' something we knew already (the patriarchal character of Roman society, or whatever); the outcome is known in advance. By contrast the aesthetic critic starts as it were from the object, without seeking in advance any definite end, but seeking the maximum responsiveness in receiving it.

Of course none of this is to exclude the operations of the critic's intellect in his encounters. I am certainly *not* arguing against the use of theory within aesthetic criticism, if the critic's reading of the work prompts it. All kind of productive thoughts may be set in motion by our encounters with poetry:

The wingèd word. The mercurial word. The word that is both moth and lamp. The word that rises above itself. The word that is itself and more. The associative word light with meanings. The word not netted by meaning. The exact word wide.[17]

In that sense there is no universal formula for writing criticism any more than for making art[18] (indeed there is no way to distinguish criticism from art within this discourse, as Wilde shows), and nothing that might be brought to bear that can be ruled out in advance. Mary Mothersill makes the point well:

'Principles of relevance'... go by the board. That Milton was blind, that Henry Moore has a collection of beach pebbles and driftwood, are thoughts that might enliven perception—thoughts, rather than information, because for the critical enterprise, it doesn't matter whether what is alleged is true. (One might say, 'In reading these lines, imagine them having been spoken by one himself deprived of sight', or 'Suppose that the creator of this sculpture was preoccupied with what wind and water can do to stone'.)[19]

For the aesthetic critic aesthetic merit, beauty, may be found anywhere, nothing should be ruled out *a priori*. 'To him all periods, types, schools of taste, are in themselves equal.'[20] Unsurprisingly,

---

[17] Winterson (1995) 137.

[18] So Mothersill (1984) 425: 'A critic may set himself a particular project and in the course of defining its scope, establish some *ad hoc* conditions of relevance, but criticism itself is not a project type, and any proposed rules of relevance must, in the light of established practice, appear arbitrary.'

[19] Mothersill (1984) 426. As an example of criticism at its best Mothersill cites, and discusses, a passage from Empson on lines from Pope's 'Epistle to a Lady' (pp. 427–8).

[20] Pater (1980) p. xxi. Wilde more than once echoes Pater's sentiments. See e.g. 'The Critic as Artist': 'The true critic will... seek for beauty in every age and in each school, and will never suffer himself to be limited to any settled custom of thought, or stereotyped mode of looking at things' (Ellmann (1970) 393; cf. ibid. 390).

The Aesthetic Turn

for Pater poetry can deal with anything it wants. This is so because there is nothing 'in' the object that automatically makes it beautiful. 'Critical efforts to limit art *a priori*, by anticipations regarding the natural incapacity of the material with which this or that artist works... are always likely to be discredited by the facts of artistic production'; and so he criticizes as useless 'the protest that poetry might not touch prosaic subjects as with Wordsworth, or an abstruse matter as with Browning, or treat contemporary life nobly as with Tennyson'.[21] Both in the 'Preface' and in the 'Conclusion' Pater gives poetically resonant lists of objects with which an aesthetic critic (himself not least) might have to do:

> To him, the picture, the landscape, the engaging personality in life or in a book, *La Gioconda*, the hills of Carrara, Pico of Mirandola, are valuable for their virtues...
> ...the function of the aesthetic critic is to distinguish...the virtue by which a picture, a landscape, a fair personality in life or in a book, produces this special impression of beauty or pleasure...
> Every moment some form grows perfect in hand or face; some tone on the hills or the sea is choicer than the rest; some mood of passion or insight or intellectual excitement is irresistibly real and attractive to us...
> ...we may well grasp at...any stirring of the senses, strange dyes, strange colours, and curious odours, or work of the artist's hands, or the face of one's friend.[22]

Here is no narrow, or sterile, aestheticism; rather Pater brings together, in a remarkable synaesthesia, aspects of life and art, art and nature, people and places and objects, the canonical and the little known—all in a mood of sweet melancholy for their value and their transience and the little knowledge we can have of them in our short lives. In his essay on Botticelli, then a painter comparatively unfamiliar, Pater expresses a certain preference for what would often be called 'lesser' artists, who 'convey to us a peculiar quality of pleasure which we cannot get elsewhere... and are often the object of a special diligence and a consideration wholly affectionate, just because there is not about them the stress of a great name and authority'.[23] We are far indeed from the iron grip of any strong version of the Western Canon.

Pater is often charged with a subjectivism that borders on the solipsistic. In a bad-tempered essay, 'Walter Pater, Matthew Arnold

---

[21] Pater (1973) 61 ('Style').
[22] Pater (1980) pp. xx–xxi, 188–9.   [23] Ibid. 48.

and Misquotation', Christopher Ricks refers contemptuously to Pater's 'fugitive noosphere'.[24] Positivistically-minded critics prefer to march under the banner of Arnold's famous statement of critical objectivity: seeing the object as it really is. In the 'Introduction' the feline Pater, averse to polemics or even overt critical contention, bows gravely to his great predecessor (without naming him), while giving the doctrine his own subjectivist turn. Characteristically he introduces his qualification with 'and' rather than 'but', so that any irony is indeed 'fugitive': ' "To see the object as in itself it really is," has been justly said to be the aim of all true criticism whatever; and in aesthetic criticism the first step towards seeing one's object as it really is, is to know one's own impression as it really is, to discriminate it, to realise it distinctly.'[25]

In 'The Artist as Critic' Oscar Wilde alludes to both Arnold and Pater as he produces his own paradoxical variant: 'The highest Criticism, then, is more creative than creation, and the primary aim of the critic is to see the object as in itself it really is not.'[26] This can be read as an attempt to go one better than Pater. For Wilde the greatest criticism, like Pater's meditation on the *Mona Lisa*, is itself a form of art, and not therefore bound to the object any more than the creator of an artwork (as normally understood) is bound to nature or 'reality'. Great criticism on this view reflects the character of the critic, and is not merely a *mimesis* of a prior object. Pater's *Mona Lisa* is obviously not *the same* as Leonardo's; in that sense it might be called an allegory of the text. In Wilde's words, 'To the critic the work of art is simply a suggestion for a new work of his own, that need not necessarily bear any obvious resemblance to the thing it criticises.'[27] Wilde inverts Arnold's statement producing a scintillating paradox to provoke us to question our customary common-sense assumptions about these things. How seriously, we have to ask, is the paradox meant? Does Wilde expect us to believe him? If not, what response is he eliciting, what conclusions should we draw?

Wilde could be read less as 'improving' on Pater, more as rebuking him for denying the integrity of the artwork. On this reading it

---

[24] Ricks (1984) 408.
[25] Pater (1980) p. xix (see also Hill's note ad. loc.); Arnold's formulation was made first in 'On Translating Homer' (1862) and repeated in 'The Function of Criticism at the Present Time' (1865).
[26] Ellmann (1970) 368-9.   [27] Ibid. 369.

is Pater who becomes the more radical and subversive of the two, since his formulation denies by implication the existence of any objective reality in respect of the artwork that we could know (something which Wilde's inversion of Arnold still requires). Of course Pater is working through the aesthetic implications of Kant's system. We cannot know the thing-in-itself, only the thing as it appears to us with our particular combination of sense and mind (a bee experiences a flower in a very different way from us, 'sees' it differently).[28] But is he also nudging Kant in the direction of a more corrosive scepticism, a more individualistic conception of the judgement of taste? We are back with the charge of solipsism.

Certainly Pater is no friend of positivism. In 'The School of Giorgione' he gently undermines what he calls a 'new Vasari',[29] that is *A History of Painting in North Italy* by Crowe and Cavalcaselle which questioned the authorship of most of the paintings attributed to Giorgione (in fact there is no surviving painting by 'Giorgione' which has always been regarded as his work— Giorgione is so to say a 'virtual painter', an idea). Pater duly and with solemn deference acknowledges their expertise, but is undeterred by it from his own aesthetic goal: the delineation of the distinctive character of a group of works which constitutes what he terms the 'Giorgionesque'. Aesthetic criticism is not dependent on 'scientific' attribution[30] (Pater would doubtless have relished the irony whereby his test case in the essay, the *Concert* from the Pitti, has since been assigned to Titian). And certainly Pater is fully alert to the question of solipsism. In the 'Conclusion' he observes that 'analysis' takes us from the flickering world of our experience of objects to 'the narrow chamber of the individual mind':

Experience, already reduced to a group of impressions, is ringed round for each one of us by that thick wall of personality through which no real voice has ever pierced on its way to us, or from us to that which we can only conjecture to be

---

[28] Of course Kant is not proposing a free-floating subjectivism: if the object is such that it will appear thus to an organism having our perceptual apparatus, the object is thus for that organism.

[29] Pater (1980) 113.

[30] See the essays by Jonah Siegel ('"Schooling Leonardo": Collaboration, Desire, and the Challenge of Attribution in Pater') and Rachel Teukolsky ('The Politics of Formalist Art Criticism: Pater's "School of Giorgione"') in Brake, Higgins, and Williams (2002) 133–50, 151–69.

without. Every one of those impressions is the impression of the individual in his isolation, each mind keeping as a solitary prisoner its own dream of a world.[31]

I suspect that this passage contributed to some famous lines in *The Waste Land*, even though in the notes Eliot refers only to Dante's Ugolino and to *Appearance and Reality* by the philosopher F. H. Bradley[32]:

> *Dayadhvam*: I have heard the key
> Turn in the door once and turn once only
> We think of the key, each in his prison
> Thinking of the key, each confirms a prison
> Only at nightfall... (411–15)

Certainly we can have absolutely no guarantee that our experience corresponds to that of anyone else, or that effective communication of that experience to others is possible. This is true both for the creative artist and for the critic. But both can strain to achieve the greatest precision of which they are capable (this is the most valuable quality in all writing, according to Pater's essay 'Style'), in the hope that such communication can take place. For no other road is possible. The aesthetic critic thus aims to 'disengage' the 'virtue' of a work of art, 'as a chemist notes some natural element, for himself *and others*' (my italics).[33] Accordingly Pater's scepticism leads him to 'an intense form of engagement with reality',[34] not to a retreat from it.

Given the stress on the formulation of subjective response as the starting-point of enquiry, 'the original facts with which the aesthetic critic has to do',[35] this kind of critic is likely to be sympathetic to autobiography (which is not to say, as Wilde seems to do on occasion, that the distinction between criticism and autobiography should simply be collapsed). The very private Pater always eschewed overt self-disclosure (as he did controversy), but it is hard to resist the view that his story 'The Child in the House' at least in part describes his own experiences and their part in his formation as an aesthete. Pater acknowledges the importance of the

---

[31] Pater (1980) 187–8.
[32] For the way Eliot suppresses the influence of Pater on his work see Lesley Higgins, 'No Time for Pater: The Silenced Other of Masculinist Modernism' in Brake, Higgins, and Williams (2002) 37–54.
[33] Pater (1980) p. xxi.   [34] Loesberg (1991) 26.
[35] Pater (1980) p. xx; the word 'fact' is doubtless artfully chosen.

The Aesthetic Turn

process of 'brain-building' that occurs during childhood, as a result of aesthetic experiences, usually in relation to quite commonplace objects that happen to present themselves, some dandelions perhaps, or 'those whites and reds through the smoke on very homely buildings':

> a system of visible symbolism interweaves itself through all our thoughts and passions; and irresistibly, little shapes, voices, accidents—the angle at which the sun in the morning fell on the pillow—become parts of the great chain wherewith we are bound.[36]

For Florian, the boy in the story (as for Pater), beauty and pain often intermingle—'the fear of death intensified by the desire of beauty'.[37] What Pater is as an aesthetic critic has its origin deep in events of his past, in the great chain wherewith he is bound. Using the psychoanalytic theories of Melanie Klein, Adrian Stokes successfully combines autobiography and criticism in *Smooth and Rough* in order to formulate with clarity his response to the classical architecture of the Renaissance and certain aspects of the machine age. I have myself made one experiment in this kind of autobiographical criticism,[38] but, as I have said elsewhere, I would not necessarily wish to repeat it or recommend it to others.[39]

The typical modern account of a Latin poem offers an interpretation, usually by reading it under the sign of some prior set of commitments (feminist, deconstructionist, generic, or whatever). The aesthetic critic by contrast might prefer to describe than to interpret.[40] Now obviously this polarity of terms can readily be deconstructed; there is no degree zero of description that is not also interpretation, and even if there were, it would hardly be very interesting (counting the number of lines or whatever). The critic has to decide what and how to describe, to produce a description that is *illuminating* in some way for a reader. Yet, as Richard Rorty likes to say, although all distinctions can be blurred, that does not remove their utility for particular purposes.[41] In a famous essay of

---

[36] Text in Carrier (1997) 55, 57, 58.   [37] Ibid. 65.
[38] Martindale (1993b).   [39] Martindale (1997b) 94.
[40] Cf. Vendler (1988) 2: 'The aim of an aesthetic criticism is to *describe* the art work in such a way that it cannot be confused with any other art work (not an easy task), and to *infer* from its elements the aesthetic that might generate this unique configuration.' Similarly Sontag (1983) calls for 'acts of criticism which would supply a really accurate, sharp, loving description of the appearance of a work of art' (p. 103).   [41] See too de Bolla (2001) 139–41.

1964 'Against Interpretation' Susan Sontag, starting from Wilde's famous aestheticist *mot* 'it is only shallow people who do not judge by appearances', calls interpretation 'the revenge of the intellect upon art' as a result of 'the hypertrophy of the intellect at the expense of energy and sensual capability'.[42] Admittedly Sontag falls too easily into the trap of formalism and of a sentimental anti-intellectualism (thoughts as well as feelings are involved in responses to art), and she ends, fashionably for the time and reductively, by calling merely for an 'erotics' of art.[43] Still, in my view, she is right in her insistence that interpretation often serves to 'tame' the artwork: 'Interpretation makes art manageable, comfortable.'[44] Art can be disconcerting, dangerous even.

I have already made clear that none of this implies any hostility to 'theory' (indeed what theory is may itself be refigured in an aesthetic encounter[45]). Indeed there is *nothing* I would want to rule out *a priori* for a critic of an aesthetic kind, except perhaps a failure of close attention to the object.[46] For example, *The Renaissance* shows how historical commentary and aesthetic perception can be combined, so that the Renaissance becomes as much a mode of perception as a historical period. This does not mean the work is simply ahistorical, as is so often said, rather that it embodies a distinctive way of achieving historical understanding (though what 'history' is changes in the process).[47] Similarly, although

---

[42] Sontag (1983) 98. Cf. Beech and Roberts (1996), who argue that the aesthetic, while claiming to be emancipatory, actually involves 'the suppression of bodily wants and needs' (p. 104).

[43] Some of the same problems vitiate Faas (2002). Faas, whose hero is Nietzsche, thinks that aesthetics from Kant onwards has been excessively ascetic, and calls for a return to the body. He tends to elide sex and aesthetic response, and believes that the future of aesthetics lies with sociobiology and neo-Darwinian cognitive science (see his afterword for a useful introduction to this important topic).

[44] Sontag (1983) 99. See Jonathan Dollimore, 'Art in Time of War: Towards a Contemporary Aesthetic' in Joughin and Malpas (2003) 36–50 for a similar argument: 'To take art seriously is to know it comes without the humanitarian guarantees that currently smother it' (p. 48).

[45] So de Bolla (2001) 130, 134–5. His argument for an aesthetic form of knowing could be seen as a version of Kant's aesthetic ideas.

[46] But it may be that on occasion this too is unnecessary. Could a critic write something illuminating on an object he had not seen? After all Winckelmann was able to intuit the character of classical Greek art he had never seen from later Graeco-Roman examples.

[47] This is the argument of Loesberg (1991). See esp. pp. 8–10, 59–60, 122–3, and p. 54: '[Pater] offers historical commentary as a part of aesthetic evaluation and aesthetic perception

I favour an aesthetic 'turn', I am not recommending a *re*turn to anything in particular, even the practices of Pater, admirable as these may have been. Indeed, as I attempt to show throughout, aesthetic criticism can incorporate a variety of other voices, and in that sense at least the aesthetic critic is not solipsistic since he sees together with others. I am sometimes accused of promoting a return to the New Criticism (within which I was partly educated). Certainly I would commend its practice of 'close reading', but I share few if any of the New Critical shibboleths and priorities: the preference for lyric over other forms of poetry, for the complex over the simple, or belief in the heresy of paraphrase, the sovereign virtue of paradox and irony and ambiguity, the self-sufficiency of the words-on-page, the biographical fallacy, and so forth.[48] That does not mean that the aesthetic critic cannot learn from the best of the New Critics, as from the best critics of other schools. Indeed one of the virtues of any New Aestheticism (as of Reception Theory) may be that it can make 'usable' again earlier works of criticism which are currently neglected or dismissed. A revised and principled Kantianism can provide theoretical underpinning for critical practices of the past which might otherwise have seemed merely impressionistic, their authors all too easily dismissed as unconscious victims of various kinds of unscrutinized assumptions and ideological conditioning. Certainly we should not neglect the past, but what we need above all is a criticism *of the future*.

Criticism, it goes without saying, usually takes the form of writing and involves choices about how and what to write.[49] To that extent there is something in Barthes' observation that 'aesthetics as a discipline could be that science which studies not the work in itself but the word, as the spectator or the reader makes it talk within himself; a typology of discourses, so to speak'[50] (though that is certainly not to say that aesthetic experience is reducible to

as a form of historic interpretation. In so doing, he informs each of his aesthetic evaluations and perceptions with the frictions within and between historic moments.'

[48] Of course not every New Critic shared all these commitments (Cleanth Brooks, for example, wrote conspicuously well about *Paradise Lost* and *The Rape of the Lock*). The New Critics are rather shabbily treated at the moment; the best of them were certainly not the fascistic form-mongers of the current representation. Their misfortune was to have immediately preceded 'theory', and therefore to have been in the front line for demonization.

[49] Of course a painting, for example, could be a form of criticism.

[50] Barthes (1988) 178.

language without any remainder). And, as Barthes says, it is difficult to talk about beauty, which may be the reason why academics talk about almost anything else (most commonly history or morality, though why they consider themselves well informed on the latter is unclear). Barthes goes on to give such a typology of discourses in relation to a painting by Cy Twombly:

There are...several subjects who are looking at Twombly (and softly speak to him, each one in his head).
 There is the subject of culture, who knows how Venus was born, who Poussin or Valéry are; this subject is talkative, he can talk fluently. There is the subject of specialization, who knows the history of painting well and can lecture on Twombly's place in it. There is the subject of pleasure, who rejoices in front of the painting, experiences a kind of jubilation while he discovers it, and cannot quite express it. This subject is therefore mute; he can only exclaim: 'How beautiful this is!' and say it again. This is one of the small tortures of language: one can never explain why one finds something beautiful; pleasure generates a kind of laziness of speech, and if we want to speak about a work, we have to substitute for the expression of enjoyment discourses that are indirect, more rational—hoping that the reader will feel in them the happiness given by the paintings of which we speak. There is a fourth subject, that of memory. In a Twombly picture a certain touch of colour at first appears to me hurried, botched, inconsistent: I don't understand it. But this touch of colour works in me, unknown to myself; after I have left the painting, it comes back, becomes memory, and a tenacious one: everything has changed, the picture makes me happy retrospectively. In fact, what I consume with pleasure is absence: a statement that is not paradoxical if we remember that Mallarmé has made it the very principle of poetry: 'I say: a flower, and musically arises the idea itself, fragrance which is absent from all bouquets.'
 The fifth subject is that of production, who feels like reproducing the picture.... As the subject of production, the spectator of the painting is then going to explore his own impotence—and at the same time, as it were in relief, the power of the artist.[51]

Of course Barthes himself can on occasion satisfactorily express the beauty of something. Most classical scholars are like Barthes's first two subjects (plus a strong dose of ideology). Thus, when it comes to Latin poetry, the aesthetic critic is likely to get little help from her colleagues. Both Richard Jenkyns and Theodore Papanghelis have shown interest in English Aestheticism, in a way that has affected their own criticism. But in terms of the politics of interpretation they have situated themselves 'on the right', and brought

[51] Barthes (1988) 178–9.

The Aesthetic Turn

a lot of that traditional baggage which it has been part of the purpose of this book to show is not entailed by a rigorous Kantianism. A more interesting case, and one more unexpected perhaps, is John Henderson. He would probably object to being enlisted in the ranks of aesthetic critics, given his own 'political' commitments. Henderson employs a new style of critical prose—new that is to Classics—which he himself calls 'writing free'[52] and which in its day caused considerable offence in some quarters, while being perceived as a source of liberation in others. Typically his strategy is not so much to set out a step-by-step argument, but to offer a series of close readings that are also provocations. In one way Henderson is a sort of New Critic run wild, who starts from formalist readings of an almost obsessive closeness, even if, within his discourse, the tenor tends to run from aesthetics to politics. The great essay on Lucan—'Lucan/The Word at War'[53]—is perhaps the single most exciting piece on the *Bellum Civile* that we have. Part of its power derives from the way it refuses to tame the text, to reduce it to something safely under our control. Any good reading of Lucan, the implication runs, should acknowledge the element of excess, of desperation, of transgression. The monstrousness of the work is accepted, indeed embodied, in Henderson's commentary on it—Henderson's voice here could well itself be described as 'Lucanian'. In general, in the post-structuralist manner, Henderson struggles to break down the normal divisions between 'art' and 'criticism' in a way that might well have pleased Wilde, to make his readings not merely describe but enact the text being read.

It is not incumbent for someone advancing arguments for a change in critical practice to be himself able to perform a new form of criticism. Indeed the very arguments I have made entail that it is not possible to say in advance what form such criticism might take or to provide models to imitate; that of course would be to make the judgement of taste into something instrumental, end-driven. I see the function of this book rather as being to prepare the ground for others, to provide a principled defence of the need for an aesthetic turn and the value of the aesthetic for classicists as for others. So I will simply repeat what I said in the prologue, that I claim nothing for the three short studies that follow except that they are the merest gestures, however feeble, in the direction of that

---

[52] Henderson (1998) p. ix. [53] Henderson (1988).

turn. The three authors are chosen simply because they give me a distinct form of pleasure that I could not obtain elsewhere.

In so doing, I shall continue to pursue my concern with the *reception* of Latin poetry, not least on the part of great poets and writers. Consideration of their responses often helps to set in motion those aesthetic ideas that are involved in the judgement of taste. Kantian aesthetics and Reception Theory have this too in common, that they pay particular attention to the subject's encounter with the work. Both also acknowledge the work's power and scope beyond the originary moment in an encounter which is always in the present. It is also always worth comparing other receivers' aesthetic responses with one's own, as a partial defence against a descent into mere solipsism.

II

Lucretius' didactic poem *De Rerum Natura* is one of the works most regularly invoked—another is Dante's *Commedia*—as creating problems for any version of art for art's sake or belief in the autonomy, or comparative autonomy, of the work of art. In the generation after Kant writers about aesthetics frequently showed hostility to didactic poetry. For Shelley it was an 'abhorrence'[54] (despite the fact that some of his own work showed strong didactic tendencies). 'Whatever in Lucretius is poetry is not philosophical, whatever is philosophical is not poetry,' wrote Coleridge, in a letter to Wordsworth (30 May 1815), one philosophical poet to another.[55] Lessing had already argued that Pope's *Essay on Man* was a better poem than *De Rerum Natura*, precisely *because* Pope was not a serious philosopher.[56] Schiller thought any such didacticism conflicted with the commitment to 'aesthetic determinability': 'No less self-contradictory is the notion of a fine art which teaches (didactic) or improves (moral); for nothing is more at variance with the concept of beauty than the notion of giving the psyche any definite bias.'[57] However a responsive reading of Lucretius does not necessarily result in the reader's conversion to

---

[54] Cited by Dalzell (1996) 3. [55] Cited by Volk (2002) 72.
[56] Dalzell (1996) 35–6. [57] Schiller (1967) 157.

Epicureanism; and if it did, we might not want to describe that reading as mainly aesthetic.

Part of the problem seemed to lie in the relationship of form and content in a didactic work. A poet who set out in verse a pre-existing philosophical system previously in prose form could only be seen as a versifier, since the indissoluble fusion of form and content that Romantics demanded of poetry was broken. This objection to didactic poetry is set out in detail by Hegel in his *Aesthetics* of 1835:

> Didactic poetry is not to be numbered amongst the proper forms of art. For in it we find, on the one hand, the content already cut and dried and developed explicitly as meaning in its therefore prosaic form, and, on the other hand, the artistic shape which yet can only be tacked on to the content in an entirely external way because the content has already been completely characterized prosaically for apprehension; and in its prosaic aspect, i.e. its universal abstract significance, and in no other aspect, the content is to be expressed for intellectual examination and reflection with the aim of instruction. Therefore, given this external relation [between form and content], art can, in the didactic poem, concern itself with nothing but externals such as metre, for example, elevated diction, interspersed episodes, images, similes, subjoined explosions of feeling, faster development, quicker transitions, etc. These do not penetrate the content as such; they stand beside it as an appendage in order by their relative vivacity to enliven the seriousness and dryness of the doctrine and to make life more agreeable. What has become prosaic in itself is not to be reshaped poetically; it can only be dressed up....[58]

Lucretius might seem to endorse something like this view of the relationship of form and content in his work, when he famously compares the function of his poetry for the reader to that of honey smeared on the rim of a cup of bitter medicine to induce a child to drink it (1. 935–50). But, as we shall see shortly, this hardly seems an adequate description of Lucretius' working procedures; on the contrary, the power and expressiveness (and beauty) of the Latin language was vastly extended by what Lucretius did with it. We might go so far as to say that the particular greatness and genius of Latin, its rightful reputation for monumental clarity, is partly Lucretius' doing. Moreover, as we saw in Chapter 2, it is better to regard 'form' and 'content' as heuristic categories than as reified entities 'in' the text. There is no reason why we should not make the judgement of taste, as a judgement of form and content together, in relation to *De Rerum Natura* or indeed any other didactic poem.

[58] Hegel (1975) i. 423.

Obviously there are also other ways of reading it. Those who seek from Lucretius to give an account of the history and development of Epicurean doctrine are doing something potentially worthwhile, but they are not reading aesthetically. In his inaugural lecture Bradley argued that some poetry was less poetical than others because for part of the time the special union of form and content that marked the greatest poetry was neglected, and cites both satire and didactic poetry as providing instances of this. But in a subsequent note he recants this view; the aim of the poet should always be to achieve such a union whatever the poetic matter.[59] And even in the lecture itself he asserted that no material could be ruled out in advance as unsuited to poetry: 'it is surely true that we cannot determine beforehand what subjects are fit for Art, or name any subject on which a good poem might not possibly be written.'[60] In this he agrees with the views of Pater, as we saw in the previous section. But the reverse is also true—no (so to say) 'unformed material', however great its value, can of itself guarantee poetic merit:

So also Shakespeare's knowledge or his moral insight, Milton's greatness of soul, Shelley's 'hate of hate' and 'love of love', and that desire to help men or make them happier which may have influenced a poet in hours of meditation—all these have, as such, no poetical worth: they have that worth only when, passing through the unity of the poet's being, they reappear as qualities of imagination, and then are indeed mighty powers in the world of poetry.[61]

One does not have to believe in the unity of the poet's being to see that Bradley obviously has a point here.

Along with the question of form and content, the 'problem of belief' seems raised by didactic poetry in a particularly acute form. For some there is no such problem, since for them, as for Sir Philip Sidney, the poet 'nothing affirms, and therefore never lieth'.[62] In a modern version of Sidney's view, I. A. Richards argued that statements in poetry are really pseudo-statements, and that therefore

---

[59] Bradley (1909) 22–3 and note D 30–2; see also above, pp. 65–8.

[60] Bradley (1909) 10. But Bradley also argues that some subjects are likely to be more productive poetically than others, since the fact that 'the subject *settles* nothing' does not mean that 'it counts for nothing': 'The Fall of Man is really a more favourable subject than a pin's head' (p. 11).

[61] Bradley (1909) 7.   [62] Vickers (1999) 370 (from *A Defence of Poetry*).

their truth or otherwise is irrelevant.[63] One can readily imagine the indignation of Lucretius if he had been told that his arguments for the mortality of the soul were simply 'pseudo-statements'. It seems obvious that he writes to persuade his reader to embrace his version of philosophical truth.[64] Now of course one does not have to be an Epicurean to take pleasure in Lucretius. C. S. Lewis makes the point with characteristic forthrightness:

> In good reading there ought to be no 'problem of belief'. I read Lucretius and Dante at a time when (by and large) I agreed with Lucretius. I have read them since I came (by and large) to agree with Dante. I cannot find that this has much altered my experience, or at all altered my evaluation, of either. A true lover of literature should be in one way like an honest examiner, who is prepared to give the highest marks to the telling, felicitous and well-documented exposition of views he dissents from or even abominates.[65]

This could be seen as a strong version of Kantian disinterestedness. Lewis is also adopting a standard Oxford English School position of the period as part of a conscious stand against the moralism of F. R. Leavis and Cambridge. Eagleton by contrast insists that 'silly, vicious or palpably wrong-headed beliefs in literature...can diminish our enjoyment of it'.[66] For example, how—to take a somewhat overworked limit case—could we make the judgement of taste about a great poem praising the Holocaust? There seem two answers to this. First one could say this is a purely hypothetical case—if there were such a poem, and we were invited to judge it 'beautiful', then and only then would there be any need to confront the problem. Secondly, were there such a poem, we might decide not to read it on moral and political grounds, which would have no bearing on its aesthetic quality (de la Mare has a telling poem called 'The Imagination's Pride', warning us not to go where 'the dark enemy spreads his maddening net'). A less extreme case might be rather more unsettling—I myself take intense pleasure in reading Dante's *Inferno*, although I regard the doctrine of the eternal

---

[63] See Eagleton (2002); Richards (1964) esp. p. 3, ch. 7, and Richards (1928) esp. ch. 35. Hume (1996) 152–3 argues that, when reading literature, we are relatively happy to accept incorrect scientific beliefs, since such 'speculative opinions' (including those regarding religion) are 'in continual flux and revolution', but have more difficulty with ethical beliefs we cannot share.

[64] Kivy (1997) 88, 114–15 is clearly right on this.   [65] Lewis (1961) 86.

[66] Eagleton (2002) 15. Clearly historical distance has an effect.

damnation of the wicked as 'wrong-headed' and indeed very possibly 'vicious'. George Santayana in his *Three Philosophical Poets* wrestles with the problem of whether Lucretius' poem would be diminished if his scientific and materialist views were shown to be wholly mistaken. This is his answer:

> Suppose, however,—and it is a tenable supposition,—that Lucretius is quite wrong in his science, and that there is no space, no substance, and no nature. His poem would then lose its pertinence to our lives and personal convictions; it would not lose its imaginative grandeur. We could still conceive a world composed as he describes.... Surely that universe, for those who lived in it, would have had its poetry. It would have been the poetry of naturalism. Lucretius, thinking he lived in such a world, heard the music of it, and wrote it down.[67]

To regard Lucretius as engaged in a straightforward act of versification is completely unsatisfactory. Like other Epicureans Lucretius aspired to be a faithful follower of his master's voice (3. 3–8), though in one crucial respect he flew in the face of his teaching—'sail past poetry with stopped ears, as from the Sirens' song', Epicurus had advised (fragment 164 Usener). In reorganizing the material, thinking through the arguments and how to present them persuasively in Latin, Lucretius brought to bear all his faculties of imagination and reason (*ratio* is a word of power in the poem). The difficulty of the task may have been increased by the deficiencies of Latin (*egestas linguae*) as a vehicle for philosophical thinking (1. 136–45), but it was the labour of overcoming those obstacles that enabled Lucretius' greatness as a writer. Or it might be better to say (as being less mentalist) that the *egestas linguae* makes the poem what it is. In general Catharine Atherton is right to point out that 'to have something to say is ... to have a way to say it',[68] so that to separate form and content, as Hegel does in the passages cited above, would be as misleading with philosophy as with poetry (one of the achievements of Derridean deconstruction is precisely to break down simplistic formulations of the distinction between philosophy and literature).[69]

---

[67] Santayana (1947) 36–7.   [68] Atherton (1998) 29.
[69] Cf. Atherton (1998), introduction p. XVII: 'Not only does he present us with supporting argumentation, in all its complexity and subtlety, for the system he recommends: he exploits to the full the special resources which poetry affords to provide, as vividly and directly as possible (and in this context vividness and directness are themselves philosophical virtues), precisely the sort of evidence, culled from perception and sensation, which is demanded by

On the whole Lucretius avoids technical vocabulary and philosophical neologism, preferring to extend the resources of the natural language—the sense of the extension of linguistic possibility is part of what makes the writing so dynamic. Lucretius at some level may have shared the view of those for whom, like Rorty, metaphor in language goes 'all the way down'. His metaphoric use of familiar language as a heuristic tool is one of the ways that the dark, superficially unappealing and anti-intuitive doctrines of Epicurus are naturalized within the poem. A good example is provided by the passage, subject of a fine analysis by Duncan Kennedy, in which Lucretius begins to introduce the idea of atoms (1. 54–61):[70]

>   nam tibi de summa caeli ratione deumque
>   disserere incipiam et *rerum primordia* pandam,   55
>   unde omnis natura creet res auctet alatque
>   quove eadem rursum natura perempta resolvat,
>   quae nos *materiem* et *genitalia corpora rebus*
>   reddunda in ratione vocare et *semina rerum*
>   appellare suëmus et haec eadem usurpare   60
>   *corpora prima*, quod ex illis sunt omnia primis.

For I will set out to discourse to you about the most high system (*ratio*) of heaven and the gods, and I will open *the first-beginnings of things*, from which nature creates all things, increases, and nurtures them, and into which nature too resolves them again when they perish, which I in rendering a rational account (*ratio*) have made it my custom to call *matter* and *the bodies that bring things to birth*, and *seeds of things*, and to speak of these same things as *first bodies*, because all things have their existence from them as first elements.   (my italics)

Lucretius does not use the Greek technical term 'atoms' (indivisibles), but a whole range of linguistic 'equivalents' that will subsequently help to advance the argument and energize the poem. Within *materies* lurks *mater*, and the idea of nature personified as mother (*natura* is linked etymologically with *nasci*, 'to be born') is to be crucial for the subsequent argument, as well as making the reader more comfortable with the poem's unfamiliar matter. Thus the unseen atoms which lack most of the features of

---

Epicureanism.... Surely it would be unfair not to see *this*, too, as philosophy: after all, what philosophy is, and how it is done, are part of Lucretius' lesson to us.'

[70] See Kennedy (2002) 75–82. Throughout this section I am indebted to two unpublished lecture series by Duncan Kennedy, one given in Bristol and one in Dublin.

the visible world are *genitalia corpora rebus*, bodies that produce life (the poem began with a paean to *Venus Genetrix*)—the emphasis is on life more than death, in a poem uncomfortably designed to show that the soul dies with the body. 'Bodies' is another anthropomorphism that further assimilates the atomic system to our normal sense of the world. Moreover the emphasis on primacy in 'first bodies' links the opening of Lucretius' poem with an epic stress on origins (as in the *Iliad*, and later Virgil's *Aeneid*)—though in reality the atoms of Epicurus have neither beginnings nor endings. 'Seeds' are miniature entities that we nonetheless know and see turn into much larger organisms, just as atoms, though unseen, compose the structure of all things (yet seeds are alive, whereas atoms are not). The passage is hardly one of the best known in the poem, but it is brimming with excitement and potentiality; in the words of Santayana, 'the imagination of Lucretius, in tracing the course of the atoms, dances and soars most congenially.'[71] Of course there are risks in Lucretius' strategy of naturalization and use of heuristic fictions, here and throughout the poem. The anthropomorphisms can work to undermine a system in which man is decentred and there is no ultimate agency or purpose. Opposing views to those advocated in the poem echo through gaps in the text, enabling recuperative interpretations by theists and others. This is a matter to which I shall be returning.

There are numerous other respects in which the Hegelian accusation that Lucretius gives a merely decorative form to a wholly pre-existing content seems peculiarly ill-judged. There is, for example, the analogy between the sweetness and pleasure that the poetry is designed to bestow and the pleasure, *voluptas*, that is the aim of the Epicurean life.[72] Scholars have pointed to the fact that Lucretius repeatedly uses the way the letters of the alphabet form into different combinations in discourse as an illustration for the atomic structure of the world: in both cases limited elements combine to produce an amazing variousness.[73] This figure implies a richer implication of form with content than the honey on the cup passage. As Katharina Volk puts it, 'if the letters are like the atoms, then the poem is like the universe that it describes'; indeed she goes

---

[71] Santayana (1947) 213. [72] So Volk (2002) 116.
[73] See Volk (2002) 86, 100–16.

The Aesthetic Turn

further: 'It is, then, no longer clear which system is the model for the other.'[74]

Similarly, Lucretius' much-admired keenness of observation can be seen as a product of the nature of philosophical enquiry as defined by Epicurus. There is indeed an intriguing kinship between the emphasis on 'seeing' in the aesthetic life as described by Pater and the Epicurean view that we must start from sense perception and, in especial, vision. Words of the kind (*videre* and so forth[75]) are common throughout *De Rerum Natura*, as indeed they are in philosophical writing generally (so in English we have words like 'evidence', 'perspective', 'insight'). As a result the French philosopher and aesthetician Victor Cousin (1792–1867) is able cunningly to appropriate a passage of Lucretius for his aesthetic theory:

> Lucretius has said, that it is not the pleasure of seeing the sufferings of the shipwrecked that constitutes the *beauty* of a Shipwreck; do not seek it either in compassion or in terror, for such feelings draw us away from the spectacle; another feeling different, and triumphing over them must make us stay on the sea-shore, this feeling is the pure sentiment of the Beautiful, caused by the grandeur of the sight, the wide expanse of water, the majestic motion of the ship and of the waves. If we think for a moment, that beneath the dreadful billows are hid the agony and the groan of dying men, we can endure the sight no longer; the sentiment of the Beautiful is gone. It is for this reason that the dramatic representation of a shipwreck is more Beautiful than an actual shipwreck, the sentiment of the Beautiful is then not overborne by terror or compassion; these may bear it company, but it rules them; it is then a sentiment altogether peculiar, and the object of it is not the pathetic.[76]

Cousin is commenting on the opening of the second book, which is given thus by Dryden:

---

[74] Ibid. 100–1; cf. 104: 'The poem appears as the ideal medium to describe the Epicurean world, not because it consists of atoms (a quality it shares, after all, with all other objects), but because its "elements" behave like atoms; not because it is born and dies... but because it describes the alternation of birth and death and thus reflects nature's cycle of growth and decay.'

[75] Conte (1994a) 16: 'in Lucretius perhaps no semantic field recurs as frequently as "seeing", "sight", "visions": the reader must see the images of things, just as the poet must know how to make the reader see them.' In this fine essay, 'Instructions for a Sublime Reader', Conte shows how Epicurus' theory of perception finds its perfect correlative in the *phantasia* of Lucretius' sublime style.

[76] Cousin (1848) 58–9.

> 'Tis pleasant safely to behold from shore
> The rolling ship and hear the tempest roar;
> Not that another's pain is our delight,
> But pains unfelt produce the pleasing sight.[77]

Lucretius is not ostensibly talking about beauty at all, but about the calm of mind with which the Epicurean can survey the undesirable contingencies of life (perhaps Cousin merely misremembered the passage). But the assimilation of aesthetic experience of art and nature to *ataraxia*, the equanimity that was sought by Epicureans, is a suggestive one. Moreover the passage from *De Rerum Natura* 2 lays particular emphasis on sight (*spectare*, 2; *cernere*, 4; *tueri*, 5; *despicere*, 9). Cousin's language is partly Kantian—though Kant would have categorized such a picture as sublime rather than beautiful—and *ataraxia* is easily conflated with a version of Kantian disinterest. We saw that for Pater an aesthetic education was precisely a form of the contemplative life.[78] Santayana's characterization of Lucretius fits well with this:

The greatest thing about this genius is its power of losing itself in its object, its impersonality. We seem to be reading not the poetry of a poet about things, but the poetry of things themselves.[79]

We have seen that recuperative accounts of *De Rerum Natura* have often been advanced. Certainly Lucretius' imagination can be fired by the positions he is attacking; indeed this happens in some of the most memorable passages in the poem (a similar phenomenon marks Pope's satiric writings). This may help to explain the persistence of the tradition of 'L'Antilucrèce chez Lucrèce', first advanced by H. J. G. Patin in 1868/9, the idea that at some level Lucretius did not fully accept the truth of the materialist doctrines he was advancing. At the end of book 1 Lucretius argues that if a certain view were correct (the centrifugal force of fire), the universe would immediately self-destruct (1102–10):

> ne volucri ritu flammarum moenia mundi
> diffugiant subito magnum per inane soluta
> et ne cetera consimili ratione sequantur

---

[77] For these versions of selected passages from Lucretius, the finest ever made into English and one of Dryden's most impressive achievements, see Hammond (1983); Hopkins (1986) 112–21, 125–30.

[78] See p. 171 above. [79] Santayana (1947) 34.

> neve ruant caeli tonitralia templa superne 1105
> terraque se pedibus raptim subducat et omnis
> inter permixtas rerum caelique ruinas
> corpora solventis abeat per inane profundum,
> temporis ut puncto nil exstet reliquiarum
> desertum praeter spatium et primordia caeca. 1110

<Moreover, if air and fire continue mounting upwards, there is a danger> lest, after the winged way of flames, the walls of the world suddenly fly apart, dissolved through the great void, and lest all else follow them in like manner, lest the thundering quarters of the sky rush upwards, and the earth in hot haste withdraw itself from beneath our feet, and amid all the mingled ruin of things on earth and of the sky, whereby the frames of bodies are loosed, it pass away through the deep void, so that in an instant of time not a wrack be left behind, except emptied space and unseen first beginnings.

It is a striking and characteristic passage, full of cosmic imagining and Lucretian words of power (*inane, ruant, primordia caeca*, and so forth). It evidently reminded Cyril Bailey, whose translation I gave above[80], of one of the most haunting evocations of the end of the world in all literature:

> These our actors,
> As I foretold you, were all spirits, and
> Are melted into air, into thin air,
> And, like the baseless fabric of this vision,
> The cloud-capped towers, the gorgeous palaces,
> The solemn temples, the great globe itself,
> Yea, all which it inherit, shall dissolve,
> And, like this insubstantial pageant faded,
> Leave not a wrack behind. We are such stuff
> As dreams are made on, and our little life
> Is rounded with a sleep.   (*Tempest*, IV. i. 148–58)

Prospero's words are occasioned by the interruption of the betrothal masque, but the insubstantiality of masque and theatrical performance slides into thoughts about transience, death, and the end of all things. That they should have come into Bailey's mind at this point is proof enough of the hold that the Lucretian passage had over his imagination. Yet, strictly the point of those lines is that in Lucretius' atomic universe such immediate destruction does *not* happen.

---

[80] Bailey (1949) i. 233.

In this instance Lucretius may to some extent be invoking through his description that eventual destruction of this and other worlds which was posited by Epicureanism. More complex is the effect of the use of the myth of Phaethon in book 5. 392–410:[81]

> tantum spirantes aequo certamine bellum
> magnis inter se de rebus cernere certant,
> cum semel interea fuerit superantior ignis
> et semel, ut fama est, umor regnarit in arvis.   395
> ignis enim superat et ambiens multa perussit,
> avia cum Phaethonta rapax vis Solis equorum
> aethere raptavit toto terrasque per omnis.
> at pater omnipotens ira tum percitus acri
> magnanimum Phaethonta repenti fulminis ictu   400
> deturbavit equis in terram, Solque cadenti
> obvius aeternam succepit lampada mundi
> disiectosque redegit equos iunxitque trementis,
> inde suum per iter recreavit cuncta gubernans,
> scilicet ut veteres Graium cecinere poetae,   405
> quod procul a vera nimis est ratione repulsum.
> ignis enim superare potest ubi materiai
> ex infinito sunt corpora plura coorta;
> inde cadunt vires aliqua ratione revictae,
> aut pereunt res exustae torrentibus auris.   410

Breathing out so great a war in equal contest, they [fire and water] strive to struggle with one another about great things; although nevertheless once fire proved somewhat superior, and once, as the story goes, moisture ruled in the fields. For fire was victorious and burnt up all things, going round them, when the rapacious force of the horses of the Sun going off the path hurled Phaethon over the whole sky and through all lands. But the almighty father, struck then with sharp anger, with a sudden thunderbolt cast down from his horses high-hearted Phaethon to the ground, and the Sun going to meet him as he fell caught up the eternal lamp of the world and brought back the scattered horses and yoked them as they trembled, then guiding them through their own path renewed all things, at least as the old poets of the Greeks sang. This, however, is utterly at odds with true reason. For fire can conquer only when more bodies of its material have arisen from the infinite; and then its strength falls conquered in some way, or else things perish burned up by its scorching blasts.

The story of Phaethon is told in the grandest epic style. We have the epicizing periphrases, *vis equorum* for 'the mighty horses' and

---

[81] Useful discussions include West (1969) 50–3; Gale (1994) 33–4.

'the eternal lamp of the world' for the sun; the etymological play *rapax/ raptavit*; the grandiose, high-sounding epithets (*omnipotens, magnanimum*—this latter suggesting the youthful high spirits of Phaethon); the succession of powerful verbs; the enlivening detail (the horses trembling after their stampede, the sun taking up the lamp like the successor in a torch race). It would be wrong to regard such impressive writing simply as epic parody as do many scholars. Of course doubts have been sown if only lightly from the first (*ut fama est*, 395), while there are details more or less obviously inconsistent with Epicurean belief—the eternal nature of the sun, the arbitrary omnipotence of Jupiter. But if we downplay the splendour of the myth's telling we lose the full sarcastic force of the rebuttal (with *scilicet* as the initial signal), when reason, *ratio*, puts myth to rights in a very different, less glamorous style, a style grand in its way but suited to rational argument. Nonetheless Lucretius wants to keep myth operating within his poem, providing points of contact with the culture of his Roman readers, the epic tradition not least (it helps that myths like this were often allegorized, so that the story of Phaethon could be figured as the destruction of the world by fire). And in keeping myth in play he acknowledges, indeed re-enacts, its potency.

Milton precisely catches the rhetorical force of this and the effect of double response when, during the catalogue of devils, he includes the myth of Vulcan's fall from heaven (*Paradise Lost* 1. 738–51):

> Nor was his name unheard or unadored
> In ancient Greece; and in Ausonian land
> Men called him Mulciber; and how he fell
> From heaven, *they fabled*, thrown by angry Jove
> Sheer o'er the crystal battlements; from morn
> To noon he fell, from noon to dewy eve,
> A summer's day; and with the setting sun
> Dropped from the zenith like a falling star,
> On Lemnos the Aegean isle: thus they relate,
> *Erring*; for he with this rebellious rout
> Fell long before; nor aught availed him now
> To have built in heaven high towers; nor did he scape
> By all his engines, but was headlong sent
> With his industrious to build in hell.   (my italics)

There was an old tradition that the classical gods were in reality devils, which Milton uses to 'correct' the fable of Hephaistos' fall—resonant word in this context—as given by Homer in *Iliad* 1. 591–5. In emulous rivalry Milton imitates the Homeric passage closely and dazzlingly, overgoing it in glamour and beauty and romance, only to shift registers dramatically for the sarcastic dismissal (briefly anticipated by the words 'they fabled').[82] Both Lucretius and Milton worked with an epic tradition with enormous literary prestige which they bent to their own novel purposes, redeeming it so to say. It is only because the myths have authority and beauty that their rejection carries such weight, as the tension between two belief systems energizes the text.

Lucretius' ability to enter imaginatively into the minds of his opponents can be illustrated by a famous passage (often cited by proponents of the 'Anti-Lucretius in Lucretius'), in which Lucretius answers the objections of those who fear death (3. 894–918):

'Iam iam non domus accipiet te laeta neque uxor
optima, nec dulces occurrent oscula nati   895
praeripere et tacita pectus dulcedine tangent.
non poteris factis florentibus esse tuisque
praesidium. misero misere' aiunt 'omnia ademit
una dies infesta tibi tot praemia vitae.'
illud in his rebus non addunt 'nec tibi earum   900
iam desiderium rerum super insidet una.'
quod bene si videant animo dictisque sequantur,
dissolvant animi magno se angore metuque.
'tu quidem ut es leto sopitus, sic eris aevi
quod superest cunctis privatu' doloribus aegris.   905
at nos horrifico cinefactum te prope busto
insatiabiliter deflevimus aeternumque
nulla dies nobis maerorem e pectore demet.'
illud ab hoc igitur quaerendum est quid sit amari
tanto opere, ad somnum si res redit atque quietem,   910
cur quisquam aeterno possit tabescere luctu.
hoc etiam faciunt ubi discubuere tenentque
pocula saepe homines et inumbrant ora coronis,
ex animo ut dicant 'brevis hic est fructus homullis;
iam fuerit neque post umquam revocare licebit.'   915
tamquam in morte mali cum primis hoc sit eorum

---

[82] For a fuller version of this argument see Martindale (1986) 72–8 (however, the influence of Lucretius is wrongly there downplayed). See Jenkyns (1982) 129–32 for the link with Lucretius.

> quod sitis exurat miseros atque arida torrat
> aut aliae cuius desiderium insideat rei.

'Never again will your fruitful home receive you nor your best of wives, nor will your sweet children anticipate you by running to snatch your kisses and touch your heart with silent joy. You will not be able to protect your flourishing affairs and your dependents. From you in your misery miserably', they say, 'has one hostile day taken away all the many rewards of life.' Yet in these matters they do not add 'nor is there present as well any longer desire of these things.' But if they saw this properly in mind and followed it through in their words, they would free themselves from great pain of mind and fear. 'You indeed as you have been put to sleep in death, will be free from all painful sorrows for all time to come. But we have lamented you insatiably standing nearby now that you have been turned to ashes in the horror-inducing pyre, and no day will take the everlasting grief from our hearts.' This man you must ask what is so bitter, if it comes in the end to sleep and rest, why anyone should waste away in everlasting lament. This too men do ever when they are at table and hold cups and shade their faces with garlands, so as to say this from the heart 'Brief is this enjoyment for us poor mortals; soon it will be over and done with and afterwards it will be impossible to recall it.' As if in death this were worst of their ills that thirst would burn the poor wretches and parch them with its dryness, or that a desire for any other thing would abide.

The passage takes the form of a dialogue between the Epicurean teacher and his opponents, with three objections by the latter that are then answered by the poet. We are plunged without warning *in medias res*, and it is not until we reach *aiunt* in 898 that we are given an indication of the speaker (the effect would have been all the more marked for the Roman reader, since in ancient texts there were no inverted commas). The debate is constructed with very great care rhetorically. Each of the speeches of the opponents is weaker than its predecessor. The third (lines 914–15) is as feeble in expression as it is sentimental in content, and it is given a strongly satirical setting in the picture of the diners shading their faces with garlands. The second (904–8) is weightier in both expression and thought, and contains one of Lucretius' most memorable lines: *insatiabiliter deflevimus aeternumque*. E. J. Kenney argues that the line is more grotesque than effective, on the grounds of its unusual rhythm (three words, a single caesura, a spondaic fifth foot, a four-syllable ending) and the fact that *insatiabiliter* is elsewhere used of pigs wallowing in filth (but words take colour from their particular contexts).[83] Admittedly the line is not elegant, but elegance is

---

[83] Kenney (1971) note ad loc.; cf. West (1969) 28–9.

hardly a special Lucretian virtue. The moving quality of the opening six lines is surely beyond doubt: the lack of sentimentality;[84] the intensification of pathos (*iam iam, misero misere, una tot*) along with the overall simplicity of diction; the precise evocation of a domestic scene, including the children rushing at their father the moment he appears; the delicate accuracy of the adjective *tacita* which contrasts the ebullience of the children with the father's restraint. Certainly there is little doubt that readers both in antiquity and since have been duly moved.[85] The lachrymose lines from Gray's *Elegy Written in a Country Churchyard* are well known (21-4):

> For them no more the blazing hearth shall burn,
> Or busy housewife ply her evening care;
> No children run to lisp their sire's return,
> Or climb his knees the envied kiss to share.

Finer still than this, in its greater economy and restraint, is the imitation in *Ode* 2. 14 (to Postumus), one of Horace's most haunting meditations on the inevitability of death:

> linquenda tellus et domus et placens
> uxor, neque harum quas colis arborum
>   te praeter invisas cupressos
>   ulla brevem dominum sequetur.   (21-4)

You must leave earth and home and the wife you love, and none of the trees you tend will follow you, their short-lived master, except the hated cypresses.

Kenneth Quinn, taking his cue from the Lucretian echo, argues that the poem is a soliloquy by another voice rather than a direct utterance of the poet (which is just possible), and that the speaker is one of Lucretius' sentimental party-goers who does not understand, as a good Epicurean should, the terms of human life and death.[86] This allows us to reconcile Horace's attitude with Lucretius', but only at the cost of making one of his most direct and moving *carpe diem* poems into something ingenious but rather frigid. It seems easier to suppose that Horace imitates Lucretius'

---

[84] Cf. Hopkins (1986) 121: 'The poet does not evoke a fireside idyll, but recalls the children's (from one point of view) tiresome pestering of their parents.' For Dryden's masterly treatment of the whole passage see Mason (1996) 217-19.

[85] Virgil also imitates the passage in *Georgic* 3. 523-4.

[86] Quinn (1963) 99-108.

words but ignores their context, thereby using the passage to articulate a very different set of feelings about death than those *De Rerum Natura* was designed to promote. But clearly he was able to do this only because Lucretius' lines can be found to have an authentic pathos. The responses of Horace and Gray illustrate the discursive problem that Lucretius necessarily faced in trying to naturalize Epicureanism; it is always possible for a reader to recuperate the poem for non-Epicurean ends, releasing the various suppressed others that *De Rerum Natura* necessarily contains.[87]

So what is the peculiar sensation, what is the peculiar quality of pleasure, which Lucretius' work has the property of exciting in us, and which we cannot get elsewhere? Two things, perhaps, might be adduced. First, here is a poet who loves things, and words, and ideas, and who conveys that triple enthusiasm with something very far from any note of *ataraxia*, rather with what Santayana calls 'a strange vehemence'.[88] Even at its most prosaic and ratiocinative his is a sublime voice, weighty, craggy, ponderous, at times even gallumphing.[89] Richard Jenkyns writes well about how grammar is put into contribution: 'Lucretius is the great master of the prefix: "con-", "dis-", "in-", "ex-", "re-", "per-"—these innocuous syllables come to express the unresting force of atomic movement, the pulls and pushes, the collisions, penetrations, tearing apart'[90] (the careful distinctions also attest to the precision of a highly analytical mind). The imagery is bold and clear[91] beyond the reach of any other Latin poet, in a way that reminds one of Aeschylus perhaps or the poetic books of the Old Testament. After reading Lucretius even the greatest Latin poets—Virgil, say—can seem

---

[87] Conte (1994a) 4 talks convincingly of 'Lucretius's peculiar tactic of insinuating himself into his opponents' positions and emptying them of their previous content so that he can fill them up with Epicurean doctrine'; the danger is that the reader will try to empty them again. Another poet, whose writings are fertilized by Lucretius aesthetically, though not doctrinally, is Pope: see e.g. *Essay on Man* I. 89 'Atoms or systems into ruin hurled'; ibid. 1. 251–6; and the entropic conclusion of *Dunciad* IV. It is always exciting when this celebrant of order is drawn, despite himself, into apocalypse and anarchy.

[88] Santayana (1947) 19.

[89] See Conte (1994a), esp. 18–19: 'One function of the sublime in Lucretius's text is to use greatness so that the listener can share in the incessant struggle against superficiality'; 'Facing the sublime, the reader sees himself as a text, and then uses the written text in front of him as a commentary on his own ego, on the emotions provoked by his reading and by the exaltation thereby produced.'

[90] Jenkyns (1998) 216. [91] West (1969) remains fundamental.

enervate, elegant merely, buttoned-up. Conte gives a tiny but utterly characteristic instance: Lucretian winds that flow (*fluunt*, 1. 280), 'as though they were currents of water', so that 'the two destructive forces—impetuous water and wind that drags along and tears off—merge in a single image of movement'.[92] The opening encomium of Epicurus is typical (1. 62–79). At the beginning of the passage Religion, *religio*—knots that bind—threatens us from the sky (superstition, *superstitio*, that which stands over us, *super instans*, 65); at the end in turn it is trampled underfoot by the 'Greek man'. In between Epicurus is figured as a Roman general, who breaks out of a city under siege and on a scouting party ranges 'in mind and spirit' over the infinite vastness of the universe, from which he returns victorious to bring us the victory and the truth of things. In this way images of epic and martial heroism, Greek and Roman, are appropriated for the new culture hero: intellectual, teacher, and sage.[93] When Virgil smoothly imitates the passage in *Georgic* 2. 490–2 he evokes the image of trampling but withdraws from its metaphoric clarity:

> felix, qui potuit rerum cognoscere causas,
> atque metus omnis et inexorabile fatum
> subiecit pedibus strepitumque Acherontis avari.

Happy is he who could know the causes of things, and threw under foot all fears and inexorable fate and the noise of greedy Acheron.

Trampling on a noise is a stroke of wit, but it is not, perhaps, quite Lucretian. Dryden, the greatest of Lucretius' English translators, can catch his energy and fire, but without his unselfconscious, monumental weight:

> If after death 'tis painful to be torn
> By birds and beasts, then why not so to burn,
> Or drenched in floods of honey to be soaked,
> Embalmed to be at once preserved and choked,
> Or on an airy mountain's top to lie,
> Exposed to cold and heaven's inclemency,
> Or crowded in a tomb to be oppressed
> With monumental marble on thy breast?

Secondly, Lucretius' poem as a whole offers us an imaginatively realized vision of the universe grounded in nature and reason. His

---

[92] Conte (1994*a*) 13.   [93] See West (1969) 57–63; Conte (1994*a*) 2–3.

mind, as we have seen, moves with the atoms (the properties of the Epicurean atoms, which are completely solid, are size, shape, weight, and movement). It is quite wrong to see merit only in the more familiar set-pieces and purple passages (which do not always show Lucretius at his most inventive). In this respect some great poets have proved among his most responsive readers. Ovid's admiration for Lucretius is shown in innumerable intertextualities (for example, the account of primal chaos in the first book of the *Metamorphoses*, or Pythagoras' sermon on flux in the last). When Ovid wants to characterize Lucretius in a single couplet (*Amores* 1. 15. 23-4), he evokes a doctrine of Epicurean physics and echoes a Lucretian image of cosmic destruction:

> carmina sublimis tunc sunt peritura Lucreti,
> exitio terras cum dabit una dies.

The poems of sublime Lucretius are destined to perish only when one day will give the lands to destruction.

Tennyson, whose 'Lucretius' (1869) is both a great poem in its own right and a profound reading of *De Rerum Natura*, catches the Lucretian note with one sounding line (mediated by Milton) that brilliantly describes the 'flaring atom-streams': 'Ruining along the illimitable inane' (40). Tennyson engages in a whole barrage of Latinate effects: 'ruin', here an intransitive verb, in its Latin sense of 'fall'; the compound adjective 'illimitable', a Spenserian/Miltonic echo, Latinate and grandiose; and the metaphrase on Lucretius' *inane*, the inane, the void. Milton too had responded to Lucretius' cosmic imaginings in depicting his war of the worlds in *Paradise Lost*, as angelic bodies hurtle through space. In this passage the lists in asyndeton are among the devices Milton uses to slow his verse and give it a Lucretian gravity:

> Before their eyes in sudden view appear
> The secrets of the hoary deep, a dark
> Illimitable ocean without bound,
> Without dimension, where length, breath, and highth,
> And time and place are lost; where eldest Night
> And Chaos, ancestors of Nature, hold
> Eternal anarchy, amidst the noise
> Of endless wars, and by confusion stand.
> For Hot, Cold, Moist, and Dry, four champions fierce
> Strive here for mastery, and to battle bring

>   Their embryon atoms; they around the flag
>   Of each his faction, in their several clans,
>   Light-armed or heavy, sharp, smooth, swift, or slow,
>   Swarm populous... (2. 890–903)

Santayana is the modern critic most responsive to this, the Lucretian 'virtue', this 'poetry of naturalism' and 'the march of things', and it is with his 'poet of matter' that we shall end: 'A naturalistic conception of things is a great work of imagination,—greater, I think, than any dramatic or moral mythology: it is a conception fit to inspire great poetry, and in the end, perhaps, it will prove the only conception able to inspire it.'[94]

III

> The gods that mortal beauty chase
> Still in a tree did end their race.
> Apollo hunted Daphne so,
> Only that she might laurel grow.
>   Marvell, 'The Garden', 27–30

Until the seventeenth century Ovid's *Metamorphoses* was a central point of reference for Western culture. Since then its importance has markedly diminished, though it has always maintained at least a subterranean presence.[95] There have been brief periods of reflorescence, at the beginning of the twentieth century with the High Modernists, for example,[96] or again in our own *fin de siècle*.[97] Ovid's reputation has also been restored within the academy in a quite dramatic way over the past thirty years (though, given the much-diminished importance of Classics, this hardly justifies the claim that we are living in a renewed *aetas Ovidiana*). When I went to

---

[94] Santayana (1947) 37, 60, 57, 21.
[95] Cf. Norman Vance, 'Ovid and the Nineteenth Century' in Martindale (1988) 231: 'Time which devours all things, as Ovid tells us (*Met.* 15. 234), did not destroy Ovid in the nineteenth century. It changed him as his Arethusa was changed into a fountain from which wayfarers could drink without always recognising the source.'
[96] So Tomlinson (1983). Though Tomlinson perhaps exaggerates somewhat when he calls him 'a chief ancestor of literary modernism' (p. 1), Ovid certainly influenced Joyce, Eliot, Pound, and Woolf in significant ways.
[97] See Hofmann and Lasdun (1994); Hughes (1997); Terry (2000); Duncan Kennedy, 'Recent Receptions of Ovid' in Hardie (2002) 320–35.

Oxford in the late 1960s, even the *Metamorphoses* barely featured on the syllabus; and Ovid was regarded as trivial, overly literary, and insufficiently committed to the graver Augustan values. Now he is again at the centre of the canon of Latin authors. The revaluation has not perhaps involved as significant a shift in how Ovid is conceived as is often supposed; it is simply that qualities previously condemned are now lauded—today's Ovid is witty and ludic, cunningly allusive, and politically subversive (is such an Ovid 'the same' or 'different' from the earlier one?). To that extent the current admiring consensus[98] is based on a rather narrow view of what constitutes Ovid's distinctive 'virtue', one that ignores much that seems to have attracted Ovid's many admirers in earlier centuries. In particular, today's Latinists are preoccupied, almost to the point of obsession, with the issue of intertextuality (often used simply as a synonym for allusion), always now regarded as evidently 'A Good Thing'. Yet the echoing of earlier poetry, both Greek and Latin, is a standard feature of the Latin poetic tradition as a whole, just as characteristic of the writings of Virgil, Horace, and the rest. Indeed it might be felt that the recognition of such intertextualities is *less* important in Ovid's case, since the world of the *Metamorphoses* can become (and for many readers indeed became) a comparatively 'autonomous' one, so to say, in relation to other Graeco-Roman texts.[99]

We might then be able to learn from earlier ages for which the *Metamorphoses* was not so much an intertextual and narratological *tour de force* as a master-poem of love, change, and nature, a mythographic work of importance and authority, a vehicle for wisdom within the spheres of morality, ontology, and metaphysics. Ovid's pre-eminence in the depiction of 'the passions', particularly those of love and desire, was constantly acknowledged; famously for Chaucer he was 'Venus' clerk' (*House of Fame*, 1487).[100] We shall need to go outside the work of professional Ovidians to find formulations which do justice to all this. For example, the poet and critic Charles Tomlinson argues that the 'wisdom' of the *Metamorphoses* (and what classicist would dare to use that word?) inheres 'in its

---

[98] This consensus is well represented by two recent collections: Hardie, Barchiesi, Hinds (1999) and Hardie (2002).
[99] Cf. Hardie (2002) 195 n. 29.
[100] So too Hughes (1997) p. ix: 'Above all, Ovid was interested in passion. Or rather, in what a passion feels like to the one possessed by it.' See also Zajko (2004).

imaginative vision of a world where all things are interrelated, where flesh and blood are near kin to soil and river, where man and animal share common instincts, where vegetarianism is poetically the only defensible philosophy of life'[101] (a description that would not perhaps have surprised Spenser). For the novelist Antonia Byatt, Ovid's 'skill is to make his readers feel in their fingers, at the roots of their hair, the bodies and creatures his imagination inhabits'.[102] An Ovid more like that was the favourite of Chaucer, Spenser, Shakespeare, and Milton, which for anyone who in any way takes seriously a reasonably orthodox version of literary history must assign Ovid a pretty central place in our poetic tradition.

This is not to deny that today's Ovid (whatever its limitations) is lacking in interest, or indeed insight. In 1994 Faber published a collection of poems inspired by the *Metamorphoses* authored by forty-two of the best-known English-writing poets of our day, entitled *After Ovid: New Metamorphoses*. Ovid, on an influential current reading of him, would have liked this title, with its exploitation of the instability of language, the slide of the signifier. The volume is chronologically 'after Ovid' obviously, and indeed any Western poet is necessarily writing after Ovid in a tradition Ovid helped to shape. It is after Ovid too in the sense that a film might be described as 'after the novel by—', thus raising the issue of the closeness, or difference, of 'original' and version. Titles of this 'After X' kind are common today, and speak also—whether in tribute, or anxiety, or lassitude—of a sense of belatedness, pastness, a feature (it is claimed) of our (post)modern condition. The 'new' of *New Metamorphoses* might be 'fresh' or 'novel' or 'modernist'; we recall the Poundian slogan 'make it new', and note the desire of the editors for an Ovid 'remade'[103] (Ovid too was a modernist in his day, and *nova* is the second word of the poem—indeed *in nova* could be taken as a quasi-imperative). *New Metamorphoses* implies

---

[101] Tomlinson (1983) 2. Cf. Lasdun (2003) 24: 'Ovid's chain reactions of transformation emit a liberating energy like nothing else in literature. Occurring always at some limit of human capacity or tolerance, they have something of death in them, something of birth, something of sex, but something else, too: a mysterious reverse flow, whereby the things people turn into—tree, rock, flower, fountain, bird, beast—miraculously release their own potentialities back into the human universe of the poem.'

[102] From 'Arachne', in Terry (2000) 133.   [103] Hofmann and Lasdun (1994) p. xii.

new versions or translations of Ovid's poem, the *Metamorphoses*, and we might read too the implication that these versions are themselves metamorphoses, that metamorphosis can be made into a figure for the act of translation itself. In all this we can see a constellation of 'Ovidian' concerns, at least as the poem is read today.

Such concerns can certainly be found in the episode to which I shall be devoting the rest of this section: the story of Apollo and Daphne (1. 452–567).[104] Like many others in the poem it is a story of beginnings, of origins. The work of literature which, perhaps, bodies forth most fully for Western Europe the validating power of origins is the *Aeneid* where Virgil plots a teleology for Roman history which unites Aeneas, refugee from the burning city of Troy, with his descendant Augustus. The poem's massive first sentence asserts Aeneas' primacy in a story that led, ineluctably, to the walls of high Troy. This narrative of beginnings underpins the hegemony of a whole culture and locates the principate—from other perspectives a betrayal of traditional Roman values—at the very centre of that culture. The *Metamorphoses* appears to accept the organizing principles of Virgilian grand narrative, and to overgo them, as the poet launches a history of the world from creation to principate. But that history quickly fragments into stories that cunningly spawn other stories, so that the teleological thrust of the opening is resisted in a series of deferrals, dispersals, slidings, which underline a lack of fixity, a changefulness-in-similarity in things, an irresolvable Derridean dialectic. The at least partly anti-hierarchical structure has usefully been compared to that of a hypertext.[105]

The poem of change (*Met amor phoses*) is also the story of love (*amor*), and indeed within the stories love is frequently the motor of change. The first love story—or sex story—is introduced by words which recall, and deform, the beginning lines of the *Aeneid* (with

---

[104] In what follows I am indebted to lectures given in Bristol by Denis Feeney, Duncan Kennedy, and Rowena Fowler.

[105] So Brown (2000). Brown points out (p. 121) that this is for Barthes the ideal form of textuality: 'the networks are many and interact, without any one of them being able to surpass the rest; this text is a galaxy of signifiers, not a structure of signifieds; it has no beginning; it is reversible; we gain access to it by several entrances, none of which can be authoritatively declared to be the main one' (from *S/Z*). For Byatt in Terry (2000) 143, Ovid's mythic world is 'a fluid, endlessly interconnected web'.

primus amor Phoebi and *saeva Cupidinis ira* compare *primus ab oris* and *saevae memorem Iunonis ob iram*).[106] The origins of the laurel tree are found in Apollo's attempted rape of the nymph Daphne and the transformation that allows her to evade him in the end—or rather in the beginning. This is a very different sort of aetiology from Virgil's, arguably one better able to resist purposes of social and political mystification or the naturalization of cultural phenomena as eternal truths. Apollo, tutelary deity of Augustus whom he had aided at Actium, is here depicted as a would-be rapist, who attempts simultaneously to boast, to cajole and flatter his victim, and to threaten her: 'I am the god of Delphi, Claros, Tenedos, and Patara,' he brags: 'my father is Jupiter' (I come of the very best family); and he delivers an account of his powers which enacts the form of hymn and prayer—he is his own self-worshipper. This hardly reads like the foundation text of a new world order.

The unVirgilian structure is matched by an unVirgilian style.[107] Virgil's writing in the *Aeneid* tends to the grave, the slow-moving, the opaque, the suggestive. Ovid, committed to narrative that swerves but never stops, lightens and quickens the movement of the verse, increasing the frequency of dactyls, reducing the number and roughness of elisions, with grammar and syntax put under contribution (e.g. double *que* on the model of Greek, use of the future participle). The seventeenth-century schoolmaster John Brinsley wrote that 'never heathen poet wrote more sweetly in such an easy and flowing vein'.[108] There is a continual witty dance of language created by a riot of figures (antithesis, syllepsis, paradox, oxymoron among the favourites), but this is not in general intimately bound to particular contexts. Springing from that dance, and despite the cruelty and heartlessness that characterizes most episodes some of the time and some episodes most of the time, is an intense joy and vitality which we might figure by the leap of the god in Titian's Ovidian *poesia*, *Bacchus and Ariadne*, now in the National Gallery, London. It is a style ideally suited to story-telling (in this like Homer's more than that of any other ancient poet). It is significant that, whereas in Virgil it is particular resonant

---

[106] *Met.* 1. 452–3; *Aen.* 1. 1 and 4. For Virgilian presences in this story and their possible significance see Nicoll (1980).
[107] For a good account see Kenney (1973).   [108] Quoted by Enterline (2000) 19.

combinations of words that we best remember, in Ovid it is rather narrative moments that depend comparatively little for their effect on their precise linguistic formulation. There seem to me at least two such in the story of Daphne: the first is when Apollo closes in pursuit and breathes down on Daphne's neck (542: *crinem sparsum cervicibus adflat*); the second when he feels her still racing heart beating beneath the bark (553–4: *positaque in stipite dextra | sentit adhuc trepidare novo sub cortice pectus*). In comparison with Virgil's we could call Ovid's a 'superficial' style, by which I mean that it depends on a supple fineness of surface, making me think of the words of Little Bilham in Henry James's *The Ambassadors* (book 5, chapter 1):

'I can only tell you that it's what they pass for. But isn't that enough? What more than a vain appearance does the wisest of us know? I commend you', the young man declared with a pleasant emphasis, 'the vain appearance'.

The story ends with the metamorphosis of Daphne, which provides an *aetion* for the association of Apollo with the laurel (or more strictly bay) and the founding of the Pythian games (where victory was rewarded with a laurel crown). With this Callimachean gesture Ovid weaves the story into his *perpetuum carmen*. The days have passed when scholars regularly argued that metamorphosis simply provided an artificial unifying theme for a disparate collection of tales. Now it is regarded as perhaps the poem's central trope ('turn', metamorphosis), involved in a complex play of sameness and difference. Totalizing accounts of its significance (like the view that it is a vehicle of clarification or concretizes metaphor[109]) fit some episodes much better than others. It may be better to regard metamorphosis in the *Metamorphoses* as an example of what Kant, as we have seen, calls an 'aesthetic idea', that is 'a representation of the imagination, annexed to a given concept, with which, in the free employment of imagination, such a multiplicity of partial representations are bound up, that no expression indicating a definite concept can be found for it'.[110] Such an aesthetic idea for Kant thus 'quickens the cognitive faculties' in a pleasure-inducing manner.

---

[109] So Solodow (1988), esp. chs. 5 and 6; see also Andrew Feldherr, 'Metamorphosis in the *Metamorphoses*' in Hardie (2002) 163–79.
[110] Kant (1952) 179 §49.

Just this one episode can send the mind racing with thoughts about metamorphosis. Daphne's transformation illustrates the point that change in the poem also involves continuity across the change (548–52):

> vix prece finita torpor gravis occupat artus,
> mollia cinguntur tenui praecordia libro,
> in frondem crines, in ramos bracchia crescunt,
> pes modo tam velox pigris radicibus haeret,
> ora cacumen habet: remanet nitor unus in illa.

Scarce has she finished her prayer when a heavy numbness seizes her limbs, the soft surface of her body is ringed with thin bark, her hair grows into leaves, her arms to branches, her foot just before so quick sticks in sluggish roots, a tree-top holds her face: brightness alone remains in her.

A woman 'changes' into a tree, but there is the same *nitor* (sheen, beauty) throughout. Deciding on the translation highlights the difficulty of identifying a precise moment of change. Indeed any translation (or imitation for that matter) can be said to involve appropriative metamorphosis bound up with paradoxes of sameness and difference. *Bracchium* is used of the human arm but also (literally? metaphorically? as a 'dead' metaphor?) of a tree's branch. Likewise *crines* is regularly used by poets to mean leaves as well as hair (or are they the same?).[111] *In ramos bracchia crescunt* would normally be translated, emphasizing difference, 'her arms grow to branches', but could also mean, asserting identity, 'her branches grow into branches'. *Pes*, like the English foot, can be used of many things, including plants, as well as persons. And what does the pronoun *illa* refer to—woman, tree, or tree-woman? Dryden, in his version of Pythagoras' speech from book 15, signals his awareness of such issues by means of a brilliant pun, taking metempsychosis as a figure for translation:

> All things are altered, nothing is destroyed,
> The shifted scene for some new show employed;
> . . . .
> Those very elements which we partake
> Alive, when dead some other bodies make,
> *Translated* grow, have sense or can discourse;
> But death on deathless substance has no force.

('Of the Pythagorean Philosophy' 388–9, 394–7, my italics)

[111] For *coma* in this episode see Hardie in Hardie, Barchiesi, Hinds (1999) 260.

The Aesthetic Turn

This fits nicely with a modern hermeneutic emphasis on meaning being not so much fixed as constantly reconstituted. Translation is a saying in other words, a constant negotiation of sameness-within-difference and difference-within-sameness. Does a translator find and reproduce something original and other that is really 'there', or does she construct Ovid in her own image? Charles Tomlinson finds the translator's world an Ovidian one of 'shifting shapes and changing identities' in which 'our major translators recover, carry over and transform the energies of past civilization'. And the stakes are high for the translator, because, as Tomlinson goes on to say, 'it will not be long before he realizes that it is *his* shape and *his* identity which are being called into question.'[112] On this occasion Dryden triumphantly passed the test; indeed his version might be thought more poetically alive than the 'original'; in what we might call the current 'revisionist' view of Dryden, he realizes himself most fully, is paradoxically at his most original, is or becomes most 'himself', in the best of his translations.

Throughout the description of Daphne's metamorphosis there is a constant slide of the signifier (the same word means differently) which allows for the expression of either change or stasis or both at once. One form of this is what we call a 'pun', for Ovid as much the fatal Cleopatra for which he lost the world and was content to lose it as it was (according to Dr Johnson[113]) for Shakespeare. Lynn Enterline finds in the poem what she calls a 'continual movement between literal and figural meanings'; those for whom metaphor goes all the way down may prefer to say 'between figural and figural meanings'.[114] Syllepsis ('dost sometimes counsel take—and sometimes tea') is perhaps Ovid's favourite figure, allowing him to glide smoothly and without seeming effort from one use of a word to

---

[112] Tomlinson (1983) 76, 73 (from ch. 4, 'Metamorphosis as Translation'). Ovid in the epilogue uses metempsychosis as a trope for poetic survival; see Hardie, 'Introduction' (2002) 3: 'The *Metamorphoses* closes with a reworking of Horace's ode on his own monumental fame (*Odes* 3. 30), in which Ovid looks forward to an eternity in which "I shall be read on the lips of the people" (*Met.* 15. 878). The Latin words, *ore legar populi*, could also be translated "I [i.e. my soul] shall be gathered on the lips of the people", hinting at an image of poetic tradition and transmission as a Pythagoreanizing re-embodiment of dead poets in the bodies of living poets—or living readers.'

[113] Wimsatt (1969) 68.   [114] Enterline (2000) 65.

another.[115] In the lines about Daphne from 'The Garden' quoted at the head of this section, the dendrophiliac Marvell not only puns on the word 'race' ('line' as well as 'racing competition'), but exploits a bilingual word play on Latin *ut* consecutive and *ut* final to confuse the result of Apollo's action with its purpose: what the story truly shows is that trees are more desirable than women.[116]

Daphne is changed into a tree. And, one could also argue, into a book, or a poem. Laurel is the outward and visible sign of the poet. Thus *liber* in Latin can be translated as both 'bark' and 'book', *pes* as both 'foot' and 'metrical foot'. *Gravis* (548), *mollis* (549), *tenuis* (549), and *novus* (554) are all also terms of style. Among the key words in the story are *forma* and *figura*—these can readily describe the shapely figure of the nymph, but *forma* can also refer to rhetorical modes of speech, literary forms, composition, *figura* to figures of speech, idioms, literary styles.[117] Apollo may lose the object of his desire, but he remains the god of poetry: 'Since you cannot be my bride, at any rate you will be my tree, my hair, my lyre, my quiver shall ever possess you, laurel' (557–9). Today's Ovid is relentlessly self-referential; the *Metamorphoses* is a meta-poem, a poem about writing poetry, already postmodern. Many of the principal characters of the poem are seen as artists, versions of their creator. For example, since spinning and weaving are metaphors for the writing of poetry, the fineness of the spider's web in the story of Arachne is easily seen as a figure for a refined modernist technique. In Tom Gunn's 'Arachne' from *After Ovid* we read that the spinner, 'exact artificer', lets out 'a fine, | And delicate yet tough and tensile line | That catches full day in the little room'—like Gunn's poetry, then, or Ovid's.[118] Earlier readers rather saw Ovid as creating a secondary world, reflecting the prior processes of creation (Ovid's creator-god is a maker, *mundi fabricator*, a craftsman of the world, *ille opifex rerum*, 1. 57, 79). Another poem in *After Ovid*, Robert Pinsky's 'Creation According

---

[115] See Hardie in Hardie, Barchiesi, Hinds (1999) 260: 'In one and the same word syllepsis fuses a metaphorical and a literal meaning, and the shuttling between the one and the other is a passage of linguistic metamorphosis, which mirrors the work performed by a narrative of metamorphosis in making concrete and giving temporal extension to the purely mental relationship of a metaphor.' There is rather too much reification in this analysis for it to be altogether Ovidian; nor are we talking only of binary oscillation.

[116] See Nuttall (1989) 92–3.   [117] Enterline (2000) 6–7, 31–2, 39, 63.

[118] Hofmann and Lasdun (1994) 145.

to Ovid', acknowledges that doubleness—creation is both outside and inside the poem:[119]

> The only sound
> A celestial humming, void of changes
> (*Playing the changes*, jazz musicians say).
> And then the warring elements churned forth
>
> The mother-father Shiva or Jehovah,
> The dancing god who took a hammer and smashed
> The atoms apart in rage and disarranged them
>
> Into a sun and moon, stars and elements,
> Ocean and land, the vegetation and creatures—
> Including even Ovid playing the changes
>
> In his melodious verses, including even
> God the creator...

Change in Ovid's poem is not, of course, restricted to the moments of bodily metamorphosis. The poem starts in grandly epical fashion with the world's creation and early history. The story of Apollo and Daphne and the appearance of Amor, god of love, triggers different generic associations, and thus introduces a tension between antagonistic genres, epic and love elegy.[120] The phrase *mutare figuram* (547) could be referred to a change of genre. As Ovid reruns features of the opening poem of *Amores* 1, we are in effect asked what such a love story is doing in an epic poem; and indeed in terms of language, topoi, and situations we seem to have changed generically and returned to an elegiac world.[121] Denied erotic satisfaction Apollo changes from the epic conqueror of the Python to the locked-out lover (*exclusus amator*) of elegy. At the end of the episode laurel trees stand guard over the house of Augustus; in an ironic reversal of the *recusatio*, elegy is returned to epic and compelled to celebrate martial triumph at the doorway (site of the rejected lover) of the emperor, a kind of inverse *paraklausithyron* (the lament of the lover at the closed door of his mistress). Thus throughout the story generic distinctions are

---

[119] Ibid. 92–3.
[120] See Nicoll (1980) 176: 'Cupid's arrow forces Apollo to abandon his epic-style arrogance.'
[121] We have seen that *primus amor* resonates with Aeneas' primacy in the story of Rome; it may also recall Propertius' *Cynthia prima* in the first poem of the *Monobiblos* (Nicoll (1980) 177).

simultaneously made and deconstructed. We recall that in Ovid's Chaos there was total sameness, a complete absence of difference (1. 6): *unus erat toto naturae vultus in orbe* ('there was one face of nature in the entire universe'). By contrast, in the world we know, meaning is conferred only by differentiation, but the price is that such differences can be endlessly reconfigured.

The word 'identity' is part of a discourse of sameness and difference. As we have seen, for centuries Ovid was admired for his insights into the human psyche. This aspect of his poetry is downplayed by classicists, fearful perhaps of self-exposure or accusations of lack of sophistication in a critical world uncomfortable with the notion of character and personality. Physical metamorphosis reminds the reader of the unstable nature of the self, 'an evanescent, fragile thing best grasped at the moment of its fading'.[122] Can a self change and yet remain in some sense the same? Questions of the kind interested Shakespeare, one of Ovid's most perceptive readers, who, according to Harold Bloom, invented human nature. In Vanda Zajko's words, for Shakespeare 'the fascination of change resides not in the shape-shifting of bodies but in its internal, psychological aspect, and in this aspect the process is continuous and potentially without end.'[123] We badly need a psychoanalytic reading of Ovid's greatest poem.

I have given above five ways of thinking about the transformation of one only of Ovid's characters. These are for exemplification merely; and myriad more will doubtless emerge as the poem's potential for meaning, its 'iterability', continues to be unfolded in the years ahead. And we should not forget the effect of metamorphosis for the tone and mood of the whole. The hybridization involved means that metamorphosis can usefully be seen as a form of an aesthetic of the grotesque, a form of doubleness found elsewhere in the culture of Augustan Rome. As Mary Barnard, who usefully examines the *Metamorphoses* under this sign, observes, the grotesque can be comic or disturbing or hallucinatory or all these things and more at the same time.[124] To quote Kant again, an aesthetic idea is a concept 'which language... can never get quite on level terms with or render completely intelligible' and 'to which no *intuition* (representation of the imagination) can be adequate'.[125]

---

[122] Enterline (2000) 18.   [123] Zajko (2004) 42.   [124] Barnard (1987).
[125] Kant (1952) 176 §49.

Apollo and Daphne is a story of attempted rape; indeed rape and 'violated bodies' are central to the poem, in such a way that beauty and sexual violence become more and more closely associated.[126] Amy Richlin's 'Reading Ovid's Rapes' confronts this issue in a powerful example of ideology critique; the *Metamorphoses* is seen as reflecting, and helping to sustain, a world of patriarchal values that encourage violence to women. The method is to read the poem against concepts in feminism (what Richlin calls 'the insertion of theory into the text'), and the result is a series of proposals for action ranging from blowing up the canon to resistance and reading against the grain.[127] Given the history of misogyny, it is hard not to have sympathy with Richlin's project, even if one doubts that the *Metamorphoses* is, in today's world, an especially powerful vector of patriarchal values and the processes that objectify women. Of course reading the poem aesthetically does not entail that we ignore its preoccupation with rape,[128] or exclude the thoughts that it may provoke about sexuality and gender—but it does mean that we should not aim merely to confirm what we already knew conceptually. We may find then that the poem can resist such attempts to master and control it. And clearly mastery and control are very much at issue in the story of Daphne, as in many others in the poem. The voluble Apollo delivers his speech on the run in a way that a reader who is not under threat can find comically incongruous; and significantly Apollo fails to interest, or persuade, the object of his desire. Ovid by contrast has been much more successful. One could say that any aetiological tale has a structure of expectation and its pleasing fulfilment that could be figured as a version of seduction[129]; the reader is satisfied only when the anticipated closure is achieved. If we continue reading, does this mean that we are necessarily acquiescing in our own seduction?

Guy Lee characterizes the story as in Ovid's 'lighter and wittier' vein,[130] and certainly it is told in characteristically sprightly fashion. As long as we decline to share the perspective of Daphne,

---

[126] Enterline (2000) 1, 31.
[127] Richlin (1992) 173, 178–9.
[128] Indeed we may think about rape—entertain it so to say—to a greater than usual extent; this is one of the reasons why aesthetics seems so dangerous to many. The *Metamorphoses* offers, in its various stories, a complex array of possible linkages between sex and violence and beauty and power and gender; no one such linkage can be privileged as finally authoritative.
[129] See Nagle (1988) esp. 32–4, 37–8, 46–7.   [130] Lee (1968) 119.

and concentrate on the somewhat absurd and pompous figure of Apollo, we may be amused and delighted. W. R. Johnson, while a sympathetic reader of Ovid, writes of 'the deceptively "lyrical" soft porn of Daphne's rape';[131] we might cite in particular the lines where the fleeing nymph's erotic allure is focalized through the desiring eyes of Apollo (527–30):

> nudabant corpora venti
> obviaque adversas vibrabant flamina vestes,
> et levis impulsos retro dabat aura capillos,
> auctaque forma fuga est.

The winds bared her body, the opposing breezes made her clothes flutter as she ran against them, and a light air flung back her streaming hair, and her beauty was increased by flight.

The eroticism and *esprit* of all this is brilliantly conveyed in Bernini's famous statue in the Villa Borghese, but he does not hesitate to depict as well the fear and horror that distort Daphne's features. And of course the story takes on a very different aspect if we adopt her point of view. Apollo's sense of her desirability seems only increased by her vulnerability and fear: 'O dear, I am afraid the brambles will tear your lovely skin'—the possible erotic frisson of this thought, as the would-be rapist pretends to be the victim's protector, hardly needs elaboration. This doubleness is enhanced by the hunting imagery where the conflation of epic and elegiac modes we have already looked at helps to create tensions in our response that are difficult to resolve.[132] Certainly the trope of the hunt of love takes on an unusually sinister aspect as Apollo is figured as wolf, lion, and hunting dog, Daphne as dove and hare.

Unsurprisingly Shakespeare was alert to such complexities. In the Induction of *The Taming of the Shrew* Sly is offered by the servants as possible entertainment a number of Ovidian pictures whose subjects prefigure the stories of sexual adventure and psychological change in the main body of the play, including one of Daphne (ii. 58–61):

---

[131] W. R. Johnson (1996) 22 n. 17.

[132] The simile of the hunting dog and the hare (533–9) ostentatiously recalls the simile from the pursuit of Turnus by Aeneas in *Aen.* 12. 749–55; but we think also of the hunt of love in elegy.

> Or Daphne roaming through a thorny wood,
> Scratching her legs that one shall swear she bleeds,
> And at that sight shall sad Apollo weep,
> So workmanly the blood and tears are shown.[133]

Unexpectedly Apollo may be outside, rather than inside, this so workmanly depiction (otherwise the 'so' would be illogical), creating a weird recess of viewing perspectives (Daphne observed by Apollo observed by the stage audience observed by the real audience); and as often female suffering is aestheticized into an art which gives pleasure, at least to men. It is unexpected too to find Apollo saddened by the spectacle of what he himself has done. But then the distribution of power within the sphere of the erotic may be a complicated matter in a way that the more upright sorts of moralizing analysis are reluctant to concede; Apollo's failure to fashion Daphne to his desires creates a painful gap that can never be filled, and this, whether she wants it or not, is a form of power. We shall see shortly that not all of the many women poets who have appropriated her story necessarily take her side.

The doubleness continues right to the episode's conclusion.[134] Has Daphne's agony ended or not? Has she retained something of herself unviolated, or has her selfhood been wholly destroyed? Is Apollo's adoption of the sign of the laurel a yet further act of appropriative violence,[135] or can it be read in a more positive spirit, as giving Daphne a kind of honourable acknowledgement (*honores*, 565)? Is the transformation in any way redeeming for her, or does her angry resistance persist to a bitter end (*refugit tamen oscula lignum*, 'the wood pulled back from his kisses', 556)? If the bark of Daphne earns a place in the book of Ovid, is that a reward or just a further instance of male arrogance?

> factis modo laurea ramis
> adnuit utque caput visa est agitasse cacumen.   (566–7)

The laurel waved her newly made branches, and seemed/was seen to move her top as though a head.

---

[133] For the analysis that follows I am substantially indebted to Zajko (2004).

[134] So R. Fowler (2005): 'The myth remains poised between horror and reassurance.'

[135] So Alice Fulton (Hofmann and Lasdun (1994) 50): 'Of course, he liked her better as a tree. "Girls *are* trees " | was his belief. Mediated | forms pleased him. "If you can't find a partner, use | a wooden chair," | he'd say.'

The equivocation of this, at once delicate and slightly wistful, is maintained by the verb *visa est* ('seemed' or 'was seen', and if the latter by whom?), while *ut* too keeps matters floating uncertainly. Is a still sentient woman making a genuine gesture of assent (or dissent), or is there merely a tree shaking in the wind, on to which Apollo, or Ovid, or we, can project our interpretative fantasies? We share these uncertainties with the rivers who come to Daphne's father Peneus, unsure whether to commiserate or offer congratulation (*nescia gratentur consolenturne parentem*, 578).[136]

Since the seventeenth century, and above all in our own time (as recent work by Rowena Fowler and Sarah Annes Brown has shown), women writers have shown an interest in the story of Apollo and Daphne as great as, or greater, than men; the list includes Aphra Behn, Elizabeth Carter, Virginia Woolf, Eavan Boland, Jorie Graham, Alice Fulton, Jenny Joseph, Phoebe Hesketh, Linda Pastan, Sylvia Plath, Anne Sexton, A. E. Stallings, and doubtless many others.[137] Of course this is partly because they want to bend the story to their own, sometimes explicitly feminist, purposes, or are writing in a spirit of opposition. But the results are still partly a product of what Ovid wrote, exploiting the doubleness that I have been presenting as part of Ovid's virtue:

> She'll tell
> her story
> rather than be held inside its web. There are holes—
> have you noticed—
> where the seams don't quite close? Daphne peers through
> those gaps.
> She scans the sky and plans to stare—you can almost hear her
> glance—
> down the air, the blank, the optical until
> a face stares back.[138]

This is from Alice Fulton's coolly fashionable and postmodern 'Daphne and Apollo', her contribution to *After Ovid*. Tree-bark may seem impenetrable and all-encompassing, but there are cracks after all—enacted here by the enjambment between 'peers through' and 'those gaps'—through which other voices can speak

---

[136] See too Feldherr in Hardie (2002) 172–4.
[137] See R. Fowler (2005) and Brown (2004).
[138] Hofmann and Lasdun (1994) 55.

(we remember the horrific image of baby Adonis breaking out through the bark of his mother, now a myrrh tree). In this way Ovid can readily be made to yield a Derridean message about textuality. Stallings's Daphne answers back Apollo—the sun god who provides the chlorophyll that enables the growth of plants, and also 'Poet, Singer, Necromancer' (Ovid, then, as well as Apollo), concluding:

> I may give in; I do not lose.
> Your hot stare cannot stop my shivering,
> With delight, if I so choose.

Apollo's hot breath has been replaced by the hot stare of the sun, a version no doubt of the male gaze, but not one to intimidate this Daphne. The reader is initially misled by the comma after 'shivering', but in the end encounters a shiver of delight. If so I choose.[139]

A number of these poets think that Daphne's choice may not have been the best one.[140] In Boland's 'The Women' Daphne, in flight from the god's hot breath, 'fell and grieved and healed into myth'.[141] But in 'Daphne with her Thighs in Bark' she regrets that she rejected Apollo, and advises others to act differently:

> I have written this
>
> so that,
> in the next myth,
> my sister will be wiser.
>
> Let her learn from me:
>
> the opposite of passion
> is not virtue
> but routine.
>
> . . . . .
>
> Save face, sister.
> Fall. Stumble.
> Rut with him.
> His rough heat will keep you warm and
> you will be better off than me,

---

[139] Stallings (1999) 67, 'Daphne'.
[140] So too Sylvia Plath, 'Virgin in a Tree,' and Anne Sexton, 'Where I Live in this Honorable House of the Laurel Tree' (included in *Complete Poems*, 1981).
[141] Boland (1995) 114.

> with your memories
> down the garden,
> at the start of March,
> unable to keep your eyes
> off the chestnut tree —
>
> just the way
> it thrusts and hardens.[142]

In the concluding phallic image woman's sexual desire is frankly acknowledged. Such concerns can be traced back to the tradition of the moralized, allegorized Ovid of the Middle Ages and Renaissance. Ovid's seventeenth-century translator, George Sandys, in his commentary, reads the story *in bono* 'to show what immortal honour a virgin obtains by preserving her chastity'.[143] By contrast John Brinsley is worried by her cult of virginity; a 'malcontent' she lives 'all alone without a husband, ranging of the unwayed woods' (after her transformation he shows more approval).[144] Through the androgynous figure of her man/woman protagonist Woolf, in her novel *Orlando*, seeks to resolve such antinomies. And again Daphne (the subject of a tapestry in the great house where Orlando lives) is put to use, her story reconfigured as a relationship of harmony and equality between male and female.[145] To hunt and be hunted, in the world of eros, can then become properly a source of delight, for both sexes:

> Then she had pursued, now she fled. Which is the greater ecstasy? The man's or the woman's? And are they not perhaps the same? No, she thought, this is most delicious.... For nothing, she thought... is more heavenly than to resist and to yield; to yield and to resist.[146]

Similarly, in an episode by an oak tree where he merges with nature, Orlando can become both lover and tree, with 'all the fertility and amorous activity of a summer's evening... woven web-like about his body'.[147] Woolf was perhaps responding not directly to Ovid, but to an Ovid mediated through Shakespearean comedy. Nonetheless, as Enterline has it, all such 'revisionary returns to Ovid's poem ask us to consider whether the "other", new meanings

---

[142] Boland (1995), 80–1.   [143] Sandys (1970) 74.
[144] Cited in Enterline (2000) 19.   [145] See also Brown (1999) ch. 11.
[146] Woolf (1993) 109. For the tapestry of Daphne and the hunters see pp. 76 and 218.
[147] Ibid. 15.

revealed in later poetry "might already have been 'meant' by the original" narrative.'[148] Metamorphosis continues, as the poem is reread and reinterpreted. To be at once the same and different, is that not somewhere near the heart of the virtue of Ovid's *Metamorphoses*?[149]

IV

Pater never indulges in negative criticism; he writes to isolate the 'virtue' only of an artist or writer. In this he can perhaps be regarded as a good Kantian. It is striking that, in the Third Critique (apart from the reference to 'pleasure or displeasure' in the opening sentence), the judgement of taste seems always to take a positive form ('this is beautiful'). One can see why this might be so. Negative aesthetic judgements characteristically operate by putting the object under a concept ('this is not beautiful because it is not unified', or whatever). Perhaps, on this model, we should say that when we do not find an object beautiful, we withhold the judgement, refrain from making it, rather than make a negative judgement (indeed, within art at least, 'ugliness' can become a positive quality). Eighteenth-century critics such as Johnson liked to list both the faults and the virtues of writers, as a sign of their judiciousness[150] (so Johnson, as we have just seen, condemns Shakespeare's fondness for verbal quibbling). The trouble is that the 'faults' are often quite as much part of what makes a work of art distinctive as the 'virtues'. With the authors—as with anyone—we love we cannot easily separate the two out. Dickens without his awkwardnesses, his sentimentality, his extravagance, would simply not be Dickens.[151]

The issue is of particular importance with Lucan, the last of the Latin poets with which this chapter will deal. The trajectory

---

[148] Enterline (2000) 58 (she is quoting Claire Nouvet).
[149] This is my second attempt to isolate the virtue of Ovid. For the first see Martindale (1988) 1–20; I think it fair to say that this has had no discernible influence on classicists.
[150] Cf. John J. Joughin, 'Shakespeare's Genius: *Hamlet*, Adaptation and the Work of Following', Joughin and Malpas (2003) 134–6.
[151] There is a theological version of this argument, advanced by Augustine and others. If God is perfection, anything created as a not-God-thing must be imperfect, creation necessarily implying differentiation; to complain about human imperfection is thus in effect to want your creation cancelled, like asking a tiger not to be tigerish.

of Lucan's reputation is comparable with Ovid's, though in a notably more drastic manner. Until the eighteenth century his epic was held in sufficient esteem for him to be compared seriously with Virgil. The introduction to Nicholas Rowe's translation published in 1719 (the finest in English of the whole work) by the Whig writer James Welwood includes a conventional rhetorical comparison (*synkrisis*) of the *Pharsalia*[152] and the *Aeneid*, which assumes at least a rough balance of advantage and disadvantage between them. But in the later nineteenth century the *Pharsalia*, condemned as rhetoric not poetry and the product of a 'silver' age of decadence, suffered a catastrophic fall from grace. And it is only in the last forty or so years—partly as a result of the questioning of institutional traditions in the 1960s and thereafter—that its reputation within the classical profession has risen significantly, with some of the ablest Latinists again treating Lucan with the kind of respect that is shown to other 'major' Latin poets.[153] The issue of good and bad taste often features in discussions of what we might call Lucan's extremist poetics and was already exercising Lucan's Whig admirers in the eighteenth century:

> What though thy early, uncorrected page
> Betrays some marks of a degenerate age,
> Though many a tumid point thy verse contains,
> Like warts projecting from Herculean veins,
> Though like thy Cato thy stern Muse appear,
> Her manners rigid and her frown austere,
> Like him, still breathing freedom's genuine flame,
> Justice her idol, public good her aim,
> Well she supplies her want of softer art
> By all the sterling treasures of the heart,
> By energy, from independence caught,
> And the free vigour of unborrowed thought.[154]

---

[152] As a student of reception I shall use this, the traditional title of the poem, throughout; probably Lucan's own title was *De Bello Civili*, echoing that of Caesar's account of the civil war which the poem contests.

[153] Meritorious studies include: Bramble (1982); W. R. Johnson (1987); Henderson (1988); Feeney (1991); Masters (1992); Hardie (1993); Bartsch (1997); Leigh (1997). For myself Lucan has been an indispensable poetic point of reference since I first read book 1 in 1967: see in particular Martindale (1976) and (1993a) 48–53, 64–72, and Brown and Martindale (1998) pp. xvii–xxx.   [154] Cited in Gillespie (1988) 146–7.

So wrote William Hayley in *An Essay upon Epic Poetry* (1782): for him Lucan's 'faults' of taste (seen as in part the result of his living in a decadent age) were offset by his commitment to liberty and independence of mind.

Appeals to taste can hide ideological factors that may be involved in the construction of an aesthetic sphere; and in the case of a poem as overtly transgressive as the *Pharsalia* it is important to scrutinize supposedly 'literary' judgements to see what concealed political subtexts they may contain. One may hate, as well as love, Lucan for political reasons. W. E. Heitland, in his essay on Lucan which served as the introduction to C. E. Haskins's useful edition of 1887, has a section entitled 'four characteristic defects'. These include the excessive use of hyperbole, long lists or enumerations, overloading with detail so that 'the clearness of a picture is marred', and lengthy narratives of a descriptive or moralizing character by which the poem becomes 'a vehicle for carrying great quantities of utterly irrelevant matter'.[155] Taken together, these defects amount to most of the qualities that make reading the *Pharsalia* a distinctive aesthetic experience. Again and again I find Heitland censuring the episodes that are my especial favourites. Among these is Caesar's visit to Troy (9. 961-99), a sardonic parody, or deformation, of Aeneas' arrival at Pallanteum in *Aeneid* 8; this Heitland describes as 'a melancholy instance of misused possibilities... where the effect of the situation is lost in the attempt to moralize and catalogue at once'.[156] To my mind it would be hard to find another episode into which Lucan has concentrated so much in such little space. Where Aeneas walks, accompanied by the dignified Evander, over the site of Rome, future capital of the world, Caesar, tourist in a hurry, is led by a garrulous cicerone around the ruins of Troy, symbolic of the Republic he is destroying. We have a whole series of ironic contrasts: Troy is a city of the past, ruined, trampled underfoot by a visitor indifferent to the resonance of its vestigial monuments; Caesar's prayer to the gods and talk of 'my' Aeneas (991) is egotistical, impious, the words of a hypocrite (the Virgilian typology which associates Aeneas and the Caesars is thereby undermined);

---

[155] Heitland (1887) p. lxxii.
[156] Ibid. p. lxxvi.

a dry tone[157] and cynicism about myth replaces Virgil's evocative contrasts between past, present, and future (we see a glimpse of the ancient 'tourist industry' as Caesar is shown the spot where, for example, the Judgement of Paris took place). 'There is no literary resurrection from these monuments'[158]—every rock is a tomb; *etiam periere ruinae* (969: 'even the ruins have perished'). Troy was the origin of the Homeric epic tradition, and Virgil had traced there, in Laomedon's treachery[159], the origins of civil war. (Throughout Lucan's epic we find a sense of sterility in respect of that tradition, a 'self-consciously terminal'[160] relationship with epic, a drive to destruction.) This is the moment Lucan chooses to offer his sardonic version of the topos that poetry confers fame and is more durable than any monument, beginning *o sacer et magnus vatum labor!* (980: 'o sacred/accursed and mighty task of bards'). *Magnus*, as the soubriquet of the shadowy Pompey, *magni nominis umbra* (1. 135: 'shade of a mighty name'), is a word that has become increasingly freighted with irony. Pompey was great, but is now a mere name, a shadow of Aeneas and of a myth of history that has failed;[161] the great name, most potent of signifiers, is and will ever be Caesar. Alexander the Great, for Lucan the type of the tyrant, had visited Troy and envied Achilles who had Homer to sing his praises; Caesar, the new Alexander, has found his bard in a Lucan who displays self-loathing and contempt for the debased currency of epic, and the two of them will be linked like siamese twins in a grim eternity of fame: *Pharsalia nostra | vivet et a nullo tenebris damnabitur aevo* (985–6: 'Our Pharsalia (i.e. fought by you, described by me) will live, and will be damned to darkness by no age'). 'The apostrophe to the immortal power of poetry', Colin Burrow writes tellingly, 'echoes in this deathly landscape with the misplaced shrillness of an erotic giggle in a catacomb.'[162] The *Pharsalia* would be worth reading for this episode alone.

In this regard it is striking how often the poets who most admired Lucan are particularly responsive to those parts of the *Pharsalia* that

---

[157] But the vocabulary is full of words that resonate with the Virgilian episode or with the rest of Lucan's poem; these include *fama, mirator, harena, vates, umbra, exustus, nomen, memorabilis, magnus, vestigium, putris, truncus, ruina, silva, saxum, fatum, visus, vetustas, caespes, sedes, pius, populus, Romanus.*
[158] Burrow (1993) 181. [159] *Georgic* 1. 502. [160] Burrow (1993) 181.
[161] W. R. Johnson (1987) 67, 69, 72–3, 95. [162] Burrow (1993) 182.

conventional twentieth-century criticism (like Heitland's in the nineteenth) censures for their excess. These include the extravagant sequence in book 9, which many have found ridiculous and disgusting[163], where Cato's army is attacked in the desert by a host of what Robert Graves calls 'fantastically unzoological serpents',[164] in a bizarre series of 'etymological deaths'.[165] For example, Nasidius, who is bitten by a *prester* (whose name is connected with the Greek words for 'to swell' and 'to burn') is burned and swollen into a featureless mass (789–804):

>   ecce, subit facies leto diversa fluenti.
>   Nasidium Marsi cultorem torridus agri   790
>   percussit prester. illi rubor igneus ora
>   succendit, tenditque cutem pereunte figura
>   miscens cuncta tumor; toto iam corpore maior
>   humanumque egressa modum super omnia membra
>   efflatur sanies late pollente veneno;   795
>   ipse latet penitus congesto corpore mersus
>   nec lorica tenet distenti pectoris auctum.
>   spumeus accenso non sic exundat aeno
>   undarum cumulus, nec tantos carbasa Coro
>   curvavere sinus. tumidos iam non capit artus   800
>   informis globus et confuso pondere truncus.
>   intactum volucrum rostris epulasque daturum
>   haud inpune feris non ausi tradere busto
>   nondum stante modo crescens fugere cadaver.

Look, a form of death came next opposite to death by liquefaction. A burning *prester* struck Nasidius, tiller of Marsian field. A fiery redness made his face light up, and a swelling that confused everything stretched the skin, as the shape perished. Now larger than the whole body and going beyond human bound, the discharge is exuded over all the limbs, as the poison grew powerful far and wide. The man himself deeply buried within his bloated body disappears, nor could his breastplate contain the growth of his swollen chest. The foaming mass of water does not pour forth as strongly from a heated cauldron, nor do sails curve such billowings in the storm wind. The shapeless mass and trunk with its matter confused can no longer contain the swollen limbs. Untouched by the beaks of birds and not without harm destined to provide feasts for wild animals, daring not to consign it to the pyre, since the quantity was not yet stationary, they fled a corpse that grew.

---

[163] Bartsch (1997) 31 (Bartsch herself does not endorse this judgement).
[164] Graves (1956), introd. 22. Graves calls Lucan 'the father of yellow journalism' (p. 13).
[165] I owe this phrase to J. C. Bramble.

The ruthless following through of the etymological implications of the snake's name fuels a kind of grotesque linguistic dance, in this grisly version of Ovidian metamorphosis (could *Nas*idius hint at Ovid's name, Publius Ovidius *Naso*?). Paradoxes abound. The terrible fate of warriors in the *Iliad* is to lie unburied, food for birds and beasts of prey; here such creatures would themselves die if they feasted on the bloated corpse. Normally dead bodies decompose and disintegrate; here one goes on growing. Traditional heroism is impossible in such a world; all one can do is flee (even philosophy is impotent) or (as a reader) look—spectacle and specularity are central to this poem.[166] In his account of civil war as a *theatrum mundi*, Lucan constantly evokes the gladiatorial arena; we can read this passage as a perverse *venatio*, in which a snake hunts a man. Possible allegorizations readily suggest themselves. The fiery death of Nasidius could figure the effects of anger or other debilitating emotions as diagnosed by Stoic writers like the younger Seneca (Lucan's uncle). The dissolution of the bounds of the male human body, a sort of effeminization of a Roman warrior transformed into a leaky flux, suits a narrative of civil war where all proper boundaries are transgressed. A preoccupation with dismemberment, fragmentation, and body parts and with the aestheticization of violence marks the whole poem (one might compare the aesthetic of the films of David Lynch).[167] Critics may worry about the reader's guilty complicity, but an art (like Virgil's) which privileges wholeness is no less free from repressive ideologies than one which aestheticizes the damage done to human bodies. Alternatively, since struggle with a serpent constitutes a common mythic pattern, the sufferings of Cato's men can, on another reading, become a modern form of epic heroism, 'a mighty work of virtue' (*magnum virtutis opus*, 9. 381), as Cato puts it in his hortatory speech: *durum iter ad leges patriaeque ruentis amorem* (9. 385: 'hard is the way to legality and love of country in her fall').

The episode of the snakes was often picked out for special obloquy by the more orthodox kind of critic of the last two centuries. By contrast Rowe's argument to book 9 calls it 'perhaps the most poetical part of this whole work'. Certainly it caught the imagination of three great poets, Dante, Milton, and Shelley. Milton used it for his description of the transformation of Satan

---

[166] See in particular Leigh (1997).   [167] See Most (1992).

('the infernal serpent') and the other devils into snakes in *Paradise Lost* 10. Partly no doubt out of admiration for Lucan's Republicanism, Shelley described the *Pharsalia* as 'a poem as it appears to me of wonderful genius, and transcending Virgil'.[168] And in *Adonais* Lucan, victim of Nero, 'by his death approved', is one of the writers untimely dead who mourn for the loss of the youthful Keats. In *Prometheus Unbound* a powerful image is made of a fusion of a particularly resonant and famous passage from *Hamlet*

> O that this too too solid flesh would melt,
> Thaw, and resolve itself into a dew...

with the memory of Lucan's Sabellus, whose bodily dissolution follows from the bite of a *seps*, another virtuoso etymological death (*seps* comes from the word to dissolve or make putrid):

> all my being,
> Like him whom the Numidian seps did thaw
> Into a dew with poison, is dissolved.   (III. i. 39–41)

This particular conjuncture in the mind of a great poet suggests that Lucan's lines—which Macaulay found 'as detestable as Cibber's Birthday Odes'[169]—may have their own peculiar power. Of course one could argue that it is wrong to take pleasure in the description of such horrors; but that is a moral, not an aesthetic objection. I suspect that, if you cannot take any pleasure in Lucan's snakes, you will never be much of an admirer of the *Pharsalia*.

For Dante Lucan was *quello grande poeta* (*Convivio* 4. 28. 13); so impressive was his Cato that he could become a figure for God Himself, and later in the *Commedia* made into the guardian of Mount Purgatory, despite having been a suicide (within Christianity a mortal sin) and an opponent of Julius Caesar whom Dante, a believer in a universal monarchy, commended as the first Roman Emperor. In *Inferno* 4 Lucan is among a small group of *auctores*, canonical classical poets, whom Dante encounters in Limbo and with whom, by implication, he claims equality. Indeed, along with Virgil and Ovid, Lucan is the Roman poet most powerfully evoked in Dante's Hell; Lucan's *terribilità*, in the combination of wickedness and violence and horror and black humour and ostentatious verbal paradox, constitutes a dominant strand within the *Inferno*.

---

[168] For Lucan and Shelley see Dilke (1972) 104–5.   [169] Cited Duff (1928) p. xii.

Dante's chamber of horrors is constructed, to a large extent, out of puns and wordplays, creating a kind of Poundian *logopoeia*[170] in a way that recalls the style of Lucan. And he appears to have grasped that parts of the *Pharsalia* can be read as a form of sardonic humour, something which, among modern critics, only W. R. Johnson and Jamie Masters have recognized. Lucan frequently substitutes for the solemnities of earlier epic an absurdist mode which Johnson calls the 'comic-ugly'.[171] When in canto 25 Dante describes the metamorphosis of some Florentine thieves into serpents, he bids the classical masters of metamorphosis be silent, in a striking version of what E. R. Curtius termed the outdoing topos which Lucan himself had used: 'Let Lucan now be silent with his tales of wretched Sabellus and Nasidius, and let him wait to hear what now comes forth! Let Ovid be silent...' Dante, whose reading of the *Pharsalia* shows an exceptional awareness of the text's possible implications, reworks the material, in a *tour de force* of imitative virtuosity, to exhibit the dissolution of personality that attends the thieves' destruction of the proper boundaries which divide self and other, what is mine from what is yours. Dante goes one better than Lucan by making an etymological death into a literary punishment that fits the crime.

The *Pharsalia* is easily construed as a political poem, so it is unsurprising that readings abound in which the movement of signification is from aesthetics to politics. It is also the case that many of the admirers of the *Pharsalia* have held to a version of Republican politics and been attracted to Lucan's apparent espousal of 'liberty' and hatred for one-man rule. (There have been exceptions, most notably Dante, a committed imperialist, who argued in his *De Monarchia* that in a universal monarchy the Emperor in possessing all would be free from all appetite.) The Dutch scholar Hugo Grotius, who edited the *Pharsalia*, called Lucan *poeta phileleutheros*, the freedom-loving poet, while Louis XIV excluded the poem from the classical texts to be edited *ad usum Delphini*, for the use of the heir to the French throne. In particular from the seventeenth to

---

[170] 'Poetry that is akin to nothing but language, which is a dance of the intelligence among words and ideas, and modification of ideas and words' (quoted in connection with Lucan by Bramble (1982) 541, from *The Little Review*, 1918).

[171] W. R. Johnson (1987) 56; cf. pp. xi–xii, 57–58. 'Grotesque', as used e.g. by Victor Hugo, would be another useful term.

the nineteenth century Lucanian aristocratic *libertas* proved easily recuperable for modern liberty and Republicanism, at the hands of cohorts of Whigs, radicals, revolutionaries, and Romantics. Among many tributes one may cite these eloquent words of the nineteenth-century man of letters Pietro Giordani, friend of Leopardi:

> So it seemed to me really sacred, and to be preferred to any other, this poem which took as its matter not the foundation or the conquest of a kingdom, not some curious or rare navigation, not the gods of a people or an age, but the funeral of Liberty, universally and eternally divine, which even if it could be driven into exile from the world, could not lose its right to reign there.[172]

At certain moments in history the *Pharsalia* thus contributed to a Republican discourse that produced political effects. A line from the poem, *ignorantque datos, ne quisquam serviat, enses* (4. 579: 'men are ignorant that the purpose of the sword is to save every man from slavery'), was inscribed on the sabres of the national guard of the First Republic in France after the Revolution.[173] Of course to admire the *Pharsalia* because you share, or think you share, in its political vision, or to pursue particular goals, is not to make a pure judgement of taste.

The Republican reading of the *Pharsalia* has often been linked to an author-centred account. According to our sources Lucan after a successful early career at court was eventually forbidden by Nero to recite or publish (whether because of ideological objections to the poem, or for more personal reasons). He joined a conspiracy to overthrow the Emperor, which was discovered, and, on Nero's orders, he committed suicide in AD 65, aged 25, his poem apparently still unfinished. Thus the sense of the *Pharsalia* as the poem of freedom was strengthened by certain events in Lucan's 'life', or what we might call 'the Lucan myth'. The precociously talented poet becomes the 'standard-bearer' of a conspiracy against Nero and dies by his own hand, the youthful victim of tyranny, declaiming, as a last act of defiance, lines from the *Pharsalia* that the jealous Emperor had forbidden him to recite. Readers less entranced by the poem often dwell on less reputable elements in the story, Lucan's

---

[172] Cited by J. H. Whitfield in Bolgar (1979) 142. For Lucan's reception see Gillespie (1988) 139–49; Martindale (1993a) 64–72; Conte (1994b) 449–51.
[173] Conte (1994b) 451.

earlier successes as a courtier, his anger at Nero's snub in walking out of a recitation, and his supposed attempt to escape the Emperor's wrath by implicating his own mother, Acilia (though whether there is any factual basis for this or any of the other stories is something we shall never know).

If we look to the poem's reception, then, Lucan's has been regarded in the main as 'a serious Republican voice'.[174] But the *Pharsalia* can be, and has been, appropriated for other political positions. Modern scholars sometimes argue that the apparent Republicanism is for rhetorical effect merely, or that Lucan intended to end with the praise of a Neronian principate. More popular are various forms of deconstructive readings, in which the poem enacts a kind of deconstruction of epic forms and styles, and is divided between a Republican and a Caesarean voice. The *Pharsalia* as an epic of the losers[175] is necessarily bound in to traditional epic even while it denounces or undoes it (is this always the case with any form of deconstructionism?). In civil war power is contested, and this produces a fragmented narrative, at war with itself; in Jamie Masters's words, 'It is...mimicry of civil war, of divided unity, *concordia discors*, that has produced this split in the authorial, dominating, legitimising persona, this one poet many poets, this schizophrenia, the fractured voice.'[176] In some versions we approach a form of nihilism. Thus for W. R. Johnson, 'In Lucan's universe great men are momentary monsters, brief, ironic patterns glimpsed in the wild kaleidoscope of history, phantoms disgorged by a chaos, which masquerades as order, to mock the arrogant lie of rational order, to reveal the delusion of rational purpose, and to unmask at last the true nature of rational violence.'[177] In the end the poem peters out, unfinished, *mediis in rebus*, without satisfying closure—this non-ending, even if the result of Lucan's enforced suicide, has a sinister appropriateness, for the poet can offer us no satisfactory conclusions (except perhaps death, or the destruction of the universe) but only the unending gladiatorial contest between

---

[174] Leigh (1997) 157.
[175] On this see Quint (1993).
[176] Masters (1992) 90; cf. 10, 214–15.
[177] W. R. Johnson (1987) 19; cf. preface, p. x: 'The *Pharsalia*...has no privileged center except for the energetic, bitter, and witty skepticism that devotes itself to demolishing the structures it erects as fast as it erects them.' By contrast, Bartsch (1997) attempts a deconstructive reading more consonant with Rortian liberal pragmatism.

Liberty and Caesar: *par quod semper habemus | libertas et Caesar* (7. 695–6).

The reception history suggests that readers turn with particular enthusiasm to the *Pharsalia* at times, like the period of the English Civil War[178] or the French Revolution, when Lucan's supposed political vision seems relevant and urgent. One might argue that if Lucan is to continue to attract readers in the conditions of the twenty-first century, when Roman Republicanism might seem rather remote from current political concerns, critics need rather to give aesthetic reasons why we should continue to read the *Pharsalia*.[179] The nearest we have to a sophisticated 'art for art's sake' reading comes from Jamie Masters in his essay 'Deceiving the Reader' of 1994, which seems significantly to modify his previous (highly influential) account of two years earlier. Masters argues that the *Pharsalia* is not a committed poem, but rather a parody of such a poem, 'a *reductio ad absurdum* of politically committed writing': 'The response of the "intelligent reader" to Lucan's political tub-thumping is to be amused by it.'[180] Part of the trouble with this is that many intelligent readers have responded very differently. More worrying is the reduction of the poem's impact to amusement, and the bracketing-off of its ostensible 'content' (once again with the danger of a reductive formalism). When Masters's argument does take a political/ethical turn, it risks mere banality: 'Its message, if it has one at all, may be irresponsible and opportunistic (everything is fair game for the satirist) or nihilistic (all existing systems are ripe for deconstruction in this senseless world). Ultimately what we will "learn" from Lucan's propagandistic excesses is that truth is a matter of interpretation; history means what you want it to mean.'[181] 'Ultimately' is not a deconstructionist's word, and Masters also seeks to ground his reading in the poem's original context and in Lucan's intentions (matters pretty speculative). But what seems most evident about his account is how redolent it is of a certain phase of postmodernism, what we might call the

---

[178] On this see Norbrook (1999), esp. ch. 1.
[179] Alternatively we might argue, with John Henderson, for the poem's continued political applicability.
[180] Masters (1994) 168.
[181] Ibid. 168–9; cf. p. 171: 'the poem itself is too radically irresponsible for it to have been intended as any kind of manifesto for rebellion, or any serious attempt to persuade anyone of the justice of any cause.'

'post-political' (and, in that sense, very far from my own project). To the victims of tyranny ancient or modern it might not seem so deep a truth that history means what you want it to mean. In an essay on *Coriolanus* William Hazlitt characterizes the poetic imagination in general (and, we might add, critical interpretation) as 'right-royal' so that it 'naturally falls in with the language of power'.[182] Its Republicanism—if we are not too swift to deconstruct it—may be what makes the *Pharsalia* so unusual among epic poems, even if it means that the writing can appear partly to run against the grain of poetry. Since cause and effect are necessarily instrumentalized (since it matters which comes first), one can see Lucan's deconstruction of cause-and-effect narrative as, *inter alia*, an aesthetic gesture.

Still, it is certainly useful to be reminded that, when we contemplate Lucan's transgressive poetics and politics, it may not be as easy as we think to determine which drives the other.[183] It is generally believed that the aesthetic occludes the political; it is just as possible that the occlusion can work the other way round. As I suggested in the first chapter, contemporary enthusiasm for Ovid and Lucan could be aesthetic in origin, using the supposedly anti-establishment politics of the two writers as a cloak that makes respectable a particular taste (I am not suggesting that this is a conscious matter, of course). And undoubtedly it is important to be alert to the aesthetic impact of the *Pharsalia*, what Masters calls its 'uncanny and perverse brilliance'.[184] In that regard how might we try to isolate the 'virtue' of Lucan? First, there is, throughout the *Pharsalia*, a peculiarly relentless drive to verbal point. Margaret Hubbard, writing of Propertius, comments:

The Latin poets nearest to him in this respect are probably Juvenal and Lucan: all three of them work within a rhetorical and poetical tradition that leads the reader to expect that *b* will follow *a*; all three of them exploit this fact and aim at the surprise of paradox, where the cultivated reader is expected to savour the collocation of *a*

---

[182] Quoted by Quint (1993) 208.
[183] So Masters (1994) 156: 'Lucan's poetics are prior to his politics.' Masters draws the conclusion that the *Pharsalia* can work, for 'the ideal reader', as 'pure literature' (p. 168). I would argue that this issue of priority is irrelevant within the aesthetic.
[184] Masters (1994) 168.

and not-*b*. This is a poetry of wit, in a sense more familiar to the seventeenth and eighteenth centuries than to our own.[185]

Propertius, in the *Monobiblos* at least, writes in a sprightly and polished vein. Lucan rather aims at a distinctive and severe 'ponderosity'[186], avoiding sensuous suggestiveness and metrical refinement (the first foot is usually a disyllabic spondee) and achieving an astringent declamatory brilliance (with frequent apostrophes, exclamations, rhetorical questions, *sententiae*); in the words of Lucan's epitaph this is the style of speaking that strikes home (*dictio quae feriet*), and in this vein Lucan has few if any peers.

Examples of such 'wit' can be found on every page, but a few, randomly selected examples will give the flavour.[187] In book 1 the senators and others desert Rome (503–4): *sic urbe relicta | in bellum fugitur* ('thus, the city left, there is a flight—to war') This is a paradoxical *sententia* of remarkable brevity: one normally flees from war, not to it. In book 4 Curio is defeated by the Moors, and his troops are so closely packed that the dead bodies cannot fall to the ground (787): *conpressum turba stetit omne cadaver* ('pressed together by the mass there stood upright every corpse'). The climactic word *cadaver* is connected etymologically with *cadere*, 'to fall', so that the abnormal situation is piquantly described in terms of something that stands falling. In book 5 a calm at sea is presented as an anti-storm, a description that climaxes in a capping sardonic paradox (455): *naufragii spes omnis abit* ('all hope of shipwreck is lost'). Later for his description of the storm that prevents Caesar from crossing the Adriatic, Lucan takes the standard tropes and pushes them to a bizarre logical extreme. Thus, in a version of the traditional 'battle of the winds', Lucan examines the logical absurdity of the hyperbole, observing that if they really all blew together, they would cancel each other out (649): *omni surgit ratis*

---

[185] Hubbard (1974) 6 (of course such wit is also common in Wilde and other 19th-century aesthetes). One could compare Dr Johnson's classicizing criticism of the English Metaphysical poets for 'thoughts so far-fetched as to be not only unexpected but unnatural' and for leaving 'not only reason but fancy behind them' in their use of 'amplification'. Johnson stresses the *intellectual* quality of the results: 'To write on their plan,' he observes, 'it was at least necessary to read and think' (S. Johnson (1905) 18–19).

[186] See Mayer (1981) 10 (Mayer borrows the word from H. E. Butler). Mayer, despite the negative slant, gives an account of this style that is not without insight, pp. 10–25; see also Bramble (1982), esp. 541–2.

[187] For a fuller account see Martindale (1976).

ardua vento ('all the winds blowing, the ship rose completely upright'). In book 6, when the witch raises a corpse of a Pompeian soldier from the dead, Lucan apostrophizes him thus (724–5):

> a miser, extremum cui mortis munus inique
> eripitur, non posse mori.

poor wretch, from whom the last gift of death is unfairly snatched, the incapacity to die.

Many scholars suppose the meaning to be that the dead soldier was not allowed to die, and take the *munus* as the ability to die; this is to ignore the *non*, and assign to Lucan a commonplace thought. The meaning is more ingenious: once a man dies he is exempt from death, but this soldier is destined to die twice. This unremitting display of verbal fireworks makes reading the *Pharsalia* an exhausting if pleasurable experience. Thus there can be said to be a—paradoxical—harmony of form and content, and the reader's experience parallels the narrative.

Lucan modernizes the style of epic to suit his *carmen togatum*, 'poem that wears the toga',[188] a poem resolutely 'Roman' in its commitment to 'history' and contempt for flowery mythological embellishment borrowed from Greece (thus he favours technical terms and vocabulary associated with prose). For all that, the style of the *Pharsalia* remains a radically reconfigured version of the *genus grande*. Thomas de Quincy found in Lucan 'an exhibition of a moral sublime',[189] which may help to explain how his work can be appropriated within a certain kind of Christian mentality. The seventeenth-century writer and antiquarian Thomas Browne ends his *Urn Burial* with a powerful meditation on death and decay, capping it with a quotation from book 7 of the *Pharsalia*:

'Tis all one to lie in St Innocent's churchyard as in the sands of Egypt, ready to be anything, in the ecstasy of being ever, and as content with six foot as the moles of Adrianus.

> —tabesne cadavera solvat
> An rogus haud refert. Lucan.

Here, as in Browne's earlier evocation of 'that duration which maketh pyramids pillars of snow', the conjunction of the massive

---

[188] This is the description of the Flavian epic poet Statius, *Silvae* 2. 7. 53.
[189] Cited Gillespie (1988) 147.

and the exiguous has a hint of that stylistic extremism which is a mark of Lucan's own writing, while the words cited come from one of the finest passages in the *Pharsalia* and one that exhibits this Lucanic sublime, as Lucan responds to Caesar's failure to allow the dead Pompeians proper burial after the battle of Pharsalus (7. 809–19):

>   nil agis hac ira: tabesne cadavera solvat
>   an rogus haud refert; placido natura receptat   810
>   cuncta sinu, finemque sui sibi corpora debent.
>   hos, Caesar, populos si nunc non usserit ignis,
>   uret cum terris, uret cum gurgite ponti.
>   communis mundo superest rogus ossibus astra
>   mixturus. quocumque tuam fortuna vocabit,   815
>   hae quoque sunt animae: non altius ibis in auras,
>   non meliore loco Stygia sub nocte iacebis.
>   libera fortunae mors est; capit omnia tellus
>   quae genuit—caelo tegitur qui non habet urnam.

You achieve nothing by this anger—it does not matter whether decay or the pyre dissolves the corpses; nature finds room for all in her gentle arms, and the bodies owe their end to themselves. If fire does not burn these multitudes now, Caesar, it will burn them later with the earth, with the surge of the sea. There remains a shared funeral pyre for the world that will mix the stars with the bones. Wherever fortune calls your spirit, Caesar, there the spirits of these men are also. You will not go higher in the air than they, you will not lie in a better place beneath Stygian darkness. Death is free from fortune; earth holds all she has created—he who lacks an urn is covered by the sky.

Lucan always writes well about the end of things—the description of the dissolution of the cosmos that prefaces the account of the causes of the war (1. 70–82) provides one possible framework for the whole poem. In our passage philosophical themes achieve a terrifying yet exhilarating poetic intensity; the allusion to the Stoic doctrine of the periodic destruction of the universe by fire (*ekpyrōsis*) produces an extreme but exact image in the intermixture of bones and stars.[190] The direct address to Caesar (apostrophe is perhaps Lucan's favourite trope) heightens the effect: distinctions of time and place dissolve, as the world becomes a theatre for Lucan and his characters to play and die in. The writing combines a certain

---

[190] So Mayer (1981) 24.

plainness, even prosiness, of diction[191] with various rhetorical features of the grand style (iteration, the final stabbing *sententia*, and so forth) to produce a kind of maimed sublimity that might plausibly be seen as religious or prophetic. Among ancient writers perhaps only Lucretius and Juvenal (together with Seneca at a lower level of poetic achievement) offer anything analogous. To adapt Samuel Johnson's judgement on Pope, if this is not poetry, where is poetry to be found?

One Janus-face sign under which the *Pharsalia* can productively be read is that of speech and silence (and related to that, of action and delay). The terms of such binary polarities are always implicated in each other, and, if pushed hard, difference can become identity. Is eloquent silence a form of speech (think of the notorious silences of Aeschylus)? Is evasive speech a form of silence? Not speaking may be culpable (as acquiescing in evil), or construed as a form of criticism (as with the Stoic opposition to the Emperors). There are many such significant silences in the *Pharsalia*. For example, there is the silence of the Muse (traditionally an external, divine guarantor of authenticity and what is valid); Nero has to replace the Muse and become the appropriate 'divinity' for a Roman song that blames the Caesars for Rome's destruction (1. 63–6). More generally there is the silence of the gods, the 'divine machinery' typical of epic. Their absence was criticized in antiquity as a failure of generic decorum, but has also been commended as suiting the temper of a modernist epic about comparatively recent historical events. But, as Denis Feeney has observed, there is rather more to be said: Lucan's 'failure to represent the gods is testimony to their poetic power, not their weakness. He has not abandoned the gods, they have abandoned him.'[192] Lucan is also addicted to various forms of narrative pause, a freezing of story time[193] (as in his use of apostrophe); *mora*, delay, is a key word (delaying

---

[191] *Cadaver*, for example, is an 'unpoetic' word (epic poets favour *corpus*)—it appears 36 times in Lucan, only twice in the *Aeneid*. Similarly *mors* is preferred by Lucan to the more poetic *letum*, while *nil agis* was originally colloquial.

[192] Feeney (1991) 285; cf. p. 301: 'The gods have not been blandly discarded, jettisoned as self-evidently irrelevant or out-of-date. As is the case with all epics, this poem's effects are inconceivable without the gods. Their presence is always being registered as absent, their absence as present; between these fractures the poem must find its unparalleled ways of speaking.' On the gods see also W. R. Johnson (1987) ch. 1.

[193] For the effect of this on temporality in the poem see Leigh (1997) 50, 79.

can, of course, be a form of action, as with Fabius Maximus Cunctator, whose delays saved Rome from Hannibal). At one crucial moment in his account of the battle of Pharsalus, using the figure of *omissio*, Lucan refuses to relate (7. 552–6);[194] at another he pours out a very torrent of words of condemnation (385–459). This passage, condemned by many as rant or irrelevant digression, is one of extraordinary originality, energy, daring, and power, a sort of dithyrambic tirade conducted in long, straggling sentences, which sometimes approaches a virtual loss of coherence, as the speaker is swept away by the feelings of the moment (its topics include: the ruins of Italy and its traditions; the failure of Roman imperialism; the loss of liberty which has migrated to foreign peoples; the deification of the Caesars).

To relate the story of civil war is, in a sense, to re-enact, repeat, and thus be implicated in Caesar's unspeakable crime (*nefas*, that which should not be spoken, is another of the poem's words of power). Hence the poet both wishes and does not wish to tell the story. Lucan's work is itself in certain significant respects Caesarean, vast, excessive, wild. Hence the poet, like Pompey a reluctant actor, must seek delay and silence. The tension is, so to say, terminal. As Rome and the universe self-implode, so the text collapses in on itself, as its massive structures are massively blocked. Lucan's tendency to build large static structures is well illustrated by the poem's opening. The *Aeneid* begins with a seven-line *propositio* (statement of theme), followed by an invocation of the Muse; the *narratio*, the narrative proper, begins in line 34 with an imperfect tense ('hardly out of sight of Sicilian land were they spreading their sails seaward'). By contrast in Lucan we have a deferral of the narrative until line 183, by which time Caesar has already acted, thereby thwarting the poet's delaying tactics: like a second Hannibal 'Caesar had already crossed/overcome the frozen Alps in his rapid course' and begun civil war. Moreover there is a strong narrative thrust to Virgil's *propositio*, as it charts a movement from Troy to Rome and from past to present, in which there is a clear sequence of cause and effect, a history of coherent advance, that links origins and beginnings to ends, to validate the present Augustan order of things. Is coherent narrative necessarily teleological, even when it seeks to contest official histories? Are fractured

[194] On this see W. R. Johnson (1987) 98–9.

narratives parasitic upon more conventional narratives? Lucan struggles with such paradoxes in his *propositio* which attempts to replace narrative with something more like stasis:

> Bella per Emathios plus quam civilia campos
> iusque datum sceleri canimus, populumque potentem
> in sua victrici conversum viscera dextra,
> cognatasque acies, et rupto foedere regni
> certatum totis concussi viribus orbis
> in commune nefas, infestisque obvia signis
> signa, pares aquilas et pila minantia pilis.

Wars more than civil over Thessalian plains and legitimacy conferred on crime we sing, and a powerful people turning on its own vitals with victorious right hand, and kindred battlelines, and, the compact of government broken, a struggle with all the strength of a shattered world to achieve a communal crime (*nefas*), and standards opposed to hostile standards, matched eagles, and javelins threatening javelins.

As in Virgil we have a seven-line opening period, composed with immense care, with cunningly varied pauses and clause lengths. Marcus Fronto, a critic of the second century AD and an enemy of the mannerist style of Neronian literature, accused Lucan of saying the same thing many times over: 'Annaeus, will there never be an end?'[195] A formalist defence is possible: what we have is a set of variations on a theme, to achieve emphasis. Moreover if we look at the clauses what we find is not inert repetition merely but an anticipation of different motifs. *Emathios* hints at the tyrannical overreacher Alexander the Great, precursor of the Caesars; *plus quam civilia* introduces the idea of excess; *ius datum sceleri* points to the contestation over words and meanings characteristic of struggles for power; the third colon characterizes civil war as an act of communal suicide, enlisting the authority of the imperial poem itself (*Aeneid* 6. 833 *neu patriae validas in viscera vertite vires*); *cognatas* reminds us that the contestants were related by blood and kinship; the fifth colon relates macrocosm and microcosm, *urbs* and *orbis*, while *rupto foedere* relates the implosion of Rome to the self-destruction of the universe, an analogy that later becomes an identity; the final phrases introduce personified weapons that achieve a sinister identity (*pares* points to the gladiatorial arena) and usurp

---

[195] For the full text see Haines (1920) 104–7.

the place of human beings. Nonetheless Fronto has focused on a crucial point about the poem—Lucan says 'civil war we sing', and then he says it again, and again, and again. In this way narrative momentum is refused, the unspeakable partly unspoken, but there is still an implied narrative and a story that both must and must not be told.

Such forms of modernist extremism, which I have identified as constituting a significant part of Lucan's virtue, affect every aspect of his poem—in Lucan's case, his 'defects', his 'faults', are precisely his virtues. (Lucan could easily be seen as a poet of the Longinian sublime, whose fiery genius in its onrush can lead him into faults of taste that are as insignificant as they are inevitable. My point, however, is a different one: that Lucan's 'faulty' writing is itself 'beautiful'.) The most compelling of his characters are similarly extreme, Caesar, monster of vice, Cato, monster of virtue, and, the very sign of monstrosity, the witch Erictho. Caesar in particular, a Nietzschean Superman, has left his mark on European literature, the forerunner, for example, of Marlowe's glittering overreacher, Tamburlaine, and of Milton's Satan. In what must be one of the most terrifying depictions in all literature of the totalitarian project (to use a distinctively twentieth-century appropriation), Caesar—the type of the absolutist charismatic leader—swallows up the world, obliterating all distinction between state and individual, as one who 're-deploys around his name all meanings, fixes a new centre from which all discourse is oriented and enforces *his* signs absolutely':[196] as Lucan more succinctly puts it, 'Caesar was all', *omnia Caesar erat* (3. 108). Even the divide between man and god is dissolved in the figure of the universal ruler. Caesar, embodiment of energy and will-to-power, is compared in his effects to a flash of lightning, the weapon of Jupiter (1. 150–7), and after his death he becomes a god. Thus in worldly terms Caesar is successful, where Lucan, like his Cato, fails. Despite all his efforts there is no escape from history for the strong poet of civil war, and indeed the poem can be seen as writing against the grain of language itself, an exercise in deconstructing the self-validating nature of historical narrative, and one that, like any such act of deconstruction, may be doomed to failure. We could say that the pathos of the *Pharsalia* is that its Republicanism is always already deconstructed—historically and

[196] Henderson (1988) 134.

politically of course, but also aesthetically. And that suggests that the Lucan 'myth' may also have its value: the myth of the glamorous young poet, the marvellous boy, who falls victim to worldly realities, but whose fractured and fragmented and defective poem remains to inspire opponents of that world with impossible hopes and dreams.

Epilogue

Pater and Kant have been deuteragonist and protagonist of this essay. It is fitting that they should have the last word:

> the function of the aesthetic critic is to distinguish, to analyse, and separate from its adjuncts, the virtue by which a picture, a landscape, a fair personality in life or in a book, produces this special impression of beauty or pleasure, to indicate what the source of that impression is, and under what conditions it is experienced. (Pater (1980) pp. xx–xxi)

> It [poetry] invigorates the mind by letting it feel its faculty—free, spontaneous, and independent of determination by nature... (Kant (1952) 191–2 §53)

The free experience of beauty, in poetry as in other things, may, or may not, be good for us (and thus, in Kant's phrase, a symbol of morality), but, crucially, it is a good in itself. It may even be one of those few and precious experiences that makes us most fully human.

BIBLIOGRAPHY

Note. The following list contains details of all works referred to in the text and notes, as well as certain other items consulted in the course of writing this book and recommended for further reading.

ADORNO, THEODOR W. (1997), *Aesthetic Theory*, ed. Gretel Adorno and Rolf Tiedemann, trans. Robert Hullot-Kentor (originally published in German 1970), London.

ALLISON, HENRY E. (2001), *Kant's Theory of Taste: A Reading of the Critique of Aesthetic Judgment*, Cambridge.

ANDERSON, R. D., PARSONS, P. J., and NISBET, R. G. M. (1979), 'Elegiacs by Gallus from Qasr Ibrim', *Journal of Roman Studies* 69, 125–55.

ARMSTRONG, ISOBEL (2000), *The Radical Aesthetic*, Oxford.

ARMSTRONG, JOHN (2000), *The Intimate Philosophy of Art*, London.

ARNOLD, MATTHEW (1964), *Essays in Criticism*, introduction by G. K. Chesterton, London.

ATHERTON, CATHERINE (1998), ed., *Form and Content in Didactic Poetry*, Nottingam Classical Literature Studies, 5, Bari.

AUERBACH, ERICH (1973), *Mimesis: The Representation of Reality in Western Literature*, trans. Willard R. Trask, Princeton, NJ.

BAILEY, CYRIL (1949), *Titi Lucreti Cari De Rerum Natura Libri Sex*, 3 vols., Oxford.

BARKAN, LEONARD (1986), *The Gods Made Flesh: Metamorphosis and the Pursuit of Paganism*, New Haven and London.

—— (1999), *Unearthing the Past: Archaeology and Aesthetics in the Making of Renaissance Culture*, New Haven and London.

BARNARD, MARY E. (1987), *The Myth of Apollo and Daphne from Ovid to Quevedo: Love, Agon, and the Grotesque*, Duke Monographs in Medieval and Renaissance Studies, 8, Durham.

BARRELL, JOHN (1986), *The Political Theory of Painting from Reynolds to Hazlitt*, New Haven and London.

——, and BULL, JOHN (1974), eds., *The Penguin Book of English Pastoral Verse*, London.

BARRINGER, TIM, and PRETTEJOHN, ELIZABETH (1999), eds., *Frederic Leighton: Antiquity, Renaissance, Modernity*, Studies in British Art, 5, New Haven and London.

BARTHES, ROLAND (1988), 'The Wisdom of Art', in *Calligram: Cambridge Essays in New Art History*, ed. Norman Bryson, 166–80, London.
—— (1990), *The Pleasure of the Text*, trans. Richard Miller, Oxford.
BARTSCH, SHADI (1997), *Ideology in Cold Blood: A Reading of Lucan's Civil War*, Cambridge, Mass. and London.
BATE, JONATHAN (2000), *The Song of the Earth*, Basingstoke and Oxford.
BATTERSBY, CHRISTINE (1989), *Gender and Genius: Towards a Feminist Aesthetics*, London.
BECKLEY, BILL (1998), ed., *Uncontrollable Beauty: Toward a New Aesthetic*, New York.
BEECH, DAVE, and ROBERTS, JOHN (1996), 'Spectres of the Aesthetic', *New Left Review* 218, 102–27.
BENEZRA, NEAL, and VISO, OLGA M. (1999), *Regarding Beauty: A View of the Late Twentieth Century*, exhibition catalogue of Hirshhorn Museum, Washington, DC.
BENJAMIN, WALTER (1992), *Illuminations*, trans. Harry Zohn with an introduction by Hannah Arendt, London.
BENNETT, TONY (1990), *Outside Literature*, London and New York.
BERNSTEIN, J. M. (1997), 'Against Voluptuous Bodies: Of Satiation Without Happiness', *New Left Review*, 225: 89–104.
BLOCH, ERNST (1988), *The Utopian Function of Art and Literature: Selected Essays*, trans. Jack Zipes and Frank Mecklenburg, Cambridge, Mass. and London.
BLOOM, HAROLD (1969), ed., *The Literary Criticism of John Ruskin*, Gloucester, Mass.
BOLAND, EAVAN (1995), *Collected Poems*, Manchester.
BOLGAR, R. R. (1979), ed., *Classical Influences on Western Thought AD 1650–1870*, Cambridge.
BOSANQUET, BERNARD (1966), *A History of Aesthetic* (first published 1892), London and New York.
BOURDIEU, PIERRE (1984), *Distinction: A Social Critique of the Judgement of Taste*, trans. Richard Nice, London.
BOWIE, ANDREW (1990), *Aesthetics and Subjectivity: From Kant to Nietzsche*, Manchester and New York.
—— (1997), 'Confessions of a "New Aesthete": A Response to the "New Philistines"', *New Left Review*, 225: 105–26.
BOYLE, A. J. (1986), *The Chaonian Dove: Studies in the Eclogues, Georgics, and Aeneid of Virgil*, Leiden.
BRADLEY, A. C. (1909), *Oxford Lectures on Poetry*, London.
BRAKE, LAUREL, HIGGINS, LESLEY, and WILLIAMS, CAROLYN (2002), eds., *Walter Pater: Transparencies of Desire*, University of North Carolina at Greenboro.

BRAMBLE, J. C. (1970), 'Structure and Ambiguity in Catullus LXIV', *Proceedings of the Cambridge Philological Society*, 16: 22–41.
—— (1982), 'Lucan', in E. J. Kenney and W. V. Clausen, eds., *The Cambridge History of Ancient Literature*, ii: *Latin Literature*, 533–57, Cambridge.
BRAND, PEGGY ZEGLIN, and KORSMEYER, CAROLYN (1995), eds., *Feminism and Tradition in Aesthetics*, Pennsylvania.
BROMWICH, DAVID (1989), *A Choice of Inheritance: Self and Community from Edmund Burke to Robert Frost*, Cambridge, Mass. and London.
BROOKS, CLEANTH (1974), *The Well Wrought Urn: Studies in the Structure of Poetry*, San Diego.
BROWN, SARAH ANNES (1999), *The Metamorphosis of Ovid: From Chaucer to Ted Hughes*, London.
—— (2000), 'Arachne's Web: Intertextual Mythography and the Renaissance Actaeon', in Neil Rhodes and Jonathan Sawday, eds., *The Renaissance Computer: Knowledge Technology in the First Age of Print*, 120–34, London and New York.
—— (2004), *Ovid's Metamorphoses*, London.
—— and Martindale, Charles (1998), eds., *Lucan, The Civil War, Translated as Lucan's Pharsalia by Nicholas Rowe*, London and Vermont.
BURROW, COLIN (1993), *Epic Romance: Homer to Milton*, Oxford.
CAMERON, ALAN (1995), *Callimachus and His Critics*, Princeton, NY.
CARNE-ROSS, D. S., and HAYNES, KENNETH (1996), eds., *Horace in English*, Harmondsworth.
CARRIER, DAVID (1997), ed., *England and its Aesthetes: Biography and Taste (John Ruskin, Walter Pater, Adrian Stokes: Essays)*, Amsterdam.
CARROLL, DAVID (1989), *Paraesthetics: Foucault, Lyotard, Derrida*, New York and London.
CASSIRER, H. W. (1970), *A Commentary on Kant's Critique of Judgment* (first published 1938), New York and London.
CAWS, MARY ANN (1985), *Reading Frames in Modern Fiction*, Princeton, NJ.
CAYGILL, HOWARD (1989), *Art of Judgement*, Oxford.
CAZEAUX, CLIVE (2000), ed., *The Continental Aesthetics Reader*, London and New York.
CHEETHAM, MARK A. (2001), *Kant, Art, and Art History: Moments of Discipline*, Cambridge.
CLARK, MICHAEL P. (2000), ed., *Revenge of the Aesthetic: The Place of Literature in Theory Today*, Berkeley.
CLARK, TIMOTHY (1997), *The Theory of Inspiration: Composition as a Crisis of Subjectivity in Romantic and Post-Romantic Writing*, Manchester and New York.
CLAUSEN, WENDELL (1994), *A Commentary on Virgil Eclogues*, Oxford.
CLINGHAM, GREG (2002), *Johnson, Writing, and Memory*, Oxford.
COHEN, TED, and GUYER, PAUL (1982), eds., *Essays in Kant's Aesthetics*, Chicago and London.

COMMAGER, STEELE (1967), *The Odes of Horace: A Critical Study*, Bloomington, Ind. and London.

CONTE, GIAN BIAGIO (1986), *The Rhetoric of Imitation: Genre and Poetic Memory in Virgil and Other Latin Poets*, ed. C. Segal, Ithaca, NY and London.

——(1994a), *Genres and Readers: Lucretius, Love Elegy, Pliny's Encyclopedia*, trans. Glenn W. Most, Baltimore and London.

——(1994b), *Latin Literature: A History*, trans. Joseph B. Solodow, Baltimore and London.

COOPER, DAVID E. (1997), ed., *Aesthetics: The Classic Readings*, Oxford.

COUSIN, VICTOR (1848), *The Philosophy of the Beautiful*, trans. Jesse Cato Daniel, London.

CRAWFORD, DONALD W. (1974), *Kant's Aesthetic Theory*, Madison.

CROCE, BENEDETTO (1995), *Guide to Aesthetics*, trans. Patrick Romanell, Indianapolis.

CROW, THOMAS (1996), *Modern Art in the Common Culture*, New Haven and London.

CROWTHER, PAUL (1989), *The Kantian Sublime: From Morality to Art*, Oxford.

——(1996), *Critical Aesthetics and Postmodernism*, Oxford.

CURTIUS, E. R. (1953), *European Literature and the Latin Middle Ages*, trans. W. R. Trask, London.

DALZELL, ALEXANDER (1996), *The Criticism of Didactic Poetry: Essays on Lucretius, Virgil, and Ovid*, Toronto.

DANSON, LAWRENCE (1997), *Wilde's Intentions: The Artist in his Criticism*, Oxford.

DANTO, ARTHUR C. (2003), *The Abuse of Beauty: Aesthetics and the Concept of Art* (The Paul Carus Lecture Series, 21), Chicago and La Salle, Ill.

DAVIE, DONALD (1990), *Collected Poems*, Manchester.

DAVIS, GREGSON (1991), *Polyhymnia: The Rhetoric of Horatian Lyric Discourse*, Berkeley.

DE BOLLA, PETER (2001), *Art Matters*, Cambridge, Mass. and London.

DE MAN, PAUL (1983), *Blindness and Insight: Essays in the Rhetoric of Contemporary Criticism*, 2nd edn., revised, Theory and History of Literature 7, Minneapolis.

——(1984), 'Aesthetic Formalization: Kleist's *Über das Marionettentheater*', *The Rhetoric of Romanticism*, 263–314, New York.

DERRIDA, JACQUES (1981), *Positions*, trans. Alan Bass, London.

——(1987), *The Truth in Painting*, trans. Geoffrey Bennington and Ian McLeod, Chicago and London.

——(1991), 'Che cos'è la poesia?', in Peggy Kamuf, ed., *A Derrida Reader: Between the Blinds*, 221–37, London and New York.

DEWEY, JOHN (1934), *Art as Experience*, New York.

DILKE, O. A. W. (1972), 'Lucan and English Literature', in D. R. Dudley, ed., *Neronians and Flavians: Silver Latin*, i, 83–112, London and Boston.

DOLLIMORE, JONATHAN (1991), *Sexual Dissidence: Augustine to Wilde, Freud to Foucault*, Oxford.
DONOGHUE, DENIS (1995), *Walter Pater: Lover of Strange Souls*, New York.
—— (2003), *Speaking of Beauty*, New Haven and London.
DOOB, PENELOPE REED (1990), *The Idea of the Labyrinth from Classical Antiquity through the Middle Ages*, Ithaca, NY and London.
DOWLING, LINDA (1996), *The Vulgarization of the Arts: The Victorians and Aesthetic Democracy*, Charlottesville, Va. and London.
DUFF, J. D. (1928), *Lucan* (Loeb Classical Library), London and New York.
EAGLETON, TERRY (1990), *The Ideology of the Aesthetic*, Oxford.
—— (1999), 'Hasped and Hooped and Hirpling' (review of Seamus Heaney's translation of *Beowulf*), *London Review of Books*, 11 November, 15–16.
—— (2002), 'A Good Reason to Murder Your Landlady' (review of *I. A. Richards: Selected Works 1919–38*, edited by John Constable), *London Review of Books*, 25 April, 13–15.
EDMUNDS, LOWELL (2001), *Intertextuality and the Reading of Roman Poetry*, Baltimore and London.
ELIOT, T. S. (1920), *The Sacred Wood: Essays on Poetry and Criticism*, London.
—— (1930), 'The Place of Pater', in Walter de la Mare, ed., *The Eighteen-Eighties: Essays by Fellows of the Royal Society of Literature*, 93–106, Cambridge.
—— (1957), *On Poetry and Poets*, London.
ELLMANN, RICHARD (1970), *The Artist as Critic: Critical Writings of Oscar Wilde*, London.
—— (1987), *Oscar Wilde*, London.
ENTERLINE, LYNN (2000), *The Rhetoric of the Body: From Ovid to Shakespeare*, Cambridge.
FAAS, EKBERT (2002), *The Genealogy of Aesthetics*, Cambridge.
FARMELO, GRAHAM (2003), *It Must Be Beautiful: Great Equations of Modern Science*, London.
FARRELL, JOSEPH (2001), ed., *The Vergilian Century*, special issue of *Vergilius*, 47, Michigan.
FEAGIN, SUSAN, and MAYNARD, PATRICK (1997), eds., *Aesthetics* (*Oxford Readers*), Oxford and New York.
FEENEY, DENIS (1991), *The Gods in Epic: Poets and Critics of the Classical Tradition*, Oxford.
FITZGERALD, WILLIAM (1995), *Catullan Provocations: Lyric Poetry and the Drama of Position*, Berkeley.
FOLDY, MICHAEL S. (1997), *The Trials of Oscar Wilde: Deviance, Morality, and Late-Victorian Society*, New Haven and London.
FOWLER, DON (1987), 'Vergil on Killing Virgins', in Philip Hardie and Michael and Mary Whitby, eds., *Homo Viator: Classical Essays for John Bramble*, 185–98, Bristol.

FOWLER, DON (1995), 'Horace and the Aesthetics of Politics', in S. J. Harrison, ed., *Homage to Horace: A Bimillenary Celebration*, 248–66, Oxford.

—— (2002), 'Masculinity under Threat? The Poetics and Politics of Inspiration in Latin Poetry', in Efrossini Spentzou and Don Fowler, eds., *Cultivating the Muse: Struggles for Power and Inspiration in Classical Literature*, 141–59, Oxford.

FOWLER, ROWENA (2005), 'This Tart Fable: Daphne, Apollo and Contemporary Women's Poetry', in Vanda Zajko and Miriam Leonard, eds., *Laughing with Medusa: Classical Myth and Feminist Thought*, Oxford.

FRASER, HILARY (1986), *Beauty and Belief: Aesthetics and Religion in Victorian Literature*, Cambridge.

FREELAND, CYNTHIA (2001), *But Is It Art?: An Introduction to Art Theory*, Oxford.

FRY, ROGER (1990), *Vision and Design*, London and New York.

FULLER, PETER (1988), *Theoria: Art, and the Absence of Grace*, London.

GADAMER, HANS-GEORG (1975), *Truth and Method*, 2nd edn., trans. revised by Joel Weinsheimer and Donald G. Marshall, London.

—— (1986), *The Relevance of the Beautiful and Other Essays*, trans. Nicholas Walker, Cambridge.

GALE, MONICA (1994), *Myth and Poetry in Lucretius*, Cambridge.

GAUT, BERYS, and LOPES, DOMINIC MCIVER (2001), eds., *The Routledge Companion to Aesthetics*, London and New York.

GAUTIER, THÉOPHILE (1847), 'Du Beau dans l'art', *Revue des Deux Mondes*, 19: 887–908.

GEERTZ, CLIFFORD (1973), *The Interpretation of Cultures*, New York.

GEUSS, RAYMOND (1999), *Morality, Culture, and History: Essays on German Philosophy*, Cambridge.

GILLESPIE, STUART (1988), *The Poets on the Classics: An Anthology*, London and New York.

GOFFMAN, ERVING (1974), *Frame Analysis*, Harmondsworth.

GOLDHILL, SIMON (1991), *The Poet's Voice: Essays on Poetics and Greek Literature*, Cambridge.

—— (1999), 'Literary History Without Literature: Reading Practices in the Ancient World', *Substance*, 88 (special issue on Literary History): 57–89.

—— (2002), *Who Needs Greek?: Contests in the Cultural History of Hellenism*, Cambridge.

GOLDING, WILLIAM (1979), *The Inheritors* (first published 1955), London and Boston.

—— (1982), *A Moving Target*, London.

GOOLD, G. P. (1983), *Catullus*, London.

GRAHAM, GORDON (1997), *Philosophy of the Arts: An Introduction to Aesthetics*, London and New York.

GRAVES, ROBERT (1956), *Lucan Pharsalia: Dramatic Episodes of the Civil Wars*, Harmondsworth.

GRIFFIN, JASPER (1986), *Virgil*, Past Masters series, Oxford and New York.
GUILLORY, JOHN (1993), *Cultural Capital: The Problem of Literary Canon Formation*, Chicago and London.
GUYER, PAUL (1993), *Kant and the Experience of Freedom: Essays on Aesthetics and Morality*, Cambridge.
HABER, JUDITH (1994), *Pastoral and the Poetics of Self-Contradiction: Theocritus to Marvell*, Cambridge.
HABINEK, THOMAS (1998), *The Politics of Latin Literature: Writing, Identity, and Empire in Ancient Rome*, Princeton, NJ.
HAINES, C. R. (1920), ed., *The Correspondence of Marcus Cornelius Fronto*, ii (Loeb Classical Library), London and New York.
HALL, EDITH (1997), 'The Sociology of Athenian Tragedy', in P. E. Easterling, ed., *The Cambridge Companion to Greek Tragedy*, 93–126, Cambridge.
HALLIWELL, STEPHEN (2002), *The Aesthetics of Mimesis: Ancient Texts and Modern Problems*, Princeton, NJ and Oxford.
HALPERIN, DAVID M. (1983), *Before Pastoral: Theocritus and the Ancient Tradition of Bucolic Poetry*, New Haven and London.
HAMILTON, PAUL (2003), *Metaromanticism: Aesthetics, Literature, Theory*, Chicago.
HAMMERMEISTER, KAI (2002), *The German Aesthetic Tradition*, Cambridge.
HAMMOND, PAUL (1983), 'The Integrity of Dryden's Lucretius', *Modern Language Review*, 78: 1–23.
HARDIE, PHILIP (1993), *The Epic Successors of Virgil: A Study in the Dynamics of a Tradition*, Cambridge.
——, ed. (2002), *The Cambridge Companion to Ovid*, Cambridge.
——, BARCHIESI, ALESSANDRO, and HINDS, STEPHEN (1999), eds., *Ovidian Transformations: Essays on Ovid's Metamorphoses and its Reception*, Cambridge.
HARRIS, ROY (2002), 'Why Words Really Do Not Stay Still' (review of Ferdinand de Saussure, *Écrits de linguistique général*, ed. Simon Bouquet and Rudolf Engler), *Times Literary Supplement*, 26 July, 29.
HARRISON, S. J. (2001), (ed.), *Texts, Ideas, and the Classics: Scholarship, Theory, and Classical Literature*, Oxford.
HEANEY, SEAMUS (1995), *The Redress of Poetry: Oxford Lectures*, London and Boston.
HEGEL, G. W. F. (1975), *Aesthetics: Lectures on Fine Art*, trans. T. M. Knox, 2 vols., Oxford.
HEIDEGGER, MARTIN (1971), *Poetry, Language, Thought*, trans. Albert Hofstadter, New York.
—— (1993), *Basic Writings*, ed. David Farrell Krell, London.
HEITLAND, W. E. (1887), *Introduction* to the edition of Lucan's *Pharsalia* by C. E. Haskins, London and Cambridge.

HENDERSON, JOHN (1988), 'Lucan / The Word at War', in A. J. Boyle, ed., *The Imperial Muse: Ramus Essays on Roman Literature of the Empire to Juvenal through Ovid*, 122–64, Victoria.
—— (1998), *Fighting For Rome: Poets and Caesars, History and Civil War*, Cambridge.
—— (1999), *Writing Down Rome: Satire, Comedy, and Other Offences in Latin Poetry*, Oxford.
HICKEY, DAVE (1993), *The Invisible Dragon: Four Essays on Beauty*, Los Angeles.
—— (2002), 'Buying the World', *Daedalus* 131.4, 69–87.
HOFMANN, MICHAEL, and LASDUN, JAMES (1994), eds., *After Ovid: New Metamorphoses*, London.
HOLLAND, MERLIN (2003), *Irish Peacock & Scarlet Marquess: The Real Trial of Oscar Wilde*, London and New York.
HOOPER, WALTER (1994), ed., *The Collected Poems of C. S. Lewis*, London.
HOPKINS, DAVID (1986), *John Dryden*, Cambridge.
HOPKINSON, NEIL (1988), *A Hellenistic Anthology*, Cambridge.
HUBBARD, MARGARET (1974), *Propertius*, London.
HUGHES, TED (1997), *Tales from Ovid (Twenty-four Passages from the Metamorphoses)*, London.
HUME, DAVID (1996), *Selected Essays*, ed. Stephen Copley and Andrew Edgar (World's Classics), Oxford.
HUTCHESON, FRANCIS (1994), *Philosophical Writings*, ed. R. S. Downie, London.
HYDE, H. MONTGOMERY (1973), *The Trials of Oscar Wilde*, New York.
ISER, WOLFGANG (1993), *The Fictive and the Imaginary: Charting Literary Anthropology*, Baltimore and London.
JACKSON, JOHN WYSE (1991), ed., *Aristotle at Afternoon Tea: The Rare Oscar Wilde*, London.
JAMES, HENRY (1986), *The Aspern Papers and The Turn of the Screw*, ed. Anthony Curtis (Penguin Classics), Harmondsworth.
JARVIS, SIMON (1998), *Adorno: A Critical Introduction*, Cambridge and Oxford.
JAUSS, HANS ROBERT (1982), *Aesthetic Experience and Literary Hermeneutics*, trans. Michael Shaw, Minneapolis.
JENKYNS, RICHARD (1982), *Three Classical Poets: Sappho, Catullus and Juvenal*, London.
——, ed. (1992), *The Legacy of Rome: A New Appraisal*, Oxford.
—— (1998), *Virgil's Experience: Nature and History Times, Names, and Places*, Oxford.
JOHNSON, BARBARA (1980), *The Critical Difference: Essays in the Contemporary Rhetoric of Reading*, Baltimore and London.
JOHNSON, SAMUEL (1905), *Lives of the English Poets*, i, ed. G. Birkbeck Hill, Oxford.
JOHNSON, W. R. (1987), *Momentary Monsters: Lucan and his Heroes*, Ithaca, NY and London.

―― (1996), 'The Rapes of Callisto', *Classical Journal*, 92: 9–24.
JOSIPOVICI, GABRIEL (1999), *On Trust: Art and the Temptations of Suspicion*, New Haven and London.
JOUGHIN, JOHN J., and MALPAS, SIMON (2003), eds., *The New Aestheticism*, Manchester and New York.
KAMUF, PEGGY (1991), ed., *A Derrida Reader: Between the Blinds*, New York.
KANT, IMMANUEL (1952), *The Critique of Judgement*, trans. James Creed Meredith, Oxford.
―― (1960), *Observations on the Feeling of the Beautiful and Sublime*, trans. John T. Goldthwait, Berkeley and London.
―― (1974), *Kritik der Urteilskraft*, ed. Wilhelm Weischedel, Wiesbaden.
―― (2000), *Critique of the Power of Judgment*, ed. Paul Guyer, trans. Paul Guyer and Eric Matthews, *The Cambridge Edition of the Works of Immanuel Kant*, Cambridge.
KELLY, MICHAEL (1998), ed., *Encyclopedia of Aesthetics*, 4 vols., New York and Oxford.
KENNEDY, DUNCAN F. (1984), review of Tony Woodman and David West, eds., *Poetry and Politics in the Age of Augustus*, *Liverpool Classical Monthly*, 9.10: 157–60.
―― (1987a), '*Arcades ambo*: Virgil, Gallus and Arcadia', *Hermathena*, 143: 47–59.
―― (1987b), review of Hans-Peter Stahl, *Propertius: 'Love' and 'War': Individual and State under Augustus*, *Liverpool Classical Monthly*, 12.5: 72–7.
―― (1989), review of T. D. Papanghelis, *Propertius: A Hellenistic Poet on Love and Death*, *Liverpool Classical Monthly*, 14.9: 141–4.
―― (1992), ' "Augustan" and "Anti-Augustan": Reflections on Terms of Reference', in Anton Powell, ed., *Roman Poetry and Propaganda in the Age of Augustus*, 26–58, London.
―― (1993), *The Arts of Love: Five Studies in the Discourse of Roman Love Elegy*, Cambridge.
―― (2002), *Rethinking Reality: Lucretius and the Textualization of Nature*, Ann Arbor.
KENNEY, E. J. (1971), ed., *Lucretius, De Rerum Natura, Book 3*, Cambridge.
―― (1973), 'The Style of the *Metamorphoses*', in J. W. Binns, ed., *Ovid*, (Greek and Latin Studies: Classical Literature and its Influence), 116–53, London and Boston.
―― (1977), *Lucretius* (New Surveys in the Classics), Oxford.
KERMODE, FRANK (1961), *Romantic Image*, London.
―― (1975a), *The Classic: Literary Images of Permanence and Change*, London.
―― (1975b), ed., *Selected Prose of T. S. Eliot*, London.
KIRWAN, JAMES (1999), *Beauty*, Manchester and New York.
KIVY, PETER (1997), *Philosophies of Arts: An Essay in Differences*, Cambridge.
―― (2001), *The Possessor and the Possessed: Handel, Mozart, Beethoven, and the Idea of Musical Genius*, New Haven and London.

KIVY, PETER (2003), *The Seventh Sense: Francis Hutcheson and Eighteenth-Century British Aesthetics*, revised and enlarged edition, Oxford.
—— (2004), ed., *The Blackwell Guide to Aesthetics*, Oxford.
KRAMNICK, JONATHAN BRODY (1998), *Making the English Canon: Print-Capitalism and the Cultural Past, 1700–1770*, Cambridge.
KRIS, ERNST, and KURZ, OTTO (1979), *Legend, Myth, and Magic in the Image of the Artist: A Historical Experiment* (first published 1934), New Haven and London.
LANSDOWN, RICHARD (2001), *The Autonomy of Literature*, Houndmills and London.
LASDUN, JAMES (2003), 'Hatching, Splitting, Doubling' (review of Marina Warner, *Fantastic Metamorphoses, Other Worlds: Ways of Telling the Self*), *London Review of Books*, 21 August, 24.
LEAVIS, F. R. (1972), *Nor Shall My Sword: Discourses on Pluralism, Compassion and Social Hope*, London.
LEBENSZTEJN, JEAN-CLAUDE (1994), 'Starting Out from the Frame', in Peter Brunette and David Wills, eds., *Deconstruction and the Visual Arts: Art, Media, Architecture*, 118–40, Cambridge.
LEE, GUY (1968), ed., *P. Ovidi Nasonis Metamorphoseon Liber I*, Cambridge.
—— (1984), *Virgil: The Eclogues* (Penguin Classics), Harmondsworth.
LEIGH, MATTHEW (1997), *Lucan: Spectacle and Engagement*, Oxford.
LEISHMAN, J. B. (1956), *Translating Horace*, Oxford.
LEMON, LEE T., and REIS, MARION J. (1965), eds., *Russian Formalist Criticism: Four Essays*, translated with an introduction (Regents Critics Series), Lincoln, Nebr.
LEVINAS, EMMANUEL (1989), *A Levinas Reader*, ed. Seán Hand, Oxford.
LEVINE, GEORGE (1994), ed., *Aesthetics and Ideology*, New Brunswick, NJ.
LEWIS, C. S. (1961), *An Experiment in Criticism*, Cambridge.
—— (1964), *Letters to Malcolm: Chiefly on Prayer*, London.
LOESBERG, JONATHAN (1991), *Aestheticism and Deconstruction: Pater, Derrida, and de Man*, Princeton, NJ.
LOUGHREY, BRYAN (1984), ed., *The Pastoral Mode: A Casebook*, London and Basingstoke.
LYAS, COLIN (1997), *Aesthetics*, London.
LYNE, R. O. A. M. (1984), 'Ovid's *Metamorphoses*, Callimachus, and *l'art pour l'art*', *Materiali e Discussioni*, 12: 9–34.
MACDONALD, MARGARET F. (2003), ed., *Whistler's Mother: An American Icon*, Aldershot.
MCGRATH, F. C. (1986), *The Sensible Spirit: Walter Pater and the Modernist Paradigm*, Tampa, Fla.
MACLEOD, CATRIONA (1998), *Embodying Ambiguity: Androgyny and Aesthetics from Winckelmann to Keller*, Detroit.
MANNING, SUSAN (2001), 'Whatever Happened to Pleasure?', *Cambridge Quarterly*, 30: 215–32.

MARKS, EMERSON R. (1998), *Taming the Chaos: English Poetic Diction Theory Since the Renaissance*, Detroit.
MARTINDALE, CHARLES (1976), 'Paradox, Hyperbole, and Literary Novelty in Lucan's *De Bello Civili*', *Bulletin of the Institute of Classical Studies*, 23: 45–54.
—— (1986), *John Milton and the Transformation of Ancient Epic*, London and Sydney.
—— (1988), ed., *Ovid Renewed: Ovidian Influences on Literature and Art from the Middle Ages to the Twentieth Century*, Cambridge.
—— (1993a), *Redeeming the Text: Latin Poetry and the Hermeneutics of Reception*, Cambridge.
—— (1993b), 'Descent into Hell: Reading Ambiguity, or Virgil and the Critics', *Proceedings of the Virgil Society*, 21: 111–50.
—— (1994), 'Professing Latin', *Council of University Classical Departments Bulletin*, 3–21.
—— (1996a), 'Canon Fodder' (review of Harold Bloom, *The Western Canon*), *History of the Human Sciences*, 9: 109–17.
—— (1996b), 'Troping the Colours, or How (Not) to Write Literary History: The Case of Rome' (review of Gian Biagio Conte, *Latin Literature: A History*), *History of the Human Sciences*, 9: 93–106.
—— (1997a), ed., *The Cambridge Companion to Virgil*, Cambridge.
—— (1997b), 'Proper Voices: Writing the Writer', in Judith P. Hallett and Thomas Van Nortwick, eds., *Compromising Traditions: The Personal Voice in Classical Scholarship*, 73–101, London and New York.
—— (1998), 'Desperately Seeking the Classic' (review of Shankman (1994)), *Comparative Literature Studies*, 35: 72–80.
—— (1999), foreword to Kenneth Quinn, *The Catullan Revolution*, 2nd edn., Bristol.
—— (2001), 'Banishing the Poets', review of Yun Lee Too, *The Idea of Ancient Literary Criticism*, *Arion*, NS 8: 115–27.
—— and Hopkins, David (1993), eds., *Horace Made New: Horatian Influences on British Writing from the Renaissance to the Twentieth Century*, Cambridge.
—— and Taylor, A. B. (2004), eds., *Shakespeare and the Classics*, Cambridge.
MASON, TOM (1996), 'Is there a Classical Tradition in English Poetry?', review article, *Translation and Literature*, 5: 203–19.
MASTERS, JAMIE (1992), *Poetry and Civil War in Lucan's 'Bellum Civile'*, Cambridge.
—— (1994), 'Deceiving the Reader: The Political Mission of Lucan *Bellum Civile* 7', in Jamie Masters and Jas Elsner, eds., *Reflections of Nero: Culture, History and Representation*, 151–77, London.
MATTHEWS, PAMELA R., and McWHIRTER, DAVID (2003), eds., *Aesthetic Subjects*, Minneapolis and London.
MAYER, R. (1981), *Lucan: Civil War VIII*, Warminster.

MEDCALF, STEPHEN (2002), 'The Dark Italics' (review of Denis Donoghue, *Adam's Curse*, and Don W. King, *C. S. Lewis, Poet*), *Times Literary Supplement*, 4 January, 6–7.

MERRILL, LINDA (1992), *A Pot of Paint: Aesthetics on Trial in Whistler v. Ruskin*, Washington and London.

MILLER, J. HILLIS (1991), *Theory Now and Then*, London and New York.

MOI, TORIL (1985), *Sexual/Textual Politics: Feminist Literary Theory*, London and New York.

MONTROSE, LOUIS ADRIAN (1983), 'Of Gentlemen and Shepherds: The Politics of Elizabethan Pastoral Form', *English Literary History*, 50: 415–59.

MORRIS, WILLIAM (1994), *Hopes and Fears for Art and Signs of Change*, introduced by Peter Faulkner, Bristol.

—— (1998), *News From Nowhere and Other Writings*, ed. Clive Wilmer (Penguin Classics), Harmondsworth.

MORTENSEN, PREBEN (1997), *Art in the Social Order: The Making of the Modern Conception of Art*, New York.

MOST, GLENN W. (1992), '*disiecti membra poetae*: The Rhetoric of Dismemberment in Neronian Poetry', in Ralph Hexter and Daniel Selden, eds., *Innovations of Antiquity*, 391–419, New Haven and London.

MOTHERSILL, MARY (1984), *Beauty Restored*, Oxford.

MURRAY, PENELOPE (1989), ed., *Genius: The History of an Idea*, Oxford.

NAGLE, B. R. (1988), 'Erotic Pursuit and Narrative Seduction in Ovid's *Metamorphoses*', *Ramus*, 17: 32–51.

NEHAMAS, ALEXANDER (2002), 'The Art of Being Unselfish', *Daedalus*, 131.4: 57–68.

NETTLE, DANIEL (2001), *Strong Imagination: Madness, Creativity, and Human Nature*, Oxford.

NICOLL, W. S. M (1980), 'Cupid, Apollo, and Daphne (Ovid, *Met.* 1. 452ff.)', *Classical Quarterly*, 30: 174–82.

NISBET, R. G. M., and HUBBARD, MARGARET (1970), eds., *A Commentary on Horace Odes Book 1*, Oxford.

——, —— (1978), eds., *A Commentary on Horace Odes Book 2*, Oxford.

NORBROOK, DAVID (1999), *Writing the English Republic: Poetry, Rhetoric and Politics, 1627–1660*, Cambridge.

NUTTALL, A. D. (1989), 'Ovid Immoralised: The Method of Wit in Marvell's "The Garden"', *The Stoic in Love: Selected Essays on Literature and Ideas*, 90–9, New York and London.

OBBINK, DIRK (1995), ed., *Philodemus and Poetry: Poetic Theory and Practice in Lucretius, Philodemus, and Horace*, Oxford and New York.

O'BRIAN, JOHN (1986), ed., *Clement Greenberg: The Collected Essays and Criticism*, i: *Perceptions and Judgments, 1939–1944*, Chicago and London.

—— (1993), ed., *Clement Greenberg: The Collected Essays and Criticism*, iv: *Modernism with a Vengeance, 1957–1969*, Chicago and London.

O'GORMAN, ELLEN (2002), 'Archaism and Historicism in Horace's *Odes*', in D. S. Levene and D. P. Nelis, eds., *Clio and the Poets: Augustan Poetry and the Traditions of Ancient Historiography*, 81–101, Leiden.

O'HEAR, ANTHONY (2001), 'Prospects for Beauty', in Anthony O'Hear, ed., *Philosophy of the New Millennium*, Royal Institute of Philosophy Supplement, 48: 175–91, Cambridge.

OLIENSIS, ELLEN (1998), *Horace and the Rhetoric of Authority*, Cambridge.

—— (2002), 'Feminine Endings, Lyric Seductions', in Tony Woodman and Denis Feeney, eds., *Traditions and Contexts in the Poetry of Horace*, 93–106, Cambridge.

PAPANGHELIS, THEODORE D. (1987), *Propertius: A Hellenistic Poet on Love and Death*, Cambridge.

PATER, WALTER (1893), *Plato and Platonism: A Series of Lectures*, London and New York.

—— (1894), *Greek Studies: A Series of Essays*, London.

—— (1973), *Essays on Literature and Art*, ed. Jennifer Uglow, London and Totowa, NJ.

—— (1980), *The Renaissance: Studies in Art and Poetry: The 1893 text*, ed. Donald L. Hill, Berkeley.

—— (1986), *Marius the Epicurean: His Sensations and Ideas*, ed. Ian Small, Oxford and New York.

PATTERSON, ANNABEL (1988), *Pastoral and Ideology: Virgil to Valéry*, Oxford.

PRETTEJOHN, ELIZABETH (1999), ed., *After the Pre-Raphaelites: Art and Aestheticism in Victorian England*, Manchester.

—— (2000), 'Leighton: The Aesthete as Academic', in Rafael Cardoso Denis and Colin Trodd, eds., *Art and the Academy in the Nineteenth Century*, 33–52, Manchester.

—— (2005), *Beauty and Art: 1750–2000*, Oxford.

—— (forthcoming), *Art for Art's Sake: Aestheticism in Victorian Art*.

PUTNAM, MICHAEL C. J. (1961), 'The Art of Catullus 64', *Harvard Studies in Classical Philology*, 65: 165–205 (reprinted in *Approaches to Catullus*, ed. Kenneth Quinn (Cambridge and New York, 1972), 225–65).

QUINN, KENNETH (1963), *Latin Explorations: Critical Studies in Roman Literature*, London.

QUINT, DAVID (1993), *Epic and Empire: Politics and Generic Form from Virgil to Milton*, Princeton, NJ.

READ, RICHARD (2003), *Art and its Discontents: The Early Life of Adrian Stokes*, Aldershot.

REED, CHRISTOPHER (1996), ed., *A Roger Fry Reader*, Chicago and London.

REED, J. D. (1997), ed., *Bion of Smyrna: The Fragments and Adonis*, Cambridge.

REGAN, STEPHEN (1992), ed., *The Politics of Pleasure: Aesthetics and Cultural Theory*, Buckingham and Philadelphia.

REYNOLDS, SIR JOSHUA (1975), *Discourses on Art*, ed. Robert R. Wark, New Haven and London.
RICHARDS, I. A. (1928), *Principles of Literary Criticism*, New York.
—— (1964), *Practical Criticism: A Study of Literary Judgment* (first published 1929), London.
RICHLIN, AMY (1992) 'Reading Ovid's Rapes', in Amy Richlin, ed., *Pornography and Representation in Greece and Rome*, 158–79, New York and Oxford.
RICKS, CHRISTOPHER (1984), *The Force of Poetry*, Oxford.
—— (1996), *Essays in Appreciation*, Oxford.
—— (2002), *Allusion to the Poets*, Oxford.
ROBINSON, PETER (2002), *Poetry, Poets, Readers: Making Things Happen*, Oxford.
ROSEN, CHARLES (1994), *The Frontiers of Meaning: Three Informal Lectures on Music*, New York.
ROSENBLATT, LOUISE M. (1981), 'On the Aesthetic as the Basic Model of the Reading Process', *Bucknell Review*, 26: 17–32.
ROSS, DAVID O. (1975), *Backgrounds to Augustan Poetry: Gallus, Elegy and Rome*, Cambridge.
RUSKIN, JOHN (1907), *Praeterita*, 2 vols., London.
RUSSELL, D. A., and WINTERBOTTOM, M. (1972), eds., *Ancient Literary Criticism: The Principal Texts in New Translations*, Oxford.
SAID, EDWARD (2001), 'Cosmic Ambition' (review of Christoph Wolff, *Johann Sebastian Bach: The Learned Musician*), *London Review of Books*, 19 July, 11–14.
SAMUELS, LISA (1997), 'Introduction to Poetry and the Problem of Beauty', *Modern Language Studies*, 27: 1–7.
SANDYS, GEORGE (1970), *Ovid's Metamorphosis Englished, Mythologized, and Represented in Figures*, ed. Karl K. Hulley and Stanley T. Vandersall, Lincoln, Nebr.
SANTAYANA, GEORGE (1947), *Three Philosophical Poets: Lucretius, Dante, and Goethe* (first published 1910), Cambridge, Mass.
SAVILE, ANTHONY (1993), *Kant's Aesthetics Pursued*, Edinburgh.
SCARRY, ELAINE (1999), *On Beauty and Being Just*, Princeton, NJ.
SCHAMA, SIMON (1995), *Landscape and Memory*, London.
SCHEID, JOHN, and SVENBRO, JESPER (1996), *The Craft of Zeus: Myths of Weaving and Fabric*, Revealing Antiquity, 9, trans. Carol Volk, Cambridge, Mass. and London.
SCHER, STEVEN PAUL (1992), ed., *Music and Text: Critical Enquiries*, Cambridge.
SCHILLER, FRIEDRICH (1967), *On the Aesthetic Education of Man, in a Series of Letters*, ed. Elizabeth M. Wilkinson and L. A. Willoughby, Oxford.
SCRUTON, ROGER (1997), *The Aesthetics of Music*, Oxford.
SEEL, MARTIN (2003*a*), 'The Aesthetics of Appearing', *Radical Philosophy*, 118: 18–24.

—— (2003*b*), *Aesthetics of Appearing*, Stanford, Calif.
SHANKMAN, STEVEN (1994), *In Search of the Classic: Reconsidering the Greco-Roman Tradition, Homer to Valéry and Beyond*, University Park, Pa.
SHERRY, PATRICK (2002), *Spirit and Beauty: An Introduction to Theological Aesthetics*, 2nd edn., London.
SINFIELD, ALAN (1994), *The Wilde Century: Effeminacy, Oscar Wilde and the Queer Movement*, London.
SMITH, BARBARA HERRNSTEIN (1988), *Contingencies of Value: Alternative Perspectives for Critical Theory*, Cambridge, Mass. and London.
SMITH, PAUL, and WILDE, CAROLYN (2002), eds., *A Companion to Art Theory*, Oxford.
SMITH, SIDONIE (1993), *Subjectivity, Identity, and the Body: Women's Autobiographical Practices in the Twentieth Century*, Bloomington, Ind. and Indianapolis.
SNELL, BRUNO (1953), *The Discovery of the Mind: The Greek Origins of European Thought*, trans. T. G. Rosenmeyer, Cambridge, Mass.
SOLODOW, JOSEPH B. (1988), *The World of Ovid's Metamorphoses*, Chapel Hill, NC and London.
SONTAG, SUSAN (1983), 'Against Interpretation', in *A Susan Sontag Reader*, introduced by Elizabeth Hardwick (first published 1964), London, 95–104.
STALLINGS, A. E. (1999), *Archaic Smile*, Evansville, Ind.
STEINER, WENDY (2001), *The Trouble with Beauty*, London (published in the USA as *Venus in Exile: The Rejection of Beauty in 20th-Century Art*).
STEWART, SUSAN (2002), *Poetry and the Fate of the Senses*, Chicago and London.
STOKES, ADRIAN (1951), *Smooth and Rough*, London.
—— (2002), *The Quattro Cento and Stones of Rimini* (*British Art and Visual Culture since 1750, New Readings*, ed. David Peters Corbett), foreword by Stephen Bann, introductions by David Carrier and Stephen Kite (first published 1932 and 1934), Aldershot.
STOPPARD, TOM (1997), *The Invention of Love*, London and Boston.
SUPER, R. H. (1960), *Matthew Arnold On The Classical Tradition*, Ann Arbor.
SWINBURNE, A. C. (1868), *William Blake*, London.
—— (1872), 'Victor Hugo: L'Année Terrible', *The Fortnightly Review*, 69: 243–67.
TANNER, MICHAEL (1997), 'Standing the Test of Time', *Spectator*, 30 August, 31.
TERRY, PHILIP (2000), ed., *Ovid Metamorphosed*, London.
THOMAS, RICHARD F. (1999), *Reading Virgil and his Texts: Studies in Intertextuality*, Ann Arbor.
THORPE, NIGEL (1994), ed., *James McNeill Whistler: Selected Letters and Writings*, Manchester.
TILLYARD, E. M. W. and LEWIS, C. S. (1965), *The Personal Heresy: A Controversy*, London.

TOMLINSON, CHARLES (1983), *Poetry and Metamorphosis* (The Clark Lectures 1982), Cambridge.

TOO, YUN LEE (1998), *The Idea of Ancient Literary Criticism*, Oxford.

TOWNSEND, DABNEY (2001), *Hume's Aesthetic Theory: Taste and Sentiment*, Routledge Studies in Eighteenth Century Philosophy, 2, London and New York.

VENDLER, HELEN (1988), *The Music of What Happens: Poems, Poets, Critics*, Cambridge, Mass. and London.

VEYNE, PAUL (1988), *Roman Erotic Elegy: Love, Poetry, and the West*, trans. David Pellauer, Chicago and London.

VICKERS, BRIAN (1999), ed., *English Renaissance Literary Criticism*, Oxford.

VOLK, KATHARINA (2002), *The Poetics of Latin Didactic: Lucretius, Vergil, Ovid, Manilius*, Oxford.

VON EICHENDORFF, JOSEPH (2002), *Life of a Good-for-nothing* (1826), trans. J. G. Nichols, London.

WARD, GRAHAM (2001), ed., *The Blackwell Companion to Postmodern Theology*, Oxford.

WEINBERG, GAIL S. (1987), 'Ruskin, Pater, and the Rediscovery of Botticelli', *Burlington Magazine*, 129, January: 25–7.

WEST, DAVID (1969), *The Imagery and Poetry of Lucretius*, Edinburgh.

—— (1995), *Horace Odes 1: Carpe Diem, Text, Translation and Commentary*, Oxford.

—— (1998), *Horace Odes 2: Vatis Amici, Text, Translation and Commentary*, Oxford.

—— (2002), *Horace Odes 3: Dulce Periculum, Text, Translation and Commentary*, Oxford.

WHISTLER, JAMES ABBOTT MCNEILL (1967), *The Gentle Art of Making Enemies*, New York.

WHITE, HAYDEN (1987), *The Content of the Form*, Baltimore and London.

WILDE, OSCAR (1986), *De Profundis and Other Writings*, introduced by Hesketh Pearson (Penguin Classics), Harmondsworth.

WILLIAMS, CAROLYN (1989), *Transfigured World: Walter Pater's Aesthetic Historicism*, Ithaca, NY and London.

WILLIAMS, GORDON (1983), *Technique and Ideas in the Aeneid*, New Haven and London.

WIMSATT, W. K. (1969), ed., *Dr Johnson on Shakespeare* (Penguin Shakespeare Library), Harmondsworth.

WINCKELMANN, JOHANN JOACHIM (1881), *The History of Ancient Art* (first published 1764, revised edn. 1776), trans G. Henry Lodge, vol. 1, London.

WINTERSON, JEANETTE (1995), *Art and Lies: A Piece for Three Voices and A Bawd*, London.

WOOLF, VIRGINIA (1993), *Orlando: A Biography*, ed. Brenda Lyons, London.

WYPIJEWSKI, JOANN (1997), ed., *Painting by Numbers: Komar and Melamid's Scientific Guide to Art*, Berkeley and London.

ZAJKO, VANDA (2004), 'Petruchio is "Kated"': *The Taming of the Shrew* and Ovid', in Charles Martindale and A. B. Taylor, eds., *Shakespeare and the Classics*, 33–48, Cambridge.

ZIOLKOWSKI, THEODORE (1993), *Virgil and the Moderns*, Princeton, NJ.

INDEX OF NAMES

Adorno, Theodor W. 127
Apuleius 149
Archilochus 133, 134
Aristotle 32, 126, 168
Armstrong, Isobel 119
Arnold, Matthew 45–7
Atherton, Catherine 186
Auerbach, Erich 92
Augustus 140
Austen, Jane 123

Bailey, Cyril 191
Barnard, Mary 210
Barrell, John 126
Barthes, Roland 119 n. 37, 122 n. 49, 179–80
Battersby, Christine 34, 35
Batteux, Abbé 31
Bell, Clive 63–4
Benjamin, Walter 29, 129
Bennett, Tony 122
Bernini, Gian Lorenzo 212
Bloch, Ernest 121
Boland, Eavan 215–16
Bourdieu, Pierre 23, 108, 120
Bowie, Andrew 42
Boyle, A. J. 141
Bradley, A. C. 65–6, 67–8, 184
Bramble, John 91
Brecht, Bertolt 8
Brinsley, John 204, 216
Bromwich, David 119
Brophy, Brigid 75
Browne, Thomas 230
Browning, Elizabeth Barrett 6
Burke, Edmund 34–5
Burne-Jones, Sir Edward Coley 111, 112
Burrow, Colin 220
Byatt, Antonia 202

Caesar 219–20, 235
Callimachus 82, 135, 141, 143
Carroll, David 128
Carson, Edward 113–15
Cato 222
Catullus 75–8, 90–100, 103
Cazeaux, Clive 107
Coleridge, Samuel Taylor 68–9, 182
Conte, Gian Biagio 197 nn. 87 & 89, 198
Cory, William 135
Cousin, Victor 189–90
Crabbe, George 152
Croce, Benedetto 25, 66 n. 30, 72 n. 52, 128 n. 67
Crow, Thomas 23–4
Crowther, Paul 26
Cunningham, J. V. 88
Curtius, E. R. 140, 224

Dante Alighieri 45–6, 150, 185–6, 223–4
Davie, Donald 89–90
Davis, Gregson 82, 83, 134–5
de Bolla, Peter 127, 129, 158
de Man, Paul 68, 143, 162
de Quincy, Thomas 230
Derrida, Jacques 44, 68, 100–1, 102, 106
Dewey, John 72, 119
Docherty, Thomas 125 n. 59
Donatus 148
Dryden, John 144, 150, 189–90, 198, 206–7
Dumas, Marlene 38
Duve, Thierry de 27 n. 80

Eagleton, Terry 12, 20 n. 53, 26, 69, 121–2, 185
Eichendorff, Joseph von 40–1
Eliot, George 43

Eliot, T. S. 3, 65, 74, 136, 138, 139, 156, 165, 176
Enterline, Lynn 207, 216–17

Faas, Ekbert 178 n. 43
Feeney, Denis 232
Finley, John H. 148
Flaubert, Gustave 69–70
Foucault, Michel 117 n. 29
Fowler, Don 136–7
Fränkel, Hermann 134–5
Fronto, Marcus 234–5
Frost, Robert 148
Fry, Roger 63, 64, 73–4
Fulton, Alice 214

Gadamer, Hans-Georg 55, 140
Gallus, Gaius Cornelius 145, 147
Gautier, Théophile 50–1, 57
Giordani, Pietro 225
Goffman, Erving 101–2
Goldhill, Simon 32, 33, 103, 124–5
Golding, William 8–9, 43
Goold, G. P. 90–1
Graves, Robert 221
Gray, Thomas 196
Greenberg, Clement 62
Griffin, Jasper 144, 150
Grotius, Hugo 224
Guerilla Girls 34
Guillory, John 123–4
Gunn, Tom 208
Guyer, Paul 29 n. 88, 160 n. 154

Habinek, Thomas 11–12, 21, 132 n. 74
Hall, Edith 121
Halliwell, Stephen 13
Hanslick, Eduard 66
Harpham, Geoffrey Galt 26
Harris, Roy 42 n. 132
Hayley, William 218–19
Hazlitt, William 228
Heaney, Seamus 150–1, 155
Hegel, G. W. F. 60 n. 13, 183
Heidegger, Martin 60–1
Heitland, W. E. 219
Henderson, John 131 n. 73, 181
Hesiod 32

Homer 45, 92, 97, 102–3, 126
Hopkins, Gerard Manley 34, 101 n. 114
Horace 12, 36–7, 49–50, 51–3, 59, 74–9, 81–6, 87–8, 90, 129–30, 131, 132–7, 145, 147, 160, 196–7
Hubbard, Margaret 105, 228–9
Hugo, Victor 110
Hume, David 17, 19
Hutcheson, Francis 21

Iser, Wolfgang 142, 153

Jacobson, Dan 43
James, Henry 50, 205
Jenkyns, Richard 92, 94, 99, 149, 180–1, 197
Johnson, Barbara 102
Johnson, Samuel 157 n. 141
Johnson, W. R. 212, 224, 226

Kant, Immanuel 9, 10, 12, 13–18, 19–20, 21, 22, 24, 27–8, 29, 30–1, 33, 34, 39, 41–3, 45, 59, 63, 64, 100–2, 107, 108–9, 110–11, 168–9, 205, 210, 237
Keats, John 94, 96
Kennedy, Duncan 4 n. 4, 11 n. 8, 27 n. 77, 123
Kenney, E. J. 195
Kermode, Frank 138, 157
Kivy, Peter 35, 67–8
Krieger, Murray 73
Kristeller, Paul Oskar 31

Landor, W. S. 78
Leavis, F. R. 19
Lee, Guy 146, 211
Leighton, Frederic 111
Lessing, Gotthold Ephraim 182
Levine, George 11
Lewis, C. S. 44, 71, 152, 185
Lindsay, Sir Coutts 111
Loesberg, Jonathan 60 n. 14, 74 n. 62, 163
Longinus 35, 39, 42
Louis XIV, king of France 224
Lucan 181, 217–36
Lucretius 103, 182–200

Index of Names

Lyas, Colin 72
Lyotard, Jean-François 127–8

Macaulay, Thomas Babington 223
Manning, Susan 40 n. 122
Marinetti, F. T. 38, 129
Marvell, Christopher 79–81, 82, 208
Marx, Karl 120–1
Masters, Jamie 224, 226, 227–8
Medcalf, Stephen 43–4
Miller, J. Hillis 1 n. 1
Milton, John 44, 46, 70 n. 48, 193–4, 199–200, 222–3
Montrose, Louis 142, 152
Moore, Albert 111
Morris, William 25–6, 72, 118–19
Mothersill, Mary 16, 27 n. 81, 172

Nehamas, Alexander 20, 25 n. 72
Nietzsche, Friedrich Wilhelm 51–2
Nuttall, A. D. 79

O'Gorman, Ellen 136 n. 86
Ovid 144, 199, 200–17, 222

Papanghelis, Theodore 180–1
Pater, Walter 25, 28, 45, 47–9, 50, 57–8, 66, 69, 70–1, 158, 163–5, 167, 168 n. 3, 169, 170–7, 178, 217, 237
Patin, H. J. G. 190
Patterson, Annabel 149
Pindar 87–8
Pinsky, Robert 208–9
Plato 21, 35, 57–8, 168
Pliny the Elder 32–3
Pope, Alexander 70, 182
Prettejohn, Elizabeth 62, 169
Propertius 103–6, 123, 228–9
Proust, Marcel 169 n. 5
Putnam, Michael 91
Puttenham, George 148

Queensberry, Marquess of 113
Quinn, Kenneth 196
Quintilian 149

Rapin, René 154

Reynolds, Sir Joshua 60, 156
Richards, I. A. 184–5
Richlin, Amy 211
Ricks, Christopher 173–4
Rorty, Richard 177
Rosenblatt, Louise A. 73 n. 59
Rowe, Nicholas 218, 222
Ruskin, John 70, 111, 169–70

Said, Edward 67 n. 33
Sandys, George 216
Santayana, George 186, 188, 190, 197, 200
Sappho 39, 77
Scarry, Elaine 29–30
Schama, Simon 151
Schiller, Friedrich 9–10, 25, 57 n. 6, 62, 72–3, 158–63, 164 n. 172, 182
Schlegel, A. W. 121
Scruton, Roger 25, 67 n. 33
Servius 148, 149, 151, 153
Shaftesbury, Lord 38
Shakespeare, William 46, 50–1, 191, 210, 212–13
Shankman, Steven 138–9, 140, 155–6
Shaw, George Bernard 117
Shelley, Percy Bysshe 182, 223
Shklovsky, Victor 72
Sidney, Sir Philip 148, 184
Sinfield, Alan 115
Smith, Adam 22 n. 62
Smith, Barbara Herrnstein 16 n. 29
Snell, Bruno 142
Sontag, Susan 177–8
Staël, Madame de 34
Stallings, A. E. 215
Steiner, Wendy 14, 38, 39 n. 120
Stevens, Wallace 40 n. 122
Stokes, Adrian 177
Stoppard, Tom 87
Swinburne, Algernon Charles 15, 109–10

Tanner, Michael 27
Tennyson, Alfred, Lord 199
Theocritus 141, 143
Titian (Tiziano Vecellio) 71, 204
Tolstoy, Leo 119 n. 34

Tomlinson, Charles 201–2, 207
Too, Yun Lee 2, 11, 12, 32, 126

Vendler, Helen 124, 177 n. 40
Veyne, Paul 31 n. 92, 141–2, 145, 147–8
Virgil 77–8, 82, 91, 92, 95, 97, 98, 139, 140–51, 152–5, 198, 203–4, 219–20, 233, 234
Volk, Katharina 188–9
Voltaire (François-Marie Arouet) 50–1

Weininger, Otto 34
Welwood, James 218

West, David 37, 132–3
Whigham, Peter 78
Whistler, James McNeill 8, 10, 53–4, 55–7, 71, 111–13
White, Hayden 58, 74
Wilde, Oscar 8, 25–6, 47 n. 145, 48, 113–17, 169, 174–5
Williams, Gordon 2, 140
Winckelmann, J. J. 38–9
Winterson, Jeanette 27, 170, 172 n. 17
Woolf, Virginia 69, 216
Wordsworth, William 171

Zajko, Vanda 1, 210
Zhou Enlai 115

INDEX OF SUBJECTS

accommodation 138–9
Aeneid (Virgil):
  and Augustan ideology 139–40
  Catullus and 77–8, 91, 92, 97–8
  Lucan and 219–20, 233–4
  Ovid and 203–4
aesthetic autonomy 26, 122
aesthetic criticism 3, 60, 167, 179
  Pater and 25, 49 n. 152, 50, 163–5, 170–7, 237
aesthetic determinability 160
aesthetic idea 121, 205, 210
aesthetic judgements 18, 217
Aesthetic Movement 2, 118, 180: *see also* art for art's sake
aesthetic preference 108
aesthetic present 27
aestheticism 114–15
aesthetics 8–9, 13, 25, 62, 158–65, 182
  classics and 10–11
  and gender 27–8, 33–9
  left and right 119–20
  Marxist 120–2
  and materialism 122
  and politics 12, 25–6, 129, 224–5, 219, 228
After Ovid: New Metamorphoses 202–3, 208–9, 214–15
Alexandrianism 144
alienation 161
allegory 68, 71
  in *Eclogues* 141, 146, 148–50
  in Lucan 222
  in Propertius 103–5
  Shankman and 138–9
amoebean poems 155
Anti-Lucretius in Lucretius 190, 194–5

apostrophe 231, 232
appropriation 138–9
Arrangement in Grey and Black (Whistler) 55–7, 71
art 30–1, 115, 168–9
  Adorno on 127
  autonomy of 60, 101, 109–16, 120–2, 127, 128, 182
  beginnings of 8–9
  definition of 128–9
  Marx on 120–1
  Marxism and 121–2, 161
  and morality 27, 110–11
  and time 127–8
  transcendence of 128–9
art for art's sake 50, 60, 109–11, 182, 227
  and Catullus 64: 92
  and formalism 60
  Gautier on 50–1, 57
  libel cases 111–14
  see also Aesthetic Movement
art theories 108–9
asymmetry 76, 93
ataraxia 190, 197
Augustan ideology:
  Aeneid and 139–40
  Odes and 131–3
autobiography 176, 177
autonomy of art 60, 101, 109–16, 120–2, 127, 128, 182

Bauhaus 22 n. 59
beauty 9, 10, 14–21, 39, 110–11
  dependent 17–18, 19, 24
  free 15, 17, 19
  Hume on 17, 19
  pure 25, 63, 168
  Scarry on 29–30
belief, problem of 184–5

Index of Subjects

Birmingham Society of Arts and School of Design 118
bucolic poetry, *see* pastoral poetry

Callimacheanism 136–7
canon, critique of 123–4
canonicity issues 25, 137–8
  classic, idea of 155–7
  classic, Shankman's definition of 138–9
  culture specificity of 24
  interpretation 14
capitalism 22–3
carpe diem poems 79–82, 196
Catullus 64: 90–100, 103
censorship 126–7
civil war 133, 218–36
class 23, 108
common sense 27 n. 80, 34–5
Communism 26, 129
content 34, 60–1, 62, 183–6
  and form, relationship with 34, 58, 183–6
  interpretations of 62
creativity 42–3
criticism 45, 179
  and autobiography 176, 177
  and politics 12
Critique of Judgement (Kant) 12, 13–14, 15, 39, 42, 63, 64, 100–2
  'Analytic of the Beautiful' 12, 17, 30, 59, 158
  'Critique of Aesthetic Judgement' (Kant) 30–1

Daily Telegraph 115
De Rerum Natura (Lucretius) 182–200
death 135, 221–4
  as Horatian theme 52, 59, 78–9, 84, 196–7
  as Lucanian theme 221–2, 230–1
  as Lucretian theme 194–6
deconstruction 186
  of Kant 100–1, 102
  in Lucan 226, 228, 235
decorative arts 61, 72, 118
defamiliarization 72
description 177

didactic poetry 182–200
  problem of belief 184–5
différance 68–70
disavowal, poems of 82–4, 87, 143
discourse 127–8
disinterest 2, 9, 12, 21–3, 170: *see also* interest
dispossession 141
drinking, images of 84, 133
drives (human personality) 161–2

Eclogues (Virgil) 82, 95, 140–51, 152–5
  allegory in 141, 146, 148–50
  politicization of 150–1
ecphrasis 93–5
elegy 142
engagement 137
English Aestheticism 2, 118, 180: *see also* art for art's sake
environmentalism 141
epic poetry 134
Epicureanism 136, 190, 192, 193, 195, 197
epiphanies 52–3
Epistles (Horace) 37, 131
epyllia 90–1, 144
erotics 85–7, 144–5, 147, 212–13
exile 141

Fascism 16, 129, 131
feminism 27–8, 33
feminist issues 211–13
  female sexuality 215–16
  male gaze 212, 215
  see also gender issues
fine arts 15, 23–4, 31–3, 72, 118
forgetfulness 133–4
form 60–1, 62
  and content, relationship with 34, 58, 183–6
  significant 64
formalism 11–12, 55–8, 60, 63–4, 106, 153
framing 101–7
friendship 135

gender issues 214–16
  aesthetics and 27–8, 33–9

Index of Subjects

Horace and 52, 53
  in Ovid 204, 211, 212–13
genius 33–6, 39–44
Georgics (Virgil) 198
Grosvenor Gallery 111

hermeneutics 107
homoeroticism 149
homosexuality 114–15
hyperbole 219, 229–30

idealism 14–15
identity issues 210
ideology criticism 1, 47, 49, 56, 60, 67, 125–7
  objections to 123–4
Iliad (Homer) 92, 97, 102–3, 126
imperialism 139
Impressionism 112, 116
inspiration 36–7, 43–4
integrationism 42 n. 132
intentionality 33
interest 14, 18, 21, 24, 56: *see also* disinterest
interpretation 14, 28, 157–8, 177–81
  framing and 102–3
  and politics 123, 180–1
intertextuality 34, 57–8, 86, 199, 201
intratextuality 85, 86
irony 82–4, 86, 88, 90

judgement of taste 9, 10, 14–18, 25, 27, 30
  criteria and 21
  culture-specific 24
  and disinterest 2, 21–2
  and form/content relationship 58
  and frames 102–7
  pure 14, 21, 22, 24, 28, 109
  types of 15, 18–19

knowledge 23, 25, 29

labyrinth, as image 97–8
language 42, 58, 68–70, 121, 128, 162, 210
  Catullus' use of 77–8, 97–8
  Horace's use of 51–3, 135

literary and non-literary 71–2
Lucan's use of 219, 229–33
Lucretius' use of 187–9, 192–3, 197–8
Marvell's use of 208
Milton's use of 199–200
Ovid's use of 204–5
  and politics 123
Pope's use of 70
Tennyson's use of 199
Virgil's use of 198
see also word play
laureatism 137
libel cases 111–14
literary criticism, in antiquity 12, 32
literary theory 3–4
literature 71–2, 128
  and aesthetics 131
  in antiquity 32
  as art form 18, 122
  and politics 131, 132
love poetry 84–7
lyric poetry 134

male gaze 212, 215
Marxism 26, 120–2, 161
materialism 122
materiality 69
meaning 65–7, 207
Metamorphoses (Ovid) 144, 199, 200–17
metamorphosis 200–17, 222–3, 224
metaphor 187–9, 205, 206, 207
  in Horace 51
metapoetics 97, 142–3, 208
mimesis 13, 153–4
misogyny 33, 34
modernism 38–9, 156
modernity 61
morality 13 n. 14, 15, 109–11, 113–14
  art and 27, 110–11
Mostra Augustea della Romanità 131
music 14 n. 16, 18, 66–7
mythology 143–5, 192–3, 214–15
  in Lucretius 192–3, 194
  in Milton 193–4
  in Ovid 203–5, 208–9

National Observer 115
nature, art and 40: *see also* science
Nazism 16
New Aestheticism 11 n. 7, 179
New Criticism 2, 64–5, 91, 123–4, 131, 179
New Historicism 132, 142, 152

Observations on the Feeling of the Beautiful and Sublime (Kant) 34
Odes (Horace) 52, 74–6, 84, 90
  Augustan ideology and 131–3
  Odes 1: 76–7, 78–9, 81–4, 85, 88, 133
  Odes 2: 49–50, 51–3, 59, 76–7, 79, 129–30, 132–6, 137 n. 89, 196–7
  Odes 3: 36–7, 85
  Odes 4: 79, 84–6, 87–8, 137
On the Aesthetic Education of Man (Schiller) 9–10, 158–63, 164 n. 172
Orientalism 116
originality 40
ornamentation 100, 102, 106

Paradise Lost (Milton) 44, 70 n. 48, 193–4, 199–200, 222–3
paradox 94–5, 98, 174, 204, 222, 229, 234
paraesthetics 128
paraphrase 64–7
parerga 100, 102, 106
pastoral poetry 140–54
  allegory in 141, 146, 148–50
  elegy and 142
  and environmentalism 141
  politicization of 141–2, 145, 148, 149–50
  Renaissance theorists on 140–1, 148
personality 161–2
Pharsalia (Lucan) 218–36
  reception history 226, 227
  and Republicanism 225–6, 227, 228
  snake imagery 221–3
Platonism 31
pleasure 9, 17, 18, 45, 49 n. 152
  and purposiveness 63

politics:
  and aesthetics 12, 25–6, 129, 219, 224–5, 228
  and interpretation 123, 180–1
  and literature 131, 132
positivism 175
postmodernism 227–8
proportionality 29
puns 134, 147, 206, 207–8
purposiveness 39–40, 45, 159
  and pleasure 63

quietism 137

reading 50
  intransitive 73–4
  politics of 137–8
  transitive 73–4
reception theory 6 n. 7, 28–9, 124, 126–7, 138–9, 179, 182
recusatio 82–4, 87, 143
religion 43–4, 198, 232
Renaissance 154–5, 178
  and pastoral poetry 140–1, 148
The Renaissance (Pater) 163–5, 168 n. 3, 169, 170–1, 173–6, 178
repetitions 59, 136, 234
representation 17, 59, 168
Republicanism 225–6, 227, 228
Res Gestae (Augustus) 140
Romantic thesis 71

scepticism 175–6
science 15, 41
  De rerum natura (Lucretius) 182–200
seeing 169–70, 174, 189
self-empowerment 37
sensus communis 27 n. 80, 34–5
sexism 33
sexuality:
  female 215–16
  homosexuality 114–15
  sexual violence 204, 211
  see also erotics
significant form 64
sociability 20, 37
socialism 118

Index of Subjects

solipsism 47, 173, 175–6, 179, 182
sophists 58
subjective universality 18, 48
subjectivity 28
sublime 13 n. 14, 17 n. 34, 34–5, 39
syllepsis 204, 207–8
symbolism 68, 149–50
synaesthesia 99, 173
synonyms 134

temporal transcendence 30, 128–9
time:
    art and 52–3, 127–8
    as Horatian theme 52
totalitarianism 131
touchstone theory (Arnold) 45–7
Trades Guild of Learning 118
tragedy 121, 126
transitions 88–9
translation 33, 203, 206–7
    and meaning 65–6
trouvailles 8–9, 33, 40

universalism 19–20, 27–8
universality 2, 19
    subjective 18, 48
untranslatability thesis 33, 65
utopias 25, 117, 118

Virgil Society 138
    the visual 168, 169, 176–7

Whistler *v.* Ruskin libel case 111–13
Wilde *v.* Queensberry libel case 108, 113–14
wine imagery 133
withdrawal 137
word play:
    puns 134, 147, 206, 207–8
    repetition 59, 136, 234
    synonyms 134
    see also language

Printed in Great Britain
by Amazon.co.uk, Ltd.,
Marston Gate.